Teología en Conjunto

A Collaborative Hispanic Protestant Theology

Edited by
JOSÉ DAVID RODRÍGUEZ
LOIDA I. MARTELL-OTERO

Westminster John Knox Press
Louisville, Kentucky

*T*he gifts he gave were that some would be apostles, some prophets, some evangelists, some pastors and teachers, to equip the saints for the work of ministry, for building up the body of Christ, until all of us come to the unity of the faith and of the knowledge of the Son of God, to maturity, to the measure of the full stature of Christ.

EPHESIANS 4:11–13

Scripture quotations from the New Revised Standard Version of the Bible are copyright © 1989 by the Division of Christian Education of the National Council of the Churches of Christ in the U.S.A. and are used by permission.

Book design by Jennifer K. Cox
Cover design by Alec Bartsch

First edition
Published by Westminster John Knox Press
Louisville, Kentucky

This book is printed on acid-free paper that meets the American National Standards Institute Z39.48 standard. ∞

PRINTED IN THE UNITED STATES OF AMERICA
97 98 99 00 01 02 03 04 05 06 — 10 9 8 7 6 5 4 3 2 1

Library of Congress Cataloging-in-Publication Data

Teología en conjunto : a collaborative Hispanic Protestant theology / edited by José David Rodríguez, Loida I. Martell-Otero.
    p.   cm.
Includes bibliographical references.
ISBN 0-664-25665-1 (alk. paper)
1. Hispanic American theology.   2. Protestant churches—Doctrines.
I. Rodríguez, José David, date.   II. Martell-Otero, Loida I., date.
BT83.575.T46   1997
230´.044´08968073—DC21   97-16944

Teología en Conjunto

Contents

Contributors

Teresa Chavez Sauceda is a Ph.D. candidate at the Graduate Theological Union, Berkeley, California.

Elizabeth Conde-Frazier is a Ph.D. candidate at Boston College and Director of the Orlando E. Costas Program at Andover Newton Theological School, Newton Centre, Massachusetts.

Justo L. González is Director of the Hispanic Summer Program and the Hispanic Theological Initiative, a program of The Pew Charitable Trusts at Candler School of Theology, Emory University, Atlanta.

Pablo A. Jiménez is Executive Director of the Asociación para la Educación Teológica Hispana (AETH), Decatur, Georgia, and the Administrator of the Hispanic Summer Program.

David Maldonado, Jr., is Associate Dean for Academic Affairs and professor of church and society at Perkins School of Theology, Dallas.

Loida I. Martell-Otero is associate pastor of the Soundview Christian Baptist Church and a Ph.D. student in systematic theology at Fordham University, New York. She is also a doctor of veterinary medicine.

Eliseo Pérez Álvarez teaches at the Seminario Teológica Presbiteriano de México in Mexico City.

José David Rodríguez is associate professor of theology and Director of the Hispanic Ministry Program at the Lutheran School of Theology at Chicago.

Samuel Solivan teaches systematic theology at Andover Newton Theological School, Newton Centre, Massachusetts.

David Traverzo Galarza teaches at Baruch College, City University of New York, Department of African American and Hispanic Studies.

Foreword

Justo L. González

In their Introduction the editors use the image of resetting broken bones as an apt reminder of the pain and brokenness of the Latino experience. It is important for us to bear in mind the origin of that brokenness, which is the result both of our history and of our present.

Our history is one of conflict, violence, and oppression. The atrocities committed against our native ancestors by our European ancestors who invaded these lands are well known and need not be repeated here. Suffice it to say that entire populations were wiped out, ancient civilizations destroyed, and millions upon millions sacrificed on the altar of the invaders' thirst for gold, land, and glory. In ancient mythology about European origins it was Zeus who, disguised as a bull, raped Europa; but the rape of our hemisphere by Europe is no myth! It was a rape of cosmic proportions, in which an entire continent and civilization vented its violence on peoples and civilizations whose only crime was to be at the wrong place at the wrong time with the wrong weapons. It was a cosmic rape that replicated itself again and again in the very physical and personal rape of our native foremothers by our European forefathers. And when, for a number of reasons, the native flesh and blood could no longer satisfy the invaders, they turned to Africa, and raped it too in quest of cheap labor and cheaper human flesh.

If that is our history, our present is also one of survival in the midst of brokenness, and joy in the midst of pain. As Latinas and Latinos in the United States, most of us find ourselves at the margins of society. Those whose ancestors were already in these lands when the United States invaded and conquered them often find themselves strangers in their own land, being told in myriad ways that they are not true Americans, and sometimes even not so subtly being told to "go home"—as if they had any other home to call their own, except this one in which they are not fully welcome. Along those lines, many of my friends in the American Southwest still remember the signs, "No Mexicans or dogs allowed." Those who came later usually fared no better.

Even those who have been able to move up the economic ladder still experience prejudice and discrimination. In schools, their culture and tradition are often not considered as worthy of study as are those that originated in Britain, France, or Germany. In many public schools, it has been traditional for Latina and Latino students not to be encouraged to prepare for college, but rather to be funneled into vocational schools. As a result, for decades one fact has remained constant in census figures: no matter how many Hispanics there are in the nation, no matter how large the total population is, and no matter the changing trends in the economy, in most negative indicators (unemployment, school dropouts, poverty) the figure for Latinos is 150 percent of that of the population at large. (In other words, when unemployment is at 8 percent, Hispanic unemployment is at 12 percent; and when 20 percent of the population are poor, 30 percent of Hispanics are poor.)

In summary, both in our history and in our present, there are many reasons for speaking of brokenness and for using the metaphor of bone fractures. Our brokenness, like that of the entire human race as depicted in Genesis, stems from our very origins. We were born in pain, violence, and oppression. Yet even out of those origins have come a measure of joy and beauty. Ancient Christian writers commented on the love of God, who immediately after expelling Adam and Eve from the garden provided them with furs with which to cover themselves. Likewise, even in the midst of our brokenness, God has provided us with the tools with which to build a life of love and beauty. For instance, one cannot but see a miracle in the manner in which, out of our history of rape and violence, emerged a society with such a deep and far-reaching sense of family. Somehow, by the grace of God and through much pain and frustration, our bones have been set, and we have managed to emerge as a people with a future and a contribution.

The image of broken bones being set brings to mind the familiar saying, "sticks and stones may break my bones . . ." And certainly many sticks and stones have broken our bones. Yet this book and the experiences it reflects show that the rest of the saying is not true: "but words can never harm me." If theo-logy is the logos about God, it is clear that the God-talk or God-discourse we have been taught has not always served to set our bones straight. We have been healed, but not all our healing has been straight.

The word that Protestant missionaries and others brought to us was in many ways a healing word. That is the point of departure of all the essays in this book—a point that may be obscured because, of necessity, its authors have to dwell on what still needs to be mended, on what was wrong rather than on what was right. It is because we have experienced healing in the Protestant faith—and in the communities that it created amid us—that we still claim that faith.

But the healing also created a new kind of brokenness, one best compared with the brokenness of a bone not properly set. We were told that

Jesus was our Savior and Liberator—and that is true. We were told that he was our Liberator from the brokenness in our lives, our culture, and our society—and that also is true. But too often those who told us these things were so immersed in their own prejudices that they could more readily see the brokenness and the sin than the beauty, the life, and the truth in our culture and traditions. From their perspective, there was little or nothing in our traditions and culture that was a sign of God's presence among us.

The anti-Catholic polemic that was so important an element in the Protestant "evangelization" of our people left us with few resources from our own history and culture. Thus, for instance, although we had studied in school that Bartolomé de Las Casas was a great defender of our Indian ancestors, as Protestants we were not taught to see him as one of our ancestors in the faith. Much less were we told that the Catholic protest against the exploitation of the Indians in Latin America was more forceful than any that Anglo Protestantism ever offered in defense of the natives of North America. According to the version of history which we learned as Protestants, Ignatius of Loyola, one of the greatest saints of the Spanish tradition, was the scheming founder of an order devoted to hypocrisy and deceit. Left with no saints, and with tarnished heroes, we were forced to look abroad—mostly to the Anglo world—for our saints and models. Thus, it is not surprising that our bones, though in a sense healed, were not set aright. (A point at which the life of Ignatius is particularly relevant, for it was in his sickbed, amid the torture of a broken leg that had to be painfully set more than once and that never healed properly, that Ignatius made his decision to follow his Lord to unexplored regions.)

What is true of the manner in which our history was told to us is also true of the entire system of theo-logy. Words have indeed harmed us. And that is what this book is about. It is about our need to reread every major heading of theology, not apart from the tradition nor necessarily against it, but rather as people who are fully grounded in our tradition and our present situation, and who are fully convinced that the gospel, properly understood, preached and lived, is still the only hope for the healing of our bones—and for the healing of the nations. So be it!

Introduction

José David Rodríguez
and Loida I. Martell-Otero

From June 8 through June 10, 1995, a group of Latina and Latino theologians, ethicists, sociologists of religion, pastors, teachers, and students gathered on the grounds of Princeton Seminary to discuss the distinctiveness of our theology in a collaborative way. This particular method of doing theology is very characteristic of Hispanic American theology and is what we call in Spanish *teología en conjunto*. Literally, *en conjunto* means "in conjunction," or "conjoined in," implying not only the coming together but also the integration and intimacy involved in such a sharing. It is reminiscent of the human body, whose various joints, tendons, muscles, and bones must be conjoined in order for it to function in an adequate way.[1] Thus, we use the term *teología en conjunto* to emphasize two fundamental aspects affecting Hispanic theology: its rich diversity and its integral collaborative spirit.[2] This book is the fruit of that collaborative venture celebrated in June of 1995, a venture that continues to be celebrated wherever and whenever Latina and Latino theologians come together to share the Word of God, and to share our stories about our continuing pilgrimage as a diaspora people in the United States. The book is unique in that it is the collaboration of Hispanic American Protestants in the United States and Puerto Rico, and it has generated much excitement on the part of all the midwives who collaborated in its birth.

The diversity of our theology springs from the diversity of those of us who constitute the people that this country has lumped under the generic title of "Hispanic" or "Latino." Both are unfortunate terms imposed from outside the community by a culture that is uncomfortable when a "norm" is not established.[3] Who are the people called Hispanics or Latinos? Of the 27.5 million Hispanics in the United States some of us are Mexican Americans, others are Puerto Ricans, Cubans, Dominicans, South and Central Americans, and others are the subsequent generations of these ethnic groups.[4] Suffice it to say that the terms Latino/Latina, Hispano/Hispana, or Hispanic American obscure the rich and sundry cultures represented. Our histories are diverse, and therefore our contexts, our language, our culture, and the particular flavor of our *pastoral* (pastoral ministry) are just as diverse. The reality of the Hispanic church is that it is multicultural. This, in turn, has implications for the way in which Hispanic *evangélicas* and *evangélicos* do theology.[5]

Although we are a culturally and ethnically diverse group, we hold in common as residents of the continental United States some socioeconomic and political realities. The statistics that underscore these realities have been consistent. They point to a people who have needed to struggle against poverty, lack of adequate housing, lack of decent health care, the phenomenon of "tracking" in the educational system, and the pervasive reality of racism.[6] Latinas, especially, have had to face the triple oppression of poverty, racism, and sexism. Nonetheless, they have often been the ones who, against overwhelming odds, have held both family and communities together.[7] These realities, which our people face daily, have led Hispanic American scholars to describe the Latino people as being "at the margins." The Latino people live on the fringes of society and are powerless and invisible. Thus, to speak of the Hispanic American church is to speak of the church of the poor. Those of us who pastor such congregations have learned to do much with very little resources, recognition, or support. To speak of a theological method based on our community life and historical memory (our praxis) is to include the stories behind these statistics, including the stories of being made less than human every day. These stories are what has led David Abalos to speak of the gods of incoherence.[8] They are death-dealing gods indeed. Hispanic Americans live under the daily threat of death of institutionalized violence. In this book we are responding to the brokenness of our communities, as a doctor treats the broken bones of the human body. In medicine, there are various ways of classifying fractures of the skeletal system. A fracture can be simple, which means a bone is broken in two, or compound, which means that the broken bone has broken through the skin and is now visible externally. This latter break is more dangerous: it creates significantly more tissue damage, affecting skin, muscle (or tendons), nerves, blood supply, and so forth. The fact that the tissue is exposed leaves it vulnerable to severe infection, which could ultimately spread through the blood system (septicemia). Such a complication, compounding the damage, can lead to death. The brokenness of our community is not a simple fracture but a brokenness compounded throughout time and affecting all systems: social, economic, psychological, political, spiritual (and therefore religious and theological), emotional, personal, and familial.[9] These are death-dealing gods of incoherence indeed!

Nonetheless, Hispanics are not just statistics. Nor are we defined solely by our poverty or our brokenness. The truth and beauty of the Latino people in the United States is that we are a brave people with a richness we share joyfully. Eldin Villafañe summarizes well who we are culturally. He speaks of our personalism, our love of music, our hospitality, our sense of community, our love of family, our sense of honor and dignity, and our passion.[10] Both he and Virgilio Elizondo point to our love of fiestas, where our joy and sharing are incarnated in a concrete and profound way.[11] The biblical images of banquets and table fellowship resonate with the Latino people for this reason. Our social life revolves around the table. Even our funerals are celebrated with a meal!

One of the most important characteristics of Latinas and Latinos is our deep religiosity. Villafañe characterizes the Hispanic American as a "homo religiosus," for whom

> there is no area of life, no matter how trivial, that is not "transmuted" by the religious sentiment. The depth of Hispanic religiosity cannot be fathomed by mere statistical quantification of church attendance, or for that matter, statistical surveys or religious profiles. The Hispanic culture and person cannot be understood apart from this religious dimension.[12]

The centrality of religion and faith in the lives of Hispanics is primarily due to the ubiquitous influence of the Catholic Church in the life of Latin America. Even Hispanic Protestants must recognize that Iberoamerican Catholic religiosity and ethics are embedded in our culture.[13] Many idioms and customs reflect this background. Loida Martell-Otero still recalls her grandmother, a Baptist Sunday school teacher, saying "Ave Maria Purísima" (Hail Mary, most pure). Villafañe cites a study by Frank Tennenbaum:

> The Church was everywhere and with every individual all of his life and filled all his days. The day began with early morning mass and ended with Ave Maria, and every occasion, every sorrow, every joy, every holiday had its own special religious symbolism to be acted out in church. . . . The church or cathedral bell dominated the community, and daily life was disciplined and ordered to its sound.[14]

In Latin American countries colonized by the Spaniards, there are always churches in the middle of the towns. This religious background, along with other factors, has created the "homo religiosus" that Villafañe speaks of so eloquently. In short, the Hispanic American community is a theological community.

In this theological, religious community, it is rare to find true atheists (not that they do not exist, but it is not common). It is therefore strange for some of us who come to the United States to study in seminaries to find ourselves needing to prove the "why" and "who" of God: Does God exist?

Is God truly God? Is Jesus truly a savior? These are not the typical questions of a Latino or Latina. Rather, our questions are based on the premise of God; thus, the questions are related to "where" and "what." If God is in the midst of my struggle, *where* is God to be found? If God is calling me to be in this place, *what* is God calling me to do? Liberation theology has even asked, What God? But overall, the community is a theological community, because God as God and Jesus Christ as Savior are presupposed. The reflections are: In what ways is God saving? In what places can I find or hear this Savior? How is this situation coherent with the God of my community, with the Spanish-speaking God? Thus, in our diversity we ask many similar questions and function with common hermeneutical premises.

Who are we, then? We are an undereducated, underserved, poor, mostly young, bilingual and multicultural people. We are a diverse people, and as such, we are a people with a rich history and a wonderful cultural background. It is out of this people that God has called many a leader and many a servant to work for the reign of God. It is out of this context that the Hispanic *iglesia evangélica* (Protestant church) is called, both to be part of that context and to serve in that context. To understand the context in which theology is done is to understand how and why we do theology.[15]

Our theology is more than just an expression of doctrine. It is the living expression of our deepest faith and most fervent hopes. In this book we hope to contribute to the healing of our brokenness by giving expression to that faith and that hope. It is our diversity and commonality (cultural, socioeconomic, religious), as well as the brokenness and the joys, that are reflected in the content and form of this book. As Elizabeth Conde-Frazier expresses it, the book shows our *disyuntiva en nuestra teología en conjunto* (our disjointedness in our theology of conjointedness, or collaborative theology). If we truly have a collaborative Protestant theology, then we must create a space for all voices to be heard. It is exciting for us to include men and women, ordained and lay, professional theologian and student, among the voices. Having said that, it is equally exciting to see that in the disjointedness of our conjointedness, we can indeed perceive the shared elements of our Protestant Hispanic theology. What each chapter ultimately witnesses to is a shared belief in the hope of our salvation, the hope that our brokenness can indeed be healed. It is our hope, therefore, that the reader will share with us the adventure of seeing the emerging vision, and will articulate with us the emerging voice of what defines the particularity the Hispanic Protestant theology.

We could not have partnered in this collaborative venture, *en conjunto*, without a wonderful team of people who have aided throughout. The chapters that follow grew out of the presentations made by those who met at Princeton and collaborated with this project in diverse ways.

Chapter 1, by José David Rodríguez, describes the goal for this project and provides a brief description of the development and present trends of Latino theology in the United States. The author focuses on the idea of *teología en conjunto*, that is, a collaborative theology, and its impact on the theological reflection of Hispanics as they struggle to understand and respond to their vocation of faith in the context of the struggles of their people. He describes some major challenges faced by those whose efforts are deepening and further articulating the promising contributions of this perspective for theological reflection. He proposes new areas for exploration and concludes by anticipating some of the tasks that lie ahead as we continue our witness of faith from a Hispanic perspective.

Chapter 2, by Teresa Chavez Sauceda, provides a Hispanic understanding of God. After a brief examination of key methodological elements of this perspective (a commitment of faith to a praxis of liberation; to the ethnic, socioeconomic, and religious diversity of the community; and to the communal nature of the theological endeavor), the author focuses on the Trinitarian and creative aspects of God's reality as two areas in which this perspective makes its most important contributions. For Latino and Latina theologians, God is revealed as a relational being whose essence is sharing (love and power), who calls us to participate in a loving community, empowered by the Holy Spirit, and to engage in the struggle for justice and liberation.

Chapter 3 provides some important dimensions of the vision of Christ emerging from a Hispanic Protestant perspective. Eliseo Pérez Álvarez explores these dimensions by focusing on the sacrament of the Eucharist. Three sections analyze the implications of following Jesus' imperative on practicing the Eucharist as remembrance of the transforming power of this gracious divine redemptive act in our lives. The first section addresses the challenge of building community through the exercise of memory. Our remembrance and practice of the Eucharist connect us with God's remnant in history (the Poor of Yahweh), who continue to witness to the liberating power of God's reign among us. The second section explores the call to practice love and solidarity as we remember Jesus' love and donation of self for us. The final section points to a remembrance of the promise of a new reality of justice and human fulfillment offered in the Eucharist, in the power and perspective of Jesus Christ's resurrection, calling us to an obedience of faith that witnesses to God's triumph over the powers that cause the suffering and death of our people.

In chapter 4, Samuel Solivan argues that in contrast to contemporary trends that lead to the depersonalization of the Holy Spirit as power, influence, or energy, for Hispanic American pneumatology, the personalization of the Holy Spirit plays an important role for the affirmation and self-esteem of our people, as well as for the empowerment of the church to deal with the challenge of diversity as the basis for Christian unity. Challenging a traditional Pentecostal reading of the second chapter of the book of Acts that reduces the meaning of Pentecost to the Spirit's enabling a person to speak in an unknown tongue, often unknown to both the speaker and the listener and therefore needing the gift of interpretation, Solivan proposes a focus on the Spirit's role as the power that enables the personal and collective witness of the church as a reflection of God's reign, recognizing in all people, races, and nations an expression of God's creation and thus God's graciousness.

In chapter 5, Pablo A. Jiménez analyzes the central place of the Bible for Hispanic Protestants. While there is a basic inherited use of the Bible among Latina and Latino Protestants influenced by the legacy of European Protestantism, there is also an important indigenous approach rooted in characteristic traits of the Hispanic situation and culture. This indigenous approach takes the social location of poverty, alienation, and discrimination against the community, its rich mystical and spiritual tradition, as well as its preferred narrative approach, to the study and exposition of scripture. This approach perceives the Bible as a liberating text offering orientation, models, types, directives, and inspiration, for the sociohistorical liberation of our community. The author also points to some metaphors (the Galilean principle, reading the Bible in Spanish, marginality, *mestizaje, mulatez*, alienness) developed by Hispanic theologians which serve to establish the correspondence of relationships between the social relations that underlay and shaped the biblical text and those that underlie and shape our experience.

In chapter 6, Justo L. González explores the notion of ecclesiology for Hispanic Protestants. While acknowledging our lack of a well-developed doctrine of the church, he argues that this is an area where we make the most significant contributions for theological reflection. First, he points to the parallelism between the development of our ecclesiology and the course of ecclesiological development in the history of Christian thought. This development reveals a process going from an early, almost unreflective stage, to a more systematic and abstract one, to a third stage that draws heavily on the images and perspectives of the first period. Second, he describes Latino Protestant biblical images that serve our understanding of the church and emphasize its mission. González concludes that the lack of an explicit ecclesiology in the Hispanic Protestant community becomes an asset rather than a deficiency, for this lack of attention on our ecclesiological consciousness leads to a focus on our more fundamental missional vocation.

Chapter 7, a study of theological anthropology by David Maldonado, Jr., establishes the need to reflect on the human condition as a task of theological reflection in its effort to understand and articulate the content of the faith and religious experience of believers. The author then examines the particular character of a Hispanic theological anthropology. He explores the contribution of three distinguished theologians (Virgilio Elizondo,

Justo L. González, and Eldin Villafañe) to provide a sample of the diverse nature of the Hispanic community and the basis for the development of a more comprehensive theological anthropology. This proposed anthropology seeks to define what it means to be human within the context of the history, culture, and social experience of the Hispanic/Latino mestizo or mulatto people. For this author, to be Hispanic is to experience life as a member of the American mestizo or mulatto population, which understands its birth in the context and outcome of conquest and which has experienced oppression and colonization throughout its history and continues today to identify with the poor and the oppressed.

In chapter 8, David Traverzo Galarza presents a study of the doctrine of sin by developing a working definition of the topic based on the scriptures. This definition includes that of moral and religious deviation and alienation from our relationship with God, leading to suffering and death. He then reviews the contributions of some major Christian thinkers (Augustine, Aquinas, Luther, Calvin), including distinguished Latin American theologians (Gutiérrez, Dussel, Támez), whose work has impacted the way this topic has been discussed in the past and continues to be addressed in the present. The author concludes by suggesting a Latino radical evangelical approach, based on the contributions of Orlando E. Costas, as a constructive paradigm to respond more adequately to the problem of sin from a Hispanic perspective. Such a radical evangelical approach combines an integral or holistic thrust, a praxis-oriented and -grounded perspective, and a fundamental commitment by the church to fulfill her mission based on a liberating gospel that proclaims (in word and deed) good news to, by, with, and for the marginalized and excluded.

Chapter 9 examines the contribution of Latino Protestantism in the understanding and expression of Christian spirituality. For Elizabeth Conde-Frazier the biblical and theological grounding of our spirituality closely follows the theological heritage of Protestantism, both in Europe and America, leading to a correlation between contemplation and social action. Yet this correlation draws its particular character from the legacy of Spanish mysticism, which emphasizes the presence and action of God in all aspects of our lives and the need to respond to the social challenges facing our people. What emerges is a spirituality that emphasizes (1) a deep relationship between doctrine and its correlation in pastoral practice, (2) a communal expression of the Christian vocation aimed at social justice rather than just social action, and (3) the prophetic dimension of worship (prayer, preaching, testimonies, singing, vigils, and so on) which serves as a resource for the struggle and survival of our people.

Chapter 10, by Loida I. Martell-Otero, reflects on some challenges facing Hispanics as we continue our theological endeavor, arguing that we need to sharpen our understanding and commitment to a contextual and collaborative theology that emerges from our pastoral practice. The product of this theological reflection must keep a dynamic tension between the broader theological tradition and the past, present, and future contributions that emerge from the religious experiences of our people. Future generations of Latina and Latino church leaders and scholars must be identified, encouraged, and supported as we seek to prepare the church to meet the challenges of the future. Additional paradigms, particularly from the experience of Hispanic women, are needed as interpretive frameworks for understanding our reality and faith experiences, to provide our own community and the church at large with a relevant word from the gospel for their witness and ministry.

Why is this project so important? First, the emphasis on our Hispanic Protestant perspective lies in the fact that our work shows an appreciation of the Protestant tradition. This includes the legacy we have inherited from the missionaries, which provided our experience and understanding of the central tenets of belief and practice of our Christian faith. On the other hand, our particular context has allowed us to contextualize that theology, so that we did not just imitate the centuries-old beliefs, controversies, and ideologies that contributed to the brokenness (the compound fractures) of the Christian community at large, and to the Latino community in particular. Second, it is in this critical and reflective understanding that we hope to meet the future with a promise: a promise of salvation and healing wrought by God through Jesus Christ through the power of the Holy Spirit. It is our hope that a holistic vision of Protestant theology will contribute to the larger theological discourse, that in a collaborative spirit we may partner in the setting of the broken bones of the Hispanic community, and of the world. In short, we hope and pray for the reign of God in our midst where, indeed, the will of the Father shall be done on earth as it is in heaven (Matt. 6:10).

As editors, we want to thank the contributors for their creative and challenging chapters, and Justo L. González for his stimulating foreword. We wish to thank the Asociación para la Educación Teológica Hispana for making this venture possible; a special word of thanks goes to its executive committee, and to its executive director, Pablo Jiménez. We want to express our gratitude to our "recorders" at the Encuentro de Teología y Ética, who provided us with essential feedback about the event, the presentations, and this written project. Finally, we wish to thank Westminster John Knox Press, especially Stephanie Egnotovich, Managing Editor, and Timothy Staveteig for believing in this project (so much so that Mr. Staveteig attended the Encuentro) and for patiently waiting for us to give birth to this book. To all, a heartfelt "God bless you." May we see such projects continue to come forth in the future.

NOTES

1. For a fuller discussion of this concept, please refer to chapter 10, "The Ongoing Challenge of Hispanic Theology," note 25.
2. See Justo L. González, *Mañana: Christian Theology from a Hispanic Perspective* (Nashville: Abingdon Press, 1990), 28–30.
3. Contrary to what has been perceived by the dominant society, we are not satisfied with these terms. Nonetheless, we use them, not only for the purpose of writing our scholarly works, but most important, as a sign of solidarity as our diverse communities face daunting challenges, marginalization, and oppression. In "Hispanic American Theology and the Bible: Effective Weapon and Faithful Ally," in *We Are a People! Initiatives in Hispanic American Theology*, ed. Roberto S. Goizueta (Minneapolis: Fortress Press, 1992), 26–27, Fernando F. Segovia writes the following: "The issue of nomenclature is complex and should be approached with care, subject to revision. . . . [T]he terms that are usually employed to distinguish this group as a whole within the United States—*Latinos* and *Hispanics*—are not terms the group uses itself, but rather terms that have been applied to the group by the dominant culture of this country. Cf. David T. Abalos, *Latinos in the United States: The Sacred and the Political* (Notre Dame, Ind.: Notre Dame University Press, 1986), 46. In order to be inclusive in regard to both culture and gender, we will alternate the terms "Hispanic American" or "Hispanic" or "Latino and Latina."
4. U.S. Bureau of the Census, *Statistical Abstract of the United States: 1996*, 116th ed. (Washington, D.C.: U.S. Government Printing Office), Table 13 and Table 53, pp. 14, 51. For other related data, please refer to Institute for Puerto Rican Policy, Inc., "Puerto Ricans and Other Latinos in the United States: March 1994," *IPR Datanote on the Puerto Rican Community* 17 (August 1995): 2.
5. *Evangélico/evangélica* is the Spanish translation of "evangelical," which still retains its original meaning of "Protestant." In Latin American countries, one is either *Católico* or *evangélico* (either Catholic or Protestant). The term does not have the specific sociopolitical nuances that exist in the United States. Cf. Loida Martell-Otero, "Women Doing Theology: Una Perspectiva Evangélica," *Apuntes* 14:3 (fall 1994): 69.
6. Our history has been fraught with struggles, from wars of aggression that have robbed people of their lands, to economic aggression that has robbed people of dignified employment. (Goizueta, ed., *We Are a People!* vii.) A good summary of what these battles meant for women is documented by Hedda Garza, *Latinas: Hispanic Women in the United States/The Hispanic Experience in the Americas* (New York: Franklin Watts, 1994). At times even the church has seemed to battle against us. For a historical anthology of the development of the Hispanic American church in tandem with the history of the Hispanic American people in the United States, refer to Antonio M. Stevens Arroyo, ed., *Prophets Denied Honor: An Anthology on the Hispanic Church in the United States* (Maryknoll, N.Y.: Orbis Books, 1980). In 1991, the *Journal of the American Medical Association*, in an emphasis spearheaded by the then Surgeon General, Dr. Antonia Novello, dedicated its January 9 issue to the problems of health care for Hispanics. The studies recorded there underscore the gravity of the health care

situation for the Latino community residing in the United States. With regard to education, Clara E. Rodríguez reports on the phenomenon of "tracking," wherein Hispanic and African American students are discouraged from continuing academic studies or from going to college, and are encouraged to enlist in vocational programs instead. See Clara E. Rodríguez, *Puerto Ricans: Born in the U.S.A.* (Boulder, Colo.: Westview Press, 1989), 132–33. From conversations with the Hispanic young people in her Bronx congregation, Loida Martell-Otero affirms that this practice continues. Many of the young people she spoke to were encouraged to drop out of high school, and take a general equivalency diploma (G.E.D.) instead. This, of course, ensures that these future generations will be employed in low-wage jobs, thus continuing the cycle of poverty and underemployment.

7. Irene I. Blea, *La Chicana and the Intersection of Race, Class and Gender* (Westport, Conn.: Praeger Publishers, 1992); Garza, *Latinas,* passim; Carol Hardy-Fanta, *Gender, Culture, and Political Participation in Boston* (Philadelphia: Temple University Press, 1993); Loida Martell-Otero, "Lifting Voices, Praising Gifts," *Apuntes* 13:3 (fall 1993): 171–79.

8. Abalos, *Latinos,* 8.

9. Please refer to chapter 10, note 25.

10. Eldin Villafañe, *The Liberating Spirit: Toward an Hispanic Pentecostal Social Ethic* (Grand Rapids: Wm. B. Eerdmans Publishing Co., 1993), 1–15. The Rev. Rafael Martell, a pastor in New York City, once described Hispanics as "un pedazo de música andante" (a piece of walking music).

11. Virgilio Elizondo, *Galilean Journey: The Mexican-American Promise* (Maryknoll, N.Y.: Orbis Books, 1983), 32.

12. Villafañe, 41; cf. Abalos, 4.

13. Orlando Espín and others have shown conclusively that the Catholicism which the Spaniards brought to the Americas was not the theological heir of Rome or Trent but of Toledo and Seville. "The Catholicism planted here was *not* the product of Trent. It was an older, medieval version of Catholicism that was responsible for our initial evangelization. . . . Moreover, it was the specifically Iberian strand of medieval Catholicism that came to this side of the Atlantic." See Orlando O. Espín, "Pentecostalism and Popular Catholicism: The Poor and *Traditio,*" *Journal of Hispanic/Latino Theology* 3:2 (November 1995): 20. Cf. Virgilio Elizondo, "Foreword," in *Mañana,* 13. This particular brand of Christianity merged with the worldviews of the Amerindians and Africans to create the biological and religious *mestizaje* which serves as a background for Latino Protestantism. See also Ada María Isasi-Díaz, "'Apuntes' for a Hispanic Women's Theology of Liberation," in *Voces: Voices from the Hispanic Church,* ed. Justo L. González (Nashville: Abingdon Press, 1992), 28–29.

14. Frank Tennenbaum, "Toward an Appreciation of Latin America," in *The United States and Latin America,* ed. Herbert L. Matthews (New York: Columbia University, American Assembly, 1959), 26; as cited in Villafañe, *Liberating Spirit,* 45–46.

15. Loida Martell-Otero, "En las Manos del Señor: Ministry in the Hispanic American Context," *The Apple Seed* 1:1 (winter 1994): 14–20.

1

On Doing Hispanic Theology

José David Rodríguez

In 1993 I participated in the meeting of the Association of Catholic Hispanic Theologians in the United States at Loyola College, in Baltimore. In his presidential address, Fernando F. Segovia shared a moving account of his twenty-year experience as a Hispanic scholar teaching New Testament in this country.[1] He assessed the status of Hispanic Americans and other racial/ethnic minorities in contemporary theological education and scholarship in the United States as a continuous struggle.

> It is my belief, after twenty years in theological education, that the life of a minority person in such a context is indeed *una lucha*—a "struggle." This is so whether one happens to be a student for the ministry, a graduate student, a beginning scholar, or a seasoned professor. The context is a difficult and trying one, largely unreceptive and unsympathetic. Indeed, I often wonder whether anything at all has been achieved in all these years, even in the aftermath of the civil rights and feminist movements.[2]

While Segovia's story of struggle is common in the experience of most Latinas and Latinos, particularly those of us seeking to provide opportunities for leadership development for members of our community in this country, he also shared signs of hope that give us a renewed sense of expectation for the present and the future.[3] Among these positive signs is an increase in the number of Hispanics in theological education and scholarship, which leads to greater access, presence, grounding, and power for members of our community. This increase is complemented by a boost in the impact of the many voices we represent that prevents our being ignored or dismissed summarily as in the past. In the increasing and irreversible globalization that characterizes both our world and theological reflection, our interests and concerns are increasingly becoming the interests and concerns of the vast majority of Christian believers. Finally, our voices and contexts increasingly find their way into learned societies, professional associations, grant foundations, and publishing houses.[4]

In this chapter, I will provide a brief but personal account of my understanding of developments and present trends of the Hispanic theological perspective. Like Segovia, I will speak about the challenges faced by those whose efforts are deepening and further articulating the promising contributions of this perspective. I also want to propose new areas for exploration and anticipate some of the tasks still ahead as we continue our work in confessing our faith from a Hispanic/Latino perspective.

Present Trends in Hispanic Theology

In a 1991 article celebrating the tenth anniversary of *Apuntes*, the journal of Hispanic theology, I analyzed the emergence and specific character of what in the United States has come to be called the "Hispanic/Latino" theological perspective. I showed the relationship of this perspective to Latin American theology. I explored its emphasis on the marginalization to which our community has been subjected by the dominant sectors of society throughout its historical development. I provided examples of the themes examined by this perspective, using *marginality* and *mestizaje* as hermeneutical keys. I also reviewed the efforts of some Latina and Latino theologians to confer doctrinal content to the witness of faith of their community, which continues to experience a deep sense of marginalization and *mestizaje*.[5]

My article was followed by the publication of an increasing number of studies aimed at deepening the examination of this perspective and its promising contribution. While many articles and books have been produced by individual scholars in this area, for the purpose of this chapter I want to briefly comment on the contribution of some important documents that have been generated by a *teología en conjunto*, or collaborative theology.[6]

One of the early examples of this methodological approach was an anthology produced by Antonio Stevens-Arroyo.[7] His goal was to provide a better understanding of the sources and richness of the emerging Hispanic/Latino church in the United States. Sensitive to the diverse nature of this phenomenon, he invited representative leaders of the Hispanic community to provide a powerful witness to the emergence of this important religious expression, offering the reader a profile of its promising contributions, not only for Hispanics but for the church as a whole. In spite of the limitations of the scope and representative nature of this work, it broke new ground in documenting the contribution of the Hispanic perspective in the socioreligious realm of North American society. Stevens-Arroyo wrote:

I wanted to show the different ways Hispanos in the United States have come to affirm both their faith and their cultural identity. . . . In these readings, Hispanos describe the catechetical, liturgical, and pastoral ways in which one can be Catholic and Hispano at the same time. Unfortunately, not every leader is given the attention and the space he or she deserves. Non-Hispano people have not been given much space, nor have Hispano Protestants. Moreover, I have left out many lay persons who, despite their silence, have accomplished more than some of the spokespersons included here.[8]

Another important early contribution was the book edited in 1988 by Ada María Isasi-Díaz and Yolanda Tarango, *Hispanic Women: Prophetic Voice in the Church*. This book began to explore the significant impact of the prophetic voice of Hispanic women for the mission, ministry, and theology of the church.[9] While mostly limited to the experience of a small group of Hispanic women from a Roman Catholic background, the book provided an insightful and unprecedented introductory examination of the religious understandings, motivations, and actions of Hispanic women, as well as a theological articulation of their experiences. The result was a theology that brings together feminist theology, cultural theology, and liberation theology:

Doing theology is a communal process. We do theology because of, for, and with other Hispanic women with whom we participate in the struggle for liberation. Those with whom we engage in the struggle are our primary community of accountability. Therefore, the Hispanic Women's Liberation Theology we begin to elaborate in this book has to be clear to them, make sense to them, be valid for them. . . . Hispanic Women's Liberation Theology also has to make sense to others who stand in solidarity with our struggle for liberation.[10]

In June 1990, at a national conference convened by ACHTUS[11] and the Aquinas Center of Theology[12] at Emory University, Hispanic/Latino theologians gathered to reflect on the challenge of articulating the complex but profound meaning of a people's historical experience and the significance of that experience for theological reflection. Some of the essays presented at the conference were later published in an anthology edited by Roberto Goizueta.[13] This document was an important contribution toward deepening our understanding of the method that grounds the interpretation of Christian ministry and doctrine in the historical experience of the Hispanic/Latino community. In examining the significance of our social location for reading history and bringing that history to bear on our theological method and our understanding of traditional Christian doctrines and Christian ministry, the various authors concluded that, in spite of the complex and conflicting nature of our people's historical experience, we may also become prophetic progenitors of a needed ministry of human reconciliation:

> To be a Hispanic living in the United States is to be a child of conflict, at
> the same time, a prophet of reconciliation. In a world where national borders are becoming increasingly fluid and porous, where communication can
> be virtually instantaneous, where "globalization" is no longer perceived as
> merely an option but as a necessity for the survival of any economic or political enterprise, the U.S. Hispanic stands as a living reminder that, in the
> face of the ever-present conflicts, human reconciliation is not an illusory
> ideal but an attainable goal, not a threat to be feared but a promise to be
> fulfilled. Mestizos, mulatos, heirs to the spiritual wealth of so many cultures, Latinos are the harbingers of a new American reality, where other
> cultures and people will no longer be perceived as threatening American
> identity, but will be welcomed as enriching that identity. If the first five
> hundred years of mestizaje (the experience of racial and cultural mixture)
> were constructed on the backs of millions of victims, or fore fathers and fore
> mothers, the next five hundred years will be constructed on the unquenchable hope that those victims embodied, a hope now bequeathed to their
> children.[14]

Allan Figueroa Deck and other Roman Catholic scholars moved this discussion forward, clarifying the need for Hispanic theologians to pursue the
implications of being a "bridge" within North American culture.[15] For
these scholars there are at least three areas where the bridge character of
Latinas and Latinos might be revealed:

> The first area has to do with the context of modernity, where U.S. Hispanic
> theologians function. The second refers to the distinctive situation of U.S.
> Latinos and their prototypal participation in the elaboration of U.S. Hispanic theology. The third area revolves around the issues of relative importance of different analytical tools of the social sciences and differing
> social science methodologies in the analysis of reality, the first moment in
> liberation methodology.[16]

With the publication of *Voces*[17] in 1992, a more ecumenical but mostly
Protestant approach to these issues was presented. The book is a collection
of articles published in the journal of Hispanic theology *Apuntes*. The goal
of the anthology was to give Hispanics the opportunity to address those
concerns related to their situation and context that, while often ignored, are
of paramount importance for life today:

> Catholics and Protestants address concerns that cut across denominational
> and confessional lines. Women speak of issues and realities that male theologians often ignore or misinterpret. Puerto Ricans, Mexican Americans and

others deal with a number of issues specific to their communities, as well as with others that are relevant to all Hispanics in the United States. Several discuss the urgent issues facing our communities or the world at large such as international migration, racism, ecology, militarism, etc. Others deal with biblical and historical research, with matters of church order and management, with counseling, music, etc.[18]

As in the other documents already mentioned, there was an intentional effort to deal with these issues from the perspective of faith. For that reason, the proposals for a new reading of scripture and history and the new interpretations of traditional doctrines and models of ministry brought a prophetic challenge to the manner in which the church in general and its theology specifically have dealt with these matters. Yet the collective commitment of the authors was to move beyond this challenge to develop a vision of the church's vocation, calling her to repentance and greater faithfulness.

Two other documents need to be added to this list. The first, *Hidden Stories: Unveiling the History of the Latino Church*, edited by Daniel Rodríguez-Díaz and David Cortés-Fuentes, presents the content and proceedings of a national conference gathering Hispanic scholars and church leaders for the study of Latino church history, held in the spring of 1993 in Chicago.[19] The other, *Lumbrera a nuestro camino*, edited by Pablo Jiménez, is a publication of the First Encuentro of Hispanic biblical scholars sponsored by AETH (Association for Hispanic Theological Education) in San Juan, Puerto Rico.[20] The former documents a first attempt at recovering and documenting the history of Latino Protestantism in the United States, Canada, and the Caribbean. The latter provides an introduction to the study and interpretation of the Bible by Latina/Latino scholars.

Continuing Challenges

Significant efforts to improve the content and depth of this Hispanic/Latino theological perspective continue. Yet there are also important challenges facing us in our task of becoming pioneers of a new theological "frontier" in the United States and the Caribbean.[21]

I want to focus on some of the areas that need continued analysis and examination. My goal is not to provide a thorough or exaustive account of these challenges, but to suggest a framework of reference from which we may attempt to continue our reflection. My comments attempt only to stimulate further reflection and show some promising directions to explore, as we try to constructively address these challenges.

Poverty and Marginality as the
Collective Social Identity of Our People

Surely the most important of the challenges we face as we attempt to bring meaning to the social identity and recognition to the contribution of Hispanics in the United States and the Caribbean relates to the fundamental poverty and marginalization of our people, which is reflected in our collective social identity. While this is a fact already established in numerous studies,[22] it remains to be seen whether this poverty and marginalization can be turned into a positive resource for the reconciliation of our community and the society in which we struggle to fulfill our human vocation.[23]

Increasingly, Hispanic scholars agree that the promise of striving for a consciousness of a pan-ethnic identity by this heterogeneous Hispanic population in pursuit of satisfying common economic, political, and religious needs, lies in the future.[24] The experience of conflict and diversity, which also characterizes the reality of our people, aggravates attempts to address this challenge constructively. Thus, for the time being, the poverty and marginalization that characterize the social experience of our people will continue to produce an important challenge for those of us striving to respond to these needs.

A Wholistic Interdisciplinary Perspective

Part of the problem of understanding the complex nature of the collective social identity of our people lies in the need to develop a more adequate perspective to analyze the reality and promise of Hispanics in the United States and the Caribbean. We need to develop a methodological tool of analysis to help us understand the existing relationships between ethnicity, class, race, and other social factors that give meaning and future to our communities. This resource would enable us to clarify and foster the fundamental unity that may lie within the great diversity of our people for developing a Hispanic/Latino sociohistorical project in the United States and the Caribbean. It may also become an important resource for developing a sociohistorical project of greater dimensions that would include our Caribbean and Central American roots, as well as the rest of the rich Latin American experience that constitutes a fundamental component of our heritage and human identity.

This wholistic interdisciplinary analysis may also prove extremely valuable in the critical rereading of our history and traditions. Such a reading may in turn help us imagine a common sociohistorical project going beyond our own community in partnership with other communities with which to share our history and future.

Becoming a "Bridge"

In order to fulfill this task we need to play the role of "bridge" between those sectors of society with whom we share a common quest for human development and fulfillment. Thus I concur with Allan Deck and other scholars in their proposal to conceive this "bridge" character of our vocation as relating to various modern cultural trends and the participation of Hispanic/Latina women and other important sectors of our society and culture in the Americas.[25]

This "bridge" role has been anticipated by Justo L. González. For him, one of the greatest promises of Hispanics in the United States, who understand both North American and Latin American idiosyncrasies, is that of becoming a bridge, a "border people," between the dreams and struggles of the people in the United States and the dreams and struggles of the people in Latin America and the third world. Our mission is to serve as a means of communication between the rich, overaffluent, and misdeveloped world of the North and the poor, exploited, and also misdeveloped world of the South.[26]

The Role of Theological Reflection

This holistic interdisciplinary tool of analysis will need to include theological reflection on the meaning and contribution of the spiritual dimension of our people in developing our sociohistorical project. This theological reflection will attempt to produce a better understanding of the way the challenges we face impact our witness of faith and how our understanding of the gospel might become an important resource in addressing these challenges. Prominent Hispanic theologians have already called our attention to the need to take a new look at scripture and at the entire history of the church and its tradition from a Hispanic/Latino perspective, with the expectation of finding in this witness of faith valuable resources, not only for Hispanics but for other ethnic communities as well.[27]

Popular Religion as an Epistemology
of Hispanic/Latina Reality and Christian Witness

This examination of Christian tradition must be done by intentionally focusing on the experience of Hispanic/Latino popular religion. Here lies what I believe to be the most important and promising contribution of Hispanic theology in participating in an interdisciplinary collaborative reflection for the advancement of a Hispanic sociohistorical project for our people. Like Orlando Espín and other Hispanic scholars in the United States, the Caribbean, and Latin America, I am convinced that popular religion is one of the fundamental ways through which our community understands its sociohistorical reality. It is also a medium through which our people have been able to endure and provide a significant and promising response to the challenges posed by that reality.

The numerous difficulties and shortcomings characteristic of Hispanic popular religiosity should be examined and addressed. But I am of the mind of an increasing number of Latina and Latino scholars, both Roman Catholic and Protestant, who are beginning to challenge the uncritically assumed premises of the "mainstream" academy in the interpretation of popular religion and who call for a new examination of Hispanic popular religion as a Hispanic "epistemology" of reality.[28]

Confessing the Faith in Spanish

I have argued that by following Justo González's challenge to read the scriptures in Spanish we can also confess our faith from a Hispanic/Latino perspective. This confession of faith will challenge us to recover not only some foundational dimensions of our sociohistorical reality that give meaning to our identity as a people but also some basic elements of our witness of faith that have made possible our survival under strenuous and difficult circumstances. I believe that Hispanic Protestant popular religion challenges representatives of mainline Protestant bodies who insist on the "proper confessional stand" of Latino and Latina church leaders and community to go beyond the theology of the confessional documents of these bodies (articulated during the sixteenth century and in later centuries) to the act of confession characteristic of these documents and of the historical experience of Christianity, to find a more adequate witness to the gospel for the present. The recovery of these elements of faith that are so important for the affirmation of the dignity and human fulfillment of our people will be a contribution from our community to the church at large and its continuous need for the renewal of its understanding and confession of the gospel.[29]

The Task Ahead

One of the goals of the First Encuentro on Theology and Ethics sponsored by AETH in 1995 was to provide the opportunity for Hispanic theologians and ethicists to meet for reflection and collegial support of our efforts to enhance the theological educational resources for the ministry and witness of the Hispanic or Latino community in the United States, Canada, and Puerto Rico. Another important goal was to engage in a collegial and disciplined reflection on how we can provide resources, not only for our community but also for the church as a whole in its efforts to witness to this faith with relevance and commitment, as we seek to respond to the needs and challenges of the present.

Planners of the Encuentro decided to invite distinguished and promising Hispanic theologians and ethicists to reflect on central teachings of the Christian faith. Their papers initiated a discussion about developing a Hispanic/Latino approach for the examination of these topics. During the meeting their proposals were discussed and further clarified to deepen the reflection on these topics and allow for a *reflexión teológica en conjunto* (a collaborative theological reflection). As we begin exploring these topics, let us keep in mind what Justo L. González warned was one of the greatest challenges for Hispanic theology:

> Professional theology is by nature elitist and therefore classist. . . . No matter how much we may regret it, most of what has been published . . . is elitist. . . . On the other hand, we claim to be speaking of things which God has hidden from the wise and understanding and revealed to babes (Lk 10:21). . . . But we, who are so wise and understanding that we know better than God, have now managed to express them in such a way that they are hidden from any but those who have the most understanding and most schooling!
>
> This is probably the greatest and most difficult challenge of the next decade—indeed of the next millennium. Will we learn to listen to the wisdom of babes, of the uneducated Salvadorean refugee, of the old man who sits quietly on a pew in our church? And will we learn to translate our speech in such a way that in it the freeing gospel of Jesus Christ may be heard by the least of God's babes? We have shown that we can do theology with the "best" and the "great"; will we be able to do it with the least and the last who are God's first?[30]

My hope is that as we carry out our individual and collective tasks, we may all do our best to try to respond to this challenge affirmatively.

NOTES

1. See Fernando F. Segovia, "Theological Education and Scholarship as Struggle: The Life of Racial/Ethnic Minorities in the Profession," *Journal of Hispanic/Latino Theology* 2:2 (November 1994): 2–25.
2. Ibid., 8–9. Segovia suggests seeing Ada María Isasi-Díaz, *En la Lucha/In the Struggle: Elaborating a Mujerista Theology* (Minneapolis: Fortress Press, 1993), esp. 11–33 (chapter 1: "Hispanic Ethnicity and Social Locality in *Mujerista* Theology"), for a better understanding of the notion of *lucha*, or "struggle," as a fundamental category in Hispanic American theology. "For her *la lucha* has to do with survival on the part of Hispanic women in the face of multiple oppression as poor

(economic), as Hispanic (cultural), and as women (gender); such survival is further described as a constant struggle 'to be fully,' a state of being involving self-identity as well as self-determination" (p. 8).

3. While Segovia appears to give a pessimistic picture of the past, present, and future status of Hispanic and other racial/ethnic minorities in theological education and scholarship, he does provide a basic strategy for struggling to transform this situation: "I do not mean to sound overly pessimistic; I only want to be brutally realistic so we can be properly equipped, both in terms of vision and strategy, for the struggle. Indeed, I would immediately add that the dream that guides and informs our resolve to struggle is more than a dream . . . change does take place, has taken place, and is taking place right before our eyes." Ibid., 23–24.

4. Ibid., 24.

5. José D. Rodríguez, "De 'apuntes' a 'esbozo': Diez años de reflexión," *Apuntes* 10:3 (winter 1990): 75–83.

6. This term refers to the contribution of intellectuals organically rooted in their communities and working in collegiality with other Hispanic theologians in their efforts to bring meaning and public hearing to the faith of their community. Roberto Goizueta, ed., *We Are a People! Initiatives in Hispanic American Theology* (Minneapolis: Fortress Press, 1992), ix. Justo L. González describes this approach as the Fuenteovejuna style of theology: "This is a contribution that Hispanics can bring to theology. . . . Ours is not a tradition that values individualism, as does that of the North Atlantic. Indeed ours is a language that does not even have a word for that 'privacy' which the dominant North American culture so values. Coming out of that tradition, our theology will result from a constant dialogue among the entire community. . . . It will not be a theology of theologians but a theology of the believing and practicing community." Justo L. González, *Mañana: Christian Theology from a Hispanic Perspective* (Nashville: Abingdon Press, 1990), 29–30.

7. Antonio M. Stevens-Arroyo, ed., *Prophets Denied Honor: An Anthology of the Hispanic Church in the United States* (Maryknoll, N.Y.: Orbis Books, 1980).

8. Ibid., xv.

9. Ada María Isasi-Díaz and Yolanda Tarango, *Hispanic Women: Prophetic Voice in the Church* (San Francisco: Harper & Row, 1988).

10. Ibid., ix.

11. The Academy of Catholic Hispanic Theologians of the United States. For a brief history of the origins and contributions of this organization, see Allan Figueroa Deck, *Frontiers of Hispanic Theology in the United States* (Maryknoll, N.Y.: Orbis Books, 1992), 21–24.

12. A center for Roman Catholic studies at Emory University.

13. Goizueta, *We Are a People*. See n. 6 above.

14. Ibid., viii.

15. See Deck, *Frontiers*. "Here one sees a clear element of contrast with Latin American theology. It is the bridge or dialogical nature of U.S. Hispanic theology that seems to set it apart from mainstream U.S. theology, from mainstream feminist theology, and perhaps even from black theology." Ibid., xv.

16. Ibid. The articles in the book provide an examination of these areas by Hispanic theologians.
17. *Voces: Voices from the Hispanic Church*, ed. Justo L. González (Nashville: Abingdon Press, 1992).
18. Ibid., vii.
19. Daniel Rodríguez-Díaz and David Cortés-Fuentes, eds., *Hidden Stories: Unveiling the History of the Latino Church* (Decatur, Ga.: Asociación para la Educación Teológica Hispana, 1994).
20. Pablo Jiménez, ed., *Lumbrera a nuestro camino* (Miami: Editorial Caribe, 1994).
21. José D. Rodríguez, "Hispanic Theology's Foundational Challenges," in *Hidden Stories*, ed. Rodríguez-Diaz and Cortés-Fuentes, 125–29. The notion of being pioneers of a new theological "frontier" is taken from Deck's introduction to *Frontiers*, ix.
22. While there is abundant literature in English about this subject, one of the most important publications in Spanish that tries to bring a global analysis to this subject is Rodolfo J. Cortina and Alberto Moncada, eds., *Hispanos en los Estados Unidos* (Madrid: Ediciones de Cultura Hispánica, Instituto de Cooperación Iberoamericana, 1988).
23. The negative impact of Proposition 187 for undocumented persons in the state of California, with the significant support given to this proposal by Hispanic U.S. citizens, is an instance of the ambiguous and controversial effect of poverty and marginalization on our Hispanic/Latino people.
24. Alejandro Portes and Cynthia Truelove, two of the most distinguished Hispanic social scientists in this country, argue that Hispanics in the United States, rather than constituting a consolidated minority, are a group whose boundaries and self-definition are in a state of continuous change. See Alejandro Portes and Cynthia Truelove, "El sentido de la diversidad: recientes investigaciones sobre las minorías hispanas en los Estados Unidos," in *Hispanos*, ed. Cortina and Moncada, 31–51. This is one of the best studies of this issue, and it includes rich bibliographical resources for further examination of this topic.
25. For a more detailed elaboration of this topic, see Deck, *Frontiers*.
26. Justo L. González, "Hacia un redescubrimiento de nuestra missión," *Apuntes* 7 (fall 1987): 51–60.
27. This is one of the most exciting and fundamental claims made by Justo L. González as he expressed the goals and commitment of Hispanic theology in the United States and the Caribbean in his article in the first issue of *Apuntes*. Justo L. González, "Prophets in the King's Sanctuary," *Apuntes* 1:1 (spring 1981): 3–6.
28. One of the most prominent scholars in this area of research is Orlando Espín. For one of his best articles on this subject, see Orlando Espín, "Popular Religion as an Epistemology (of Suffering)," *Journal of Hispanic/Latino Theology* 2:2 (November 1994): 55–78.
29. José D. Rodríguez, "Confessing Our Faith in Spanish: Challenge or Promise?" in *Hispanic Theology: Challenge and Promise*, ed. Ada María Isasi-Díaz and Fernando F. Segovia (Minneapolis: Fortress Press, 1996), 183–97.
30. Justo L. González, "The Next Ten Years," in his *Voces*, 170–71.

2

Love in the Crossroads

Stepping-Stones to a Doctrine of God in Hispanic/Latino Theology

Teresa Chavez Sauceda

One of the foundational claims of North American Hispanic/Latino theology is that all theology is contextual. Our knowledge and understanding of who God is and how God acts is filtered through multiple lenses of language, culture, history, socioeconomic status, religious tradition, and faith experience. Thus, the theological task of reflection on the nature of God begins with a reexamination of our own self-understandings of the social location that shapes our efforts.

Latina and Latino theologians also engage in the process of self-examination and theological reflection with a set of shared commitments that function as a set of operating guidelines for the development of this theology. First is the commitment to engaging in a faith praxis of liberation, a commitment to speaking from the margins of U.S. society, to giving voice to the perspective and experience of the Latino community. Second, Hispanic theologians are committed to honoring the ethnic, socioeconomic, and religious diversity of the Latino community of faith in the context of a growing sense of unity and shared identity among Latino peoples. Third, Hispanic/Latino theology is a communal theology. While there is a lively, ongoing methodological discussion about the relationship between the "professional theologian," who works in the academy, and the Latino community of faith, there is a common understanding that the source of Hispanic theology is the faith praxis or lived experience of the Latino community of faith. This also extends to a commitment among the "professional theologians" to work as a community. Thus, Hispanic theology is fundamentally a dynamic, unifying dialogue, a *teología en conjunto*, a "new ecumenism" of Roman Catholic, Protestant, and Pentecostal.

The Hispanic/Latino community is a marginalized and, in many ways, invisible community in the United States. Despite population figures that show the Hispanic community well on its way to being the largest racial/ethnic subgroup in the United States, Hispanics continue to face a complex web of ethnocentrism, racism, classism, and sexism which keeps them on the periphery of U.S. society. This marginalization impacts all aspects of life: economic, political, social, cultural, and religious. While these factors cannot be separated or isolated from one another, the issue of racism and the tension between race and ethnicity has emerged as a critical point of reflection for Hispanic theologians.

Latino people typically identify themselves in ethnic terms, as Cuban, Puerto Rican, or Mexican American. Yet in U.S. society Latinas and Latinos are generally perceived and treated as one broadly homogeneous racial group. They often describe their experience of oppression and marginalization in the United States in terms of race and racism. It is a reality that crosses class and gender lines, whether one's first language is English or Spanish, whether one is a first-generation immigrant or fourth-generation U.S. native.

Racism permeates our daily lives and is institutionalized in the social structures of our society. The church is not exempt as a social institution. Both Virgilio Elizondo and Justo González cite personal experiences as well as the statistical absence of Hispanic women and men in leadership at the upper levels of their denominations as evidence of the racism within. Latina and Latino Roman Catholics are not only questioning the limited presence of Latinas and Latinos in official positions of leadership in their church, they are asserting the legitimacy of their cultural heritage, their expressions of popular religious faith practices that have been shunned by the North American church. For mainline, historic Protestant churches in the United States, stagnating membership rolls in Spanish-speaking congregations force Hispanic theologians to ask similar questions about their denomination's stated commitments to inclusivity and diversity.

It is far easier, in the words of Elizondo,

> to cross the legal boundary between Mexico and the United States than to cross through many of the long-established and deeply entrenched sociocultural borders that very effectively maintain a segregated existence. It is far easier to pass laws of desegregation than to create a desegregated culture. And today, the culture of segregation still reigns throughout the Americas: in the United States, in Latin America, and in my own city of San Antonio.[1]

The culture of segregation also means a life of poverty for a large majority of Latinas and Latinos. With poverty come the incumbent ills of inadequate education, poor health care, inadequate housing, high unemployment, and a future with little hope of anything better. The culture of segregation makes it easy to blame the poor for their condition, but Hispanic theologians maintain that the connection between being Latina or Latino and being poor is not strictly coincidental, nor do they accept the notion that poverty stems from some cultural or moral failure on the part of the poor.

For Latinas and Latinos, the experience of racism is inextricably linked with sexism. As Ada María Isasi-Díaz has argued, gender oppression may be a universal experience among women, but its particular forms and expressions vary with history, culture, and socioeconomic status. While Hispanic women confront the sexism within their own cultures as well as the sexism of the dominant culture, the reality of racism and ethnic prejudice they experience as Latinas influences their perceptions and their goals. For example, for Latinas and Latinos, helping their families to survive poverty and cultural exclusion is seen as essential to their own survival and the survival of their community. "Therefore," Isasi-Díaz asserts, "we are not willing to accept fully the Anglo feminist understanding of the family as the center of women's oppression."[2]

Hispanic theologians have begun to challenge the assumptions of cultural superiority in the dominant culture as an expression of the perception of racial superiority, assumptions that have become embedded and perpetuated in the social structures of our society. At the same time, those cultural norms and values which nurture and strengthen who we are as a community have taken on new meaning as a means of resistance. As second-, third-, and fourth-generation Latinas and Latinos seek to rediscover their cultural roots, Hispanic theologians assert that the loss of ethnic identity and culture is too high a price to pay for full participation in the social, economic, and political life of the United States.

As Hispanic theologians reflect on this particular confluence of culture, history, and social locality, and the contribution that their particular cultural perspective and experience brings to the theological task of reinterpreting our understanding of who God is, there are two major areas in which Hispanic theologians are making contributions that challenge traditional Western/Eurocentric understandings of God. These categories are the doctrine of creation and the doctrine of the Trinity.

Justo González lays the foundation for developing a doctrine of God in a chapter of *Mañana* titled "Let the Dead Gods Bury Their Dead."[3] Tracing the development of Christian doctrine from the first efforts of the early church to interpret the gospel to the Greco-Roman world, through the onset of Constantinianism, to its manifestations in the church today, González identifies the immutable, impassible, changeless God of Western tradition as the product of the importation of philosophical language and logic to define God, which has resulted in a god who functions as an idol for a static social order, a preserver of the status quo.

Scripture does not reveal God to us through definitive statements of who or what God is. Instead, scripture reveals God to us "in relation to a creation and a people."[4] God is revealed as God acts in creation and redemption, and ultimately, through the incarnation. Thus, it is the incarnation, González claims, which should be the basis of our doctrine of God. In so doing, González rejects the notion of the incarnation as a "last minute remedy for human sin," understanding it instead as "the very goal of creation."[5]

Hispanic/Latino theology critiques the traditional doctrine of God through the lens of oppression. Like its Latin American counterpart, this critique suggests that idolatry is a greater danger than atheism. Idols have socioeconomic consequences. Idols are used "to serve the interests of those who profit from it."[6] González suggests that the social structure most like the omnipresent, omnipotent, omniscient God of traditional theology is the transnational corporation. Those who contend that what is wrong in the church and in our society today is that we have turned away from this God are not seeking a biblical movement of spiritual renewal. They seek the preservation of an oppressive status quo. Similarly, Elizondo, using the experience of *mestizaje* as a hermeneutical key, exposes the idolatry of efforts to preserve racial purity as another means of attempting to maintain the status quo, which depends on a static understanding of God and creation.

The Trinity

The doctrine of the Trinity, which most Christians hold to be central to Christian belief, is a doctrine that many find confusing. Reviewing the history of creedal debates, González argues that the problem lies in the attempt to reconcile an absolute, immutable God who cannot therefore relate or communicate directly with a mutable world, with the God of scripture who loves and acts in and through history. We need to clear away, he argues, the "stale metaphysical language in which [the doctrine of the Trinity] has been couched," and affirm "belief in a God whose essence is sharing."[7]

In response to the traditional efforts to define or explain the "paradox" of the Trinity, González suggests that perhaps we need to ask a different question. The internal workings of God within God's self are a mystery we cannot know. What we can discern and understand is "God's revelation and relations with the world." Thus the question to be asked is, What are the socioeconomic consequences of the doctrine of the Trinity? In response to this question, González cites a number of fourth-century theologians who denounced private property and the accumulation of wealth as contrary to the laws of God. These same theologians were also among the strongest defenders of the doctrine of the Trinity. What might be the connection?

González maintains that the economic views of these fourth-generation theologians reflect their understanding of the Trinity. For Tertullian, who first used the classic formulation "one substance and three persons," the Trinity "is the doctrine of a god whose life is a life of sharing." Noting that Tertullian has been criticized in the tradition for using legal, rather than metaphysical terms, González suggests that perhaps Tertullian should instead be commended. "What Tertullian is saying," he continues, "is that the one God exists according to an inner order, and that this order is best understood in terms of the sharing of a *substancia*—which in the legal terminology of that time could mean 'property'—by three persons."[8]

Orlando Espín describes this internal relationship of the Trinity as "an eternal community of love."[9] Sixto Garcia, citing both fourth-century theologian Gregory of Nazianzus and contemporary theologian Walter Kasper, describes the relationship of the Trinity as "the interpenetration (without confusion) of the three persons" which constitutes a "dialogue of love, which supports both diversity and unity, or better yet, the diversity in the unity."[10] This understanding of the Trinity expresses the identity of God. God is love (1 John 4:16). Espín asserts, "The very essence of divinity is love and, as a consequence, there is nothing God can be or do that is not loving. . . . God is love without limits, without exceptions, without conditions, and eternally."[11] God is the "One who lives as Three," whose divine reality is sharing—sharing love, sharing power.[12]

The significance of this "relational and dialogical reality" of the Trinity, as González concludes, is in its meaning for Christian discipleship and ecclesiology. "The commonality that exists within the Trinity is the pattern and goal of creation," he asserts, and "is therefore the example that those who believe in the Trinity are called to follow." In the words of the Tanzanian Roman Catholic bishop Christopher Mwoleka, the Trinity is not "a puzzle to be solved," but rather "an example to be imitated."[13]

The example that the Trinity offers for us to imitate is that of forotherness, the sharing love of God. "For if God is love," González maintains,

> life without love is life without God; and if this is a sharing love, such as we see in the Trinity, then life without sharing is life without God; and if this sharing is such that in God the three persons are equal in power, then life without such power sharing is life without God.[14]

It is the sharing love of God which is revealed in Jesus. "God is love" not only means "that God loves Godself within the divine Trinity," González asserts, but it "also means that God is being-for-the-world." Indeed, González maintains, "the central point of the incarnation" is that "divine and human are not two opposite poles. . . . Actually, it is precisely in his being for others that Jesus manifests his full divinity, and it is also in his being for others that he manifests his full humanity."[15]

Sharing Love and Sharing Power

The sharing love of the Trinity is inextricably linked with the shared power of the "Three who live as One." As a model for human relationships this connection between love and power has far-reaching implications. Aída Besançon Spencer proposes an understanding of shared power as fundamental to our being human in her exegetical study on the role of women in the church, *Beyond the Curse*.[16] She argues that the creation story reveals that God's intention is for women and men, created together in the image of God, to share in both the responsibility and authority of stewardship. The power accorded them by God is a shared power. Moreover, it is the power and authority of love, to care for, to nurture and sustain, not to exploit, the blessings of creation.

The introduction of power conflicts between men and women, and the subordination of women, Spencer argues, are the consequence of sin. God's intention for humanity and the vision of God's reign are embodied in the ministry of Jesus. Jesus ignores the artificial barriers created between women and men by the social customs of his day. Women are included among his disciples, admittedly on the margins, not among the Twelve. Women are among the first to recognize and give witness to Jesus as the Messiah. Women continue to be found in leadership roles in the early church. The church, argues Spencer, ought to live "beyond the curse," to embody the vision of shared power and mutual responsibility which is God's intention for humanity.

While Spencer's study is focused on the question of women's leadership in the church, the biblical paradigm of shared power found in the story of Adam and Eve has implications for all human relationships. As González observes, "the married couple exemplified in the story of Adam and Eve is just one of many ways in which humans fulfill one another." The story of Adam and Eve, created as male and female in the image of God, reveals that "'man' is not complete by himself. . . . To be fully human is to be for others, and therefore God's human creature is not complete until there is another to be for."

There is no disparity in power, no subjection of one by the other, until sin enters the story. "It is significant," González observes, "that the man is quick to assert this power resulting from sin. . . . From the very beginning of life after sin, the man uses his power to subject and dehumanize the woman. But in so doing he dehumanizes himself." The "intended for-otherness" of man and woman, "based on their being 'fit' for each other, . . . is now disrupted."[17]

Created out of God's for-otherness, our humanity is expressed in our own for-otherness "for God as well as for creation and for other human beings," González asserts. Thus, he concludes, "sin is the violation of God's image in us, which is precisely the image of God's for-otherness." The alienation we experience between ourselves and God, between each other as human beings, is not simply the result of the absence of love or the emotional distance created by inherent differences (e.g., divine/human, male/female, rich/poor). Alienation, so central to the human condition, is the consequence of sin, the violation of our for-otherness, "wrongful dominance and the thirst for it."[18]

Power is neither something to be grasped, in order to exercise dominance over another, nor something to be shunned, as a way to evade responsibility for another. It is precisely because we are created as beings-for-others that the use of power has social consequences. The violation of our for-otherness in the use of power gives birth to "societies of dominance," to oppression and exploitation, to social structures of sin. Similarly, the call to imitate God's sharing love has social implications. As González observes, the institutional church and Western society have tended to privatize and sexualize sin, so much so that for many people in our society the word "sin" is almost exclusively related to sexual improprieties. Yet a thorough reading of scripture would find that "the texts which seek to limit and regulate property rights" far outweigh "the texts which seek to regulate sexual practice."[19]

The implications of imitating God's for-otherness in our societal and ecclesiastical life go far beyond the redistribution of private property, although that alone would be a radical enough project to keep the church busy for generations. Giving witness to God's presence among us through the imitation of God's sharing power and sharing love suggests that the church ought to envision and embody human structures built on relationships of mutuality and social structures that empower the powerless.

The concept of shared power calls into question the legitimacy of all hierarchical structures of power. Adam and Eve are given dominion over creation, but with that power comes the responsibility to be stewards, that is, caretakers of creation. Failure to uphold this responsibility results in wrongful dominance and injustice, creating excessive wealth for a few, poverty and hunger for the many. If in any arena (social, political, or economic) the disparate distribution of power might be conceived as just, it must be recognized that with power comes responsibility.

Creation

"God is love" is the fundamental affirmation of Christian faith and the basis for developing a doctrine of creation in Hispanic/Latino theology, as well as the doctrine of the Trinity. "God's for otherness," González asserts, "is such that this is the reason why the world and humankind were made." Or as Espín states, "Creation exists as the first sacrament of God's love and life, and as the first other that God loves."[20] González notes two consequences to this affirmation. One is the goodness of God's creation, which includes humankind. The second is that "God and creation are two distinct realities."[21] God the Creator exists apart from creation, and all of creation exists equally under the dominion of God. Anything that is a part of creation is not God. Yet, as the living, loving Creator God, God's role in creation is ongoing and dynamic, not indifferent, static, or occasional.

Using the experience of *mestizaje* as a hermeneutical key, Elizondo affirms the diversity of peoples and cultures in the world as part of the goodness of creation, even a sign of God's blessing on creation. Thus, he argues, "God created us that even in our differences we might enrich one another. Linguistic, racial, and cultural differences are not meant to be a source of division, but elements of a universal harmony."[22] The seeming unavoidable tendency in human nature to divide people on the basis of difference, to derive some kind of superiority or power of one group over another, to establish borders and boundaries that separate and exclude one group from another contradicts the universality of God's love.

Elizondo defines *mestizaje* as "the process through which two totally different peoples mix biologically and culturally so that a new people begins to emerge."[23] In segregated societies, where people are divided by race or culture, the mestizo or mestiza becomes particularly vulnerable, rejected on all sides, invisible, a non-being. Elizondo finds in the *mestizaje* of Jesus "the rejected one who becomes the source of solidarity among the rejected of society."

In the incarnation, not only does God choose to become human as one of us, but human as one of the poorest, the weakest, the most marginalized of human society. A Jew from Galilee, living under Roman rule, at minimum Jesus was part of a cultural and linguistic *mestizaje*. Elizondo also notes that to Jesus' contemporaries, his birth and parentage were suspect; many undoubtedly assumed he had a Roman father. Jesus, as the incarnation of Love, breaks all human boundaries. Jesus transcends difference. Pointing to Jesus' own words, Elizondo concludes, Jesus came as a mestizo, "that all might be one." Jesus reveals what Elizondo calls God's "universalizing love."[24] The new *mestizaje*, the *mestizaje* of inclusion, redefines the mestizo or mestiza, not as outsider, or outsider/insider, but as one who is "fully both" and "exclusively neither," an insider/insider.[25]

Efforts to establish, maintain, or preserve racial, ethnic, or national purity are among the most insidious forms of this very human tendency to create boundaries. Such efforts usually hold up the image of some idealized past (usually mythical, for true racial purity has rarely existed) as the perfection of God's intention for humanity. In so doing, they deny the goodness of God's creation, the humanity of those who are different, and set a vision of their own making above creation. In essence, they make an idol of themselves, or their idealized vision of themselves. The imposition of rigid, socially defined gender roles as being the will of God, and the associated supposition of gender superiority, function in much the same way. Such views assume a static understanding of creation. González states that

> creation, properly understood, is not something that took place sometime in the past . . . and that now is a matter of antiquarian curiosity or fanatical orthodoxy. Creation has to do both with the beginning and with the continued existence of heaven and earth. One should not suppose that God was Creator only in the beginning and has now relinquished that role in favor of Sustainer. Creation subsists, even now, because God has called it and continues calling it out of nothingness into being. Without the sustaining and creating Word of God, heaven and earth would not subsist for an instant. The doctrine of creation, therefore, is not merely a statement about origins; it is also and foremost a statement about present reality and present responsibility.[26]

The Living God who is active in creation is the God whose love is universalizing. The unity and harmony of God's love is found not in excluding difference but in embracing difference, even celebrating difference, imitating the mutual sharing love of the Triune God. Elizondo points to the model of Jesus in table fellowship. "By freely eating with everyone, [Jesus] breaks and challenges all the social taboos that keep people apart." Elizondo suggests that it was Jesus' "unquestioned joy of table fellowship with everyone and anyone" which was so revolutionary and so threatening to the established power structures, and that this revolutionary table fellowship "so scandalized all the good and religious people of his times" that his journey to the cross was hastened.[27] The goal of the new *mestizaje* is not a homogenization of humanity but a unity of the human family symbolized in the table fellowship of Jesus.[28]

This point cannot be overemphasized, and it may perhaps be the greatest risk in using the metaphor of *mestizaje*. To define *mestizaje* as "fully both and exclusively neither" implies in the definition that there are two distinct realities that exist on their own. Between those two realities, rather than building a wall that cannot be surmounted or a gap that cannot be bridged, *mestizaje* creates a new social space in which the mestiza/mestizo can move freely, openly, with a kind of dual cultural citizenship. In the words of poet-philosopher Gloria Anzaldua, who has written of the pain and the ambivalence of the mestiza, as well as the hope:

> To survive in the Borderlands
> you must live *sin fronteras*
> be a crossroads.[29]

This new space may blur the distinctions between the two original realities, but it does not obliterate them. Instead of being divided and separate, there is a linkage, an open channel that connects them in a mutual relationship of dialogue. This dimension of mutual dialogue between differences is critical to the understanding of *mestizaje*, if it is not to become simply another way of promoting sameness as somehow better or superior to difference.

Related to these comments on *mestizaje* and creation is a comment by González on the current debate about evolution. "The ultimate rule of creation is the victory of love," González asserts, not the Darwinian survival of the fittest. "Hispanics must denounce the simplistic evolutionary schemes that so often pass for science," González argues, "because they have gone beyond the point of biological theory and have become the justification of social policy." The theological understanding of *mestizaje* is not about social Darwinism, but about creating a society that is truly inclusive, truly just.

Both the doctrine of the Trinity and the doctrine of creation in Hispanic/Latino theology, in emphasizing the loving, sharing essence of God, recover for Christian faith and praxis the centrality of justice as the embodiment of love. Hispanic theology challenges the trend toward privatization of spirituality in U.S. society. God's radical call to imitate the being-for-otherness of God is a call not only to be in relationship with God but to participate in the community of love, in the life of the Spirit and to be engaged in the struggle for justice and liberation.

For future development of the doctrine of God in Hispanic theology, I want to make two recommendations. The first is that as the community of faith seeks to imitate the mutuality of the One God who lives as Three, we need to ask, Where the are the feminine faces of God and where are the feminine voices in the family of God? We must acknowledge the church's complicity in perpetuating and legitimizing the oppression of women within our own cultures as well as in the dominant culture. At the same time, we need to open our language and imagery for God and to refuse to allow our understanding of God to be diminished by the limitations of our own prejudices. We should continue to explore the images of God expressed in popular religion and, from a Protestant perspective particularly, ask ourselves, What elements of indigenous religious expression have been lost? What has survived? Are there elements that, if they can be recovered, would enrich or strengthen the praxis of the faith community?

Second, we should begin to develop an economy of the Trinity. What are the implications of imitating the shared love and shared power of God in the socioeconomic and political life of our congregations, our community, and our society? What might an economic system based on the norms of mutuality and inclusivity look like? How should our political life be structured in order to truly empower full participation rather than limiting it? What kinds of concrete steps might we begin to take toward living the hope of God's reign?

NOTES

1. Virgilio Elizondo, *The Future Is Mestizo: Life Where Cultures Meet* (Bloomington, Ind.: Meyer Stone, 1988), 47.
2. Ada María Isasi-Díaz, *En la Lucha/In the Struggle: Elaborating a Mujerista Theology* (Minneapolis: Fortress Press, 1993), 19.

3. Justo L. González, *Mañana: Christian Theology from a Hispanic Perspective* (Nashville: Abingdon Press, 1990), 89–100.

4. Ibid., 92.

5. Ibid., 91.

6. Ibid., 100.

7. Ibid., 115.

8. Ibid., 112–14.

9. Orlando O. Espín, "Grace and Humanness: A Hispanic Perspective," in *We Are a People! Initiatives in Hispanic American Theology*, ed. Roberto S. Goizueta (Minneapolis: Fortress Press, 1992), 137.

10. Sixto J. Garcia, "A Hispanic Approach to Trinitarian Theology: The Dynamics of Celebration, Reflection, and Praxis," in *We Are a People!* ed. Goizueta, 108–9. See also "United States Hispanic and Mainstream Trinitarian Theologies," in *Frontiers of Hispanic Theology in the United States*, ed. Allan Figueroa Deck (Maryknoll, N.Y.: Orbis Books, 1992), 88–103.

11. Espín, "Grace," 136–37.

12. Ibid., 115.

13. Quoted in González, *Mañana*, 113.

14. Ibid., 115.

15. Ibid., 152–53.

16. Aída Besançon Spencer, *Beyond the Curse: Women Called to Ministry* (Nashville: Thomas Nelson Publishers, 1985).

17. González, *Mañana*, 132–34.

18. Ibid., 136–37.

19. Ibid., 135.

20. Espín, "Grace," 137.

21. González, *Mañana*, 118–19.

22. Elizondo, *Future Is Mestizo*, 81.

23. Ibid., 17 note.

24. Ibid., 82–83.

25. Ibid., 26.

26. González, *Mañana*, 123.

27. Elizondo, *Future Is Mestizo*, 82–83.

28. Ibid., 108–11.

29. From Gloria Anzaldua, *Borderlands/La Frontera: The New Mestiza* (San Francisco: Spinsters/Aunt Lute Book Co., 1987), 195. (*Sin fronteras* = "without borders.")

3

In Memory of Me
Hispanic/Latino Christology beyond Borders

Eliseo Pérez Álvarez

It takes nine months to make bread . . .
Wheat is sown in November and reaped and threshed in July . . .
It also takes nine months for the grapes to ripen,
from March to November . . .
It took the same time to make a man.

Ignazio Silone[1]

In this examination of the doctrine of Christ, I will discuss some important dimensions of the Christology that is emerging from the Protestant Hispanic/Latino perspective in the United States. I will focus on the Eucharist because it is my conviction that this sacrament provides a meaningful correlation between the life and ministry of Jesus Christ and our Hispanic/Latino experience.

The Eucharist is the sacrament in which in a very significant way we meet and are called to follow Jesus Christ. The host of this table gathering, having himself experienced many situations characteristic of the mestizo people—such as the crossing of linguistic, cultural, gender, and national borders—addresses us today in radical and significant ways. First, he calls us to build community through the exercise of memory. As we respond to Christ's imperative, "Do this in remembrance of me . . .," our remembrance of the eucharistic practice connects us with God's remnant in history (the Poor of Yahweh), who continue to witness to the liberating power of God's reign among us. As Hispanic/Latino people with our more oral than written memory, our more social than individualistic memory, and our more joyful than gloomy memory, we come to the awareness that by remembering we become a people.

Second, Jesus Christ challenges us to become a border people as well as a community of love and solidarity. To be a border people means to be in a position of tension with respect to the dominant sectors of society. The goal of being a border people is to seek, following Jesus' example, to overcome those geographical, sociological, cultural, and other limitations that deny God's love as it was manifested in the event of Christ. To be a community of love and solidarity is to be connected to a community that practices sharing as an act of love, for the sake of a more human and just society.

Third, he promises a new reality of justice and human fulfillment. From a Protestant Hispanic/Latino perspective, participation in the Eucharist anticipates overcoming the powers that are the present cause of the suffering and death of our people. Viewed from the perspective of the resurrection, the Eucharist becomes the promise that the social prejudice and injustice to which our people are currently subjected will be transformed into an order of justice and human fulfillment already anticipated in Jesus Christ's presence and ministry among us.

I hope this brief discussion of the Christology emerging from the Protestant Hispanic/Latino perspective in the United States will contribute toward strengthening our understanding and commitment to the witness of faith of the Christian community as a whole.

The Memory of Liberation:
Scripture and Culture

It goes without saying that the Eucharist is related to the commemoration of the Israelites' liberation from the yoke of Egypt. In many ways, the Passover was the national celebration of 430 years of independence from political domination. Jesus Christ reinterpreted the Passover, broadening and deepening its horizon. While the Jewish celebration took place first at the temple with the sacrifice, and then at home with an elaborate family meal ceremony,[2] the emphasis Jesus gave to the Last Supper with his followers focused on the bread and wine, as the broken body of Jesus Christ (Luke 22:7ff.), a symbol of his preferential but not exclusive option for the poor and downtrodden of his society.

In his life and ministry Jesus of Nazareth became the new liberator who brought down the divisive walls among people that had been established throughout history. One of the many barriers that he brought down was the one separating the rich from the poor. Jesus was not an *hijodalgo* (son of somebody, that is, bourgeois). Rather, the content of many of Jesus' after- and over-dinner conversations (or parables) shows the Nazarene as a menial worker, not only as a carpenter but as a bricklayer (Matt. 7:24).[3] In any event, Christ was incarnated in a poor person (Luke 2:24) to avoid legitimizing the system that produced such social and economic disparities. Galilee was a region of both poor people and mighty landowners, such as

Herod the Great, who owned from half to two thirds of the land. State and temple taxes ranged from 30 to 40 percent of people's income.[4] The economic and political superiority of the province of Judea caused it to overshadow the other province, Galilee. In Christ's incarnation exactly the opposite took place. Jesus Christ took the side of the Galileans, the side of the poorest of the poor.[5]

It is not fortuitous, then, that Jesus celebrated the Last Supper in a borrowed house since he was homeless (Luke 9:58)? No wonder that during the meals the Gospels report, we find Jesus denouncing the wealthy.[6] Moreover, Jesus' proclamation showed a close relationship with the egalitarian tradition characteristic of the Old Testament:

> When the Israelites saw it, they didn't know what it was and asked each other "What is it?" Moses said to them, "This is the food that the Lord has given you to eat. The Lord has commanded that each of you is to gather as much of it as he needs, two quarts for each member of his household." The Israelites did this, some gathering more, others less. When they measured it, those who gathered much did not have too much, and those who gathered less did not have too little. Each had gathered just what he needed. (Ex. 16:15–18)

Jesus' ministry was also rooted in the prophetic vein of the Old Testament that rejected the commonly held relationship between worshiping God and exploiting God's creatures (Jer. 7:8–10; Isa. 1:3–4). The eucharistic Jesus Christ became the companion sensitive to the physical needs of people. To Jesus, monopolizing the resources needed to sustain people's lives was unworthy (1 Cor. 11:27). Hungry people became the negation of Jesus Christ's compassionate presence (1 Cor. 11:20–22). That is why the Eucharist becomes a constant remainder of Jesus' prayer, "Give us this day our daily bread."

The *homo consumens* of today's consumerist society feels comfortable with a docetic[7] Christology that emphasizes Jesus' spirituality. The Christ of the rich talks smoothly about spiritual nourishment but remains deaf and blind before the 800 million undernourished of our own population.[8]

In contrast, the perception of Jesus Christ by our Hispanic/Latino people is that of the *carnalito* (of the same flesh) who sides with those at the margin. As Caleb Rosado argues, "The Bible (Heb. 2:17) tells us that Jesus is our brother, and by taking on human flesh he became our *carnal*. That's the meaning of the incarnation, becoming one flesh with humanity."[9]

Our Hispanic/Latino people don't go so far as asserting that God is food, but certainly we differ from classical Christology in its spiritualization of bread. We tend to resonate with the position of church leaders such as Dom Helder Câmara, whose prophetic ministry challenges the roots of the unfair distribution of the resources of the world.[10] In the midst of this society ruled by the principles of a capitalist economy, the eucharistic Jesus Christ continues to oppose the unfair distribution of bread among people. Justo L. González's comment about the contradictory use of bread by different sectors of society makes this point: "Bread probably rejected by those who, in the great palaces, ate instead the most exquisite delicacies. Bread from the wheat harvested in Galilean fields, the product of Galilean sweat. Bread, like the lettuce harvested by our overworked people, that ends up on elegant banquet tables.[11]

The historical Jesus also faced class struggles and cultural oppression. Galilee was a mixed region in which several cultures merged. Nathanael the apostle used to ridicule Galileans (John 1:46). In his borderland, the Arabs, Greeks, Syrians, Phoenicians, and other cultures mingled. Galilee was influenced by the conquering empires of Egypt, Syria, Assyria, and Rome. This explains why Galilee was so well known as the place of foreigners (Isa. 9:1).

The eucharistic Jesus of the upper room was a time- and space-bound person. The Galilean was not only rejected by the members of the refined culture of his time but also murdered for inverting the values of the ruling class. The culture in power always tries to control the souls and bodies of its subjugated people. Nonetheless, the intangible cultural elements of thinking, imagining, feeling, and valuing and the tangible ingredients of our particular way of talking, walking, dressing, eating, greeting, and so on manifest a resistance to this controlling attempt.[12]

The patriarchal character of Western culture that subordinates the female to the male is also challenged by the eucharistic Jesus. Many Christians and church bodies have justified their misogynist tendencies by referring to the Last Supper held by Jesus with his followers. This position plays fast and loose with the biblical legacy.[13] Whether the Holy Meal was a Passover meal for men that later included women and children is still on the theologians' table. What has already been sufficiently proven is the decisive role women played in Jesus' agenda. However, when at the Communion table we listen to the Paschal Lamb say, "this is my blood shed for you . . . ," isn't this also evidence of the natural presence of women at the Eucharist? Blood is a metaphor of life (Lev. 17:11) and has a close relationship to the experience of women. It is a metaphor that can be related to Mary's placenta, which nourished Jesus during nine long months before his birth. This metaphor of life can also serve as an image of the all-embracing cosmological womb in which our solar system's nine planets are but dots in the long, long line of creation.

The permanent call of the eucharistic Jesus is to renew the baptism and commitment of that community which has shattered the barrier between male and female (Gal. 3:27–28). Furthermore, if patriarchalists are going to be consistent with their sexist, literalist reading of the Gospel account of the Last Supper, then it may follow that all of them must wear robes, lie down, be circumcised, kiss among men, eat with the fingers instead of with silverware, and follow all other cultural and social characteristics of Jewish society at the time of Jesus.

From the Protestant Hispanic/Latino perspective the eucharistic Jesus is also the antithesis of the Gnostic Christ. Gnostics believed that the differentiation of sexes, as well as the act of procreation, was a consequence of the Fall. For this reason sexuality was considered a negative expression of our human condition. In contrast to this position the apostle Paul argued that being single was a vocation that enabled the person to be free to serve the gospel.

Hispanics have repudiated Apollinarian Christology as well. This heresy supported a partial incarnation of Jesus Christ that conceived him as psychologically divine and bodily human. Justo L. González's translation of this position into sociological language reveals "that the ruling powers— the 'mind'—of a society are not in need of redemption, that they are not part of the 'problem,' for the 'problem' is posed by those who perform the physical tasks the society needs for survival."[14] However, we can add that we still keep some vestiges of Apollinarianism every time we reduce Hispanic women to senses, feelings, and emotions, in contrast to the characterization of Hispanic men as rational and less bodily.

Protestant Latinas and Latinos of Mexican background, consciously or not, are deeply attached to the figure of Mary revealed as Guadalupe. In this respect, Roberto Gómez notes, "after Christmas and Easter, the most holy day for all the mestizo churches, Roman Catholic or Protestant, is *el día de las madres*."[15] However, it is no less true that in our Christology we are still struggling against our misogynist heritage.

Finally I must point out that the Protestant Hispanic/Latino reading of the scriptures allows us to recognize Jesus as taking the side of the mestizos, such as the people emerging out of the experience of mixed blood in the Galilee region. In our case, we represent the bloodstreams of ancient America, Africa, and Europe. Our American ancestors emigrated from Asia and ended up in numerous native populations in America—the Caribs, Arawaks, Taínos, Mayas, Chibchas, Incas, and so on. The newcomer Spaniard brought to America in the sixteenth century not only the people from Africa but also a heritage that combined Iberian, Greek, Arab, Gothic, and Gypsy *mestizaje*. Not surprisingly, the mestizo Jesus represents an operative theological paradigm within our Protestant Hispanic/Latino community.

But—and this is an important but—we have to qualify the notion of mestizaje. While we prefer to use *mestizaje* rather than terms that call to mind veterinarian nomenclature—*la raza*, half-breed, cross-breed—we do acknowledge that this term has been associated with the oppression of the native people by the seventeenth-century conquistadores as well as by the oligarchies that later ruled these lands. For this reason we need to take seriously Alberto Rembao's observation on how the mestizos' inferiority complex led us to a exert a stronger cruelty over our own people than the cruelty whites exercised against them.[16]

The Hispanic/Latino perspective on Jesus, described above, that stresses his Galilean mestizo character, emphasizes the need to challenge every kind of ethnic rivalry for the sake of inclusivity. Edwin Sylvest is right when he states,

> We are very early in the formation of a new American cultural and biological mestizaje. We do not see the end of the process, but in the flesh and cultures of Hispanic-Americans emerges a new humanity that embraces all the ancient races, a humanity that is perfected, not by exclusion, by degrees of *limpieza de sangre* [blood cleanliness], but by inclusion.[17]

The Memory of Sharing

Jesus Christ's command, "Do this . . . ," leads us to meet and know him in practice. The experience of the Eucharist, in this respect, establishes a sharp contrast with classical christological interpretations that have dominated in the history of Christian tradition. Christology, and theology at large, have been traditionally dressed in metaphysical terms and in technical and difficult epistemological language that leads to confusion and misinterpretations. This domestication of Christology can be clearly appreciated in the wrapping of the Eucharist in the Aristotelian categories of substance and accidents. The dominant theologians of the classical tradition talked about the accidents of bread and wine, that is, their material properties of color, weight, aroma, form, flavor, consistency, texture. They also talked about their substance, that is, what supported the aforementioned accidents.[18] In doing this, theologians dealt with the ontological and existential presence of Jesus Christ in the Eucharist but avoided facing the fact that the substance of bread and wine becomes an important resource to meet the physical needs for the survival of human beings. By stressing the transcendent dimension of the Eucharist they downplayed its equally significant concrete aspect. This emphasis led to a negative spiritualization of the Eucharist. Obviously, the fact that this concrete aspect of the Eucharist played a central role in Jesus' ministry was underemphasized to the detriment of the link that exists between the transcendental dimension of the Eucharist, or a meal for the fallenness of life, and the more concrete life-giving aspect of the Eucharist expressed by Jesus' participation in meals with the outcasts and despised of the earth.

The Eucharist, therefore, leads us to the Jesus who sat countless times at the table, surrounded by relatives and friends. This man spent his teens and youth working at the shop "earning bread." Jesus was a people person who advocated familism over individualism. Furthermore, in his effort to strengthen the community, the eucharistic Jesus of the Table expanded family ties to a new community of interdependence (John 19:25–27; Luke 8:21). The eucharistic Jesus, like the hen cuddling her chicks under her wings, and as head of this new community, continues to unite what is often divided by the self-interest of the ruling sectors of society.

The Hispanic perspective on the eucharistic Jesus is that Jesus is also the family person who goes beyond the blood ties that bind people to each other through the *compadrazgo* (compaternity).[19] The eucharistic Jesus reminds us of the hen and her chicks and the importance of being related to a community of support for resisting the evil forces of the dominant sectors of society that systematically try to divide us.

The Table is the grand theme of the New Testament. Around the Table the slaves washed the feet of the guests (John 13:2–11). The Table was also the place where people fought for the positions of honor (Luke 14:7–11). Around it an endless list of rules for eating was followed (Luke 7:36, 44–46). And it is precisely at the Table that Christians must discern the real presence of Christ (1 Corinthians 11) by giving preference to the weaker, less honorable, less respectable members of the body (1 Cor. 12:12–27), and by sharing their material possessions in the task of building a more compassionate society.[20]

In Old Testament times the priests would sacrifice a victim in God's honor. However, at the eucharistic table, Jesus Christ becomes the priest as well as the victim. He is the *hostia* (sacrifice) whose donation of himself (Gal. 2:20; Eph. 5:2, 25) was carried out as an act of love. After having supper, Jesus' close followers sang a hymn, after which Jesus went to the Mount of Olives (Mark 14:26; Matt. 26:30), not to calm God's anger but to give himself to this new sharing community. The logic of the dominant Jewish establishment leaders of the time, in their quest for peace and order in the eyes of the Romans, led to the sacrifice of one person for the sake of the whole nation (John 11:50). Their plans were successfully assisted by Judas, a follower of Jesus.

The Eucharist today also represents a place of tension. The divine act of re-creating us by feeding us has been twisted into an act of inhuman annihilation by starvation. While hundreds of millions are subjected to hunger, others overeat. The holy activity of eating has been perverted in many of our Christian churches, where it is regarded as a mere physiological need. Surely one cannot live by bread alone (Matt. 4:4; Deut. 8:3). Yet Luther was right in his interpretation of the phrase "give us this day our daily bread." For Luther, food is not enough for a fulfilling life. It is also necessary and legitimate to have access to health services, education, recreation, clothing, housing, and many other resources to meet basic human needs.[21] All these resources are represented in the metaphor of bread, which exists to be shared. Bread, in this context, becomes a constant reminder of the social implications of the eucharistic Jesus Christ.

Protestant Hispanics are people who value loving and sharing. They are constantly giving from their scarcity. The sharing of Jesus Christ, even unto his death, finds resonance with Protestant Latinas and Latinos who sacrifice themselves for the sake of a more just society. This Jesus Christ is the one who lives in the conscious or unconscious mind of our people. The blood of the grapes (Gen. 49:11; Deut. 32:14) that César Chávez denounced as murder of the Hispanic agricultural workers is still crying out for a different society.

La Ultima Cena, a film about the reenactment of the Lord's Supper in a sugar mill of La Habana illustrates my point well. His Excellency, the Count, is interested in resting his soul by instructing his slaves in the Christian faith. Consequently, on Maundy Thursday the slaveholder goes to church. He washes and kisses the feet of twelve chosen slaves. After that, and in the intimacy of his home, he shares his table as Jesus did with his twelve slaves. The overseer, Don Manuel, who does the dirty work for the Count, and the priest, who provides moral validation to the whole enterprise, are well aware of the risks of seating the slaves at the master's table. The next day, the slaves are not allowed to have the day off as promised. In retaliation, some slaves organize a revolt. By Sunday, the Count regains control of the situation. To avoid further rebellions he hangs his former table guests except for one, Sebastian, who was not caught. This runaway slave finally achieves freedom and in so doing sends his brothers and sisters a message of hope.[22]

The Memory of Tomorrow

Some people might be tempted to experience the sacrament of the Eucharist as such a private and personal event that they become blinded to the present and future sociohistorical dimensions of this experience. This tendency goes against the true spirit of the Eucharist. While bread and water were indispensable for the Jewish religious tradition (Isa. 21:14), Jesus added the festive enjoyment of wine. Jesus began his ministry, according to John's Gospel, at the Cana wedding table by providing a fine wine, of noble quality and unique aroma (John 2:1–11). At Cana he was remembered for his festive character.[23] At the upper room, where the Eucharist took place, Jesus was about to close his ministry by clinking glasses with a final "cheers," in Spanish *salud*, or *salvación* (health, or salvation). No wonder

Calvin argued that wine was good not only in cases of necessity, but also to make us merry.[24] I am not trying to reinforce the unsubstantiated stereotype of Jesus as "glutton and drunkard," which contrasts with his austere life (Luke 9:58), or to promote the negative stereotype of Hispanics as amusement lovers. Quite the opposite. The *Jesús Fiestero* (that is, the joyful and party-loving Jesus) points to the fact that life is worth living, that tomorrow will be better. Justo L. González highlights this ambiguous nature of wine when he writes, "And he (Jesus) took wine. Like the wine Herod used to get drunk during his orgies. Wine made out of grapes that were harvested and pressed in Galilean blood. The wine of happiness and the wine of sorrow—like those wines from California that are sold so cheaply, yet have cost so much."[25]

This does not mean that Jesus proclaimed a purely otherworldly, inner-worldly, or afterworldly hope. Rather than undervaluing the present order, he set it in clear contrast with the divine order. Within the reign of God, which in Jesus' resurrection has already taken place, is a future for those who are despised by society. The great reversal is inaugurated, those who are now the last will be the first, and vice versa (Luke 13:29–30). Physicality plays a major role (Rom. 8:32). There is a *mañana* for the poor Galilean crowd, in contrast to the counter crowd of Jerusalem (Mark 11:17) who requested Jesus' crucifixion.[26]

Some may raise objections at this point. Some claim that those who followed Jesus, instead of looking for heavenly bread, were just interested in earthly bread. This position can lead to the conclusion that there is no connection between social analysis and faith in God. Some assume that the gospel cannot be reduced to biological existence. Furthermore, it has been argued that the Old Testament concepts of the messiah and the reign of God were too material. Finally, for some others this reading of Jesus' ministry led to a horizontal humanistic Jesuolatry. In response to these objections I would argue that the party spirit of the Supper led us into the eschatological dimension of Jesus' ministry without removing its earthly dimensions.

The *Jesús Fiestero* reminds us of the new sunrise inaugurated at the Table of the new covenant (Mark 14:24). The eucharistic table is above all the messianic meal of the proclamation of the reign of God (Luke 22:14–18). Now, the reign of God, instead of fleeing from this world, has its site in the same material world. Justo González clarifies this issue when he writes,

> It (the Reign of God) has to do with "the last days," with "those days," with "the day of the Lord." The reign for which we long and pray (thy kingdom come) is not "up there," but "out ahead." The distance between us and the Reign is best described not as that between "here" and "there," but rather as that between "now" and "then."[27]

The Jesus of the traditional, dominant, well-fed theologians is somber. He seems to be incapable of reversing the present social order (John 18:36), which is taken as a God-willed order. While in Jesus' time, under the *pax Romana* banner, the rich brutally repressed nations in order to keep their privileges, actions many times worse have continued happening throughout the past five hundred years of history, this time under the flag of a "new world order."

The Hispanic/Latino perspective cannot have communion with this modern Marcionite version of the status quo. For Marcion, God was a spiritual being different from Yahweh, the lesser being who by mistake created this imperfect material world. The Apostles' Creed combated that heresy by declaring God as *Pantocrator*, that is, all-ruling, or ruling over spiritual, earthly, and political matters.[28] The Christology of the ruling class, then, not only denies the eschatological proviso that states that we must commit ourselves to God's reign in spite of the fact that it will never be fully reached in our time, but it also encourages us to abandon our attempts to take care of creation and to focus our attention on a rugged individualistic salvation.

The Hispanic perspective on the eucharistic Jesus emphasizes the all-embracing reality of God's reign as the central thrust of Jesus' teaching and practice (Luke 4:43; 9:60; 16:16; 22:16, 18). At the Table, Jesus Christ strengthens us through his Spirit to remain united with the entire society, in order to shape our future in a different way. Our *mañana* mentality is in clear contradiction with the way things are today.[29] The Hispanic perspective is oriented toward the reign of God, and this is vividly dramatized by our sitting at the eucharistic table with Jesus and with each other to foretaste the definitive triumph over the powers of death. Daisy Machado expresses this point eloquently when she writes,

> The borders and margins that humans have created to keep and control wealth, power and status have now lost their meaning and usefulness before God's table. To enter and sit at the feast table of the kingdom does not require a green card nor speaking with the "right" accent of the dominant tongue. The biblical message is that Jesus has broken down every wall and has rejected the marginality of any of God's children.[30]

Because in the Eucharist God's will and Jesus' obedience meet,[31] our witness to the present actualization of God's reign and its justice (Matt. 6:33) is guaranteed by the very same God. Our confession of faith in this reality is not in vain, and we must continue our efforts of witnessing to the ongoing presence of God's reign among us until Jesus Christ returns (1 Cor. 11:26).

At this stage of our reflection, it is already apparent that Christology is by its very nature linked with the study of the Trinity, the study of the Holy Spirit, ecclesiology, and theological anthropology. Nonetheless, when we approach the theme of the cosmic Christ, this connection becomes more perceptible. The eucharistic Jesus has to do with the redemption of all creation (Gen. 22:18) through his donation of self for everyone and everything (Rom. 1:16; Heb. 10:10).

In order to better comprehend the interplay between Christology and the cosmos, or to have a better understanding of the place of Jesus in the whole universe, let us examine the traditional titles given to him, such as Wisdom of God, Lord, and God's eternal Word.[32]

The cosmological dimension of the crucified Christ of the Eucharist is well appreciated in the Paul's female image of Wisdom (Sophia, 1 Cor. 1:22–24, 30). Jesus as the Wisdom of God is directly associated with the Creator (Prov. 8:22–31), preserver (Prov. 8:35), and sovereign of any principality or authority (Col. 1:15–18). Not surprisingly the Wisdom Woman Banquet presents an image similar to that of the eucharistic Jesus:

> She has had an animal killed for a feast, mixed spices in the wine, and set the table. She has sent her servant girls to call out from the highest place in town: "come in, ignorant people!" And to the foolish man she says, "come, eat my bread and drink the wine that I have mixed." (Prov. 9:2–5).

The cosmic Jesus Christ is also present in the declaration of him as Lord (*Kyrios*, an imperial title), not only of the individual but of the whole creation (Rom 10:9; Acts 2:36). The Lordship of Jesus Christ means he is the ruler of spiritual as well as earthly matters. His Lordship reminds us that Christology includes the whole cosmos and all cosmological theories (Phil. 2:8–11).

The christological cosmic perspective is also present in the eternal Word of God as it was incarnated in Jesus of Nazareth and commemorated in the Holy Supper. The Gospel assertion that in the beginning was the Word (John. 1:1–16), and in the beginning God created heaven and earth (Gen. 1:1), are but two sides of the same coin. The two natures of the second person of the Trinity are referred to when the creator of the universe is said to appear both at the dawn of time and as the human being who assumed that very creation on himself in his incarnation. The incarnation of God in Jesus of Nazareth is an affirmation of the goodness of creation. It shows us the sacramental substance of the universe. Bread and wine are powerful symbols that remind us of the sacred presence of Christ. Pablo Neruda, the poet from Chile, asserts the same point in one of his poems:

> Pan, con harina, agua y fuego te levantas. Espeso y leve, recostado y redondo, repites el vientre de la madre, equinoccial germinación terrestre (Bread, with flour, water and fire you rise. Heavy and light, lying down and circular, you repeat the womb of the mother, equinoctial earthly germination).[33]

Yet to affirm the cosmic Jesus Christ is quite different from adopting a Gnostic position. The latter relies not on the memory of the Word of God

but on the dictum: "Remember that you are a God." Gnostic Christology
is of the opinion that the spirit of the human being is of divine nature, and
it is compared to a beam of light that was trapped by matter.[34] The act of
anamnesis (remembering) leads to the consciousness of the divine origin
and the consequent *fuga mundi* (flight from the world). This Christology
also represents a temptation for avant-garde theologians, who by denying
the secular order support the present anti–reign of God.

Our human hope for redemption needs to be understood in terms of a
cosmic eschatology in which creation, incarnation, and consummation in-
tersect. Jesus Christ holds all things together, past, present, and the final
consummation point.

It is not easy to resist the dominant ideas of an era built on scientific
knowledge that is considered the only way to explain reality. However, the
eucharistic Jesus reminds us of a deeper and broader dimension of reality
which can be apprehended through the mystical union.[35]

God the Creator (Father) indwelt his Spirit in everyone (Jer. 31:33;
Ezek. 36:26; Joel 3:1–2; John 1:1, 9, 10, 14), establishing a new covenant
(Jer. 32:36–44; Heb. 8:8). Pagans know God, but not all of them acknowledge God (Rom. 1:21, 28). Jesus Christ gave himself for all humanity (Mark
10:45; Isa. 53:10). Nevertheless, the "white man's burden" of sharing
Christianity with the "pagans" did not take into account the dimension of
the cosmic Christ. They ignored what the same Scriptures cite from other
religious sources (Acts 17:28). Westerners were blind to the fact that God's
presence is always present in all places where there is love (Matt. 25:40).
Consequently, we endorse Justo González's sharp observation: "The Eu-
ropeans did not bring the Word to the Western Hemisphere. That Word
was here since creation, and that Word was the light that produced the values that were already here."[36]

The proper way of knowing the cosmic eucharistic Jesus is by loving,
sharing, and doing justice. The values of the Beatitudes (Luke 6:20ff.) will
resound within everyone in harmony, every time they are reproduced at the
level of practice.

The criterion for eternal salvation for all humans is to actualize the values of God's reign already written in our hearts. As a whole, humankind
lacks God's full self-revelation in Jesus Christ. However, the vital revelation of justice and love are God's universal gracious gift in Christ through
the Spirit. In this sense, our knowledge of Christ helps clarify and deepen
what God has revealed in many ways and forms to people in their own contexts. As Tissa Balasuriya argues, far too often Christians have failed to
respect the honest search and self-sacrifice of many other faiths and ideologies in the cause of human liberation and hence God's kingdom.[37]
Galileans, with their exposure to a plurality of religions, were able to better
understand Jesus' radical affirmation, "whoever is not against you is for

you" (Luke 9:50). For them, as well as for Protestant/Latinas and Latinos today, to do God's will is to have our hearts attuned with God's reign.

Hispanics embrace the cosmic Jesus Christ because we realize that he is the ultimate mediator of God's love for all humankind. We are convinced that consciously or not, openly or anonymously, the name of Jesus Christ is blessed every time justice flows like a stream, and righteousness like a river that never goes dry (Amos 5:24). But, above all, Hispanics feel at home with the cosmic Jesus Christ because our hope is for a holistic liberation seeking justice for all. For this reason Harold Recinos argues that "Latinos, Blacks, Native Americans, Asians, women and progressive White communities must forge an alliance with each other and with the justice struggles of the global poor."[38]

Conclusion

As I have mentioned, it is by remembering that we become aware of our Hispanicness. We need to remember not only with our minds but, above all, with our hearts. In this sense, the Eucharist, as a rich event where crucial existential issues confront us, contributes to our remembrance of a deeper and more meaningful Christology.

To share the meal is a call to equality. Jesus' friends lay down for the celebration of the Last Supper (Luke 22:14). It was the Greek-Roman custom for free persons to receive their guests lying down.[39] Jesus did not want his followers to eat standing up, for this was compulsory for slaves (John 6:10).

Jesus' community is always open, especially for those who are denied entrance to exclusive tables (Luke 14:15–24). The breaking of bread was not an invitation to pay your own way, but rather an invitation that said, I'll pick up the tab. In fact, it was celebrated with the door open, as was the Passover.[40] The Jewish feast was not exclusively a family celebration; it was an evening meal (1 Cor. 11:23) where many people mingled. Hispanics, whose sense of territoriality is less marked, will do right in never distancing themselves from the people who live "on the wrong side of the tracks," the untouchables, the poor.

The eucharistic Jesus is the advocate of the right of life; of the primacy of human beings above national borders; of togetherness in contrast to the law of the market which tends to make a profit at the expense of the well being of others. Pablo Neruda captures this point well when he writes,

> Todos los seres tendrán derecho a la tierra y a la vida, y así será el pan de mañana, el pan de cada boca, sagrado, consagrado, porque será el producto de la más larga y dura lucha humana (All beings will have the right to the land and life, and this will be the bread of tomorrow, the bread of each mouth, sa-

cred, consecrated, because it will be the product of the longest and hardest human struggle).[41]

Churches with empty crosses avoid dealing with the uncomfortable memory of the brutal execution of Jesus Christ. Other churches got rid of the altar and in so doing they spiritualized Jesus Christ's painful sacrifice. Some congregations prefer that their pastors wear a business suit in order to transform the church into a mere enterprise, and they have also abandoned the use of kneelers, in order to have a more optimistic view of life. Some communities still talk of the Eucharist bread as "food of angels" to romanticize Jesus' humble socioeconomic status as well as the sociopolitical dimensions of his ministry. Nevertheless, the symbol of the Twelve around the Holy Supper points toward our present responsibility as the body of Christ, to share, serve, and love the people who are taken for granted (Matt. 25:40), the dregs of society who, like the wine dregs, are thrown out as being undesirable.

Finally the *manteles largos* (festive tablecloths) remind us of the cosmic Jesus Christ, the creative Word of God who has not aborted the original divine plan for the redemption of the whole universe. The Bakerwoman is still mixing the flour and the divine yeast into the dough of this world until the whole batch rises (Matt. 13:33). The reign of Christ continues to emerge in contrast to the current antidivine system of massive planet destruction. The banquet room is a constant reminder that the final overthrow of the dominion of death has already happened while we continue praying, "Come, Lord Jesus."

NOTES

The original manuscript of this chapter was edited for publication by José David Rodríguez, but a strong effort was made to maintain the style and content provided by the original author.

1. Ignazio Silone, *Bread and Wine* (1936; New York: Penguin Books, 1986), 265.
2. Herber Haag, *De la antigua a la nueva pascua: Historia y teología de la fiesta pascual* (Salamanca: Ediciones Sígueme, 1980), 121.
3. William Barclay, *The Gospel of Matthew*, vol. 1, 2d ed. (Philadelphia: Westminster Press, 1958), 295 ff.
4. Joseph A. Grassi, *Broken Bread and Broken Bodies: The Lord's Supper and World Hunger* (Maryknoll, N.Y.: Orbis Books, 1985), 7.
5. See Virgilio Elizondo, *Galilean Journey: The Mexican-American Promise* (Maryknoll, N.Y.: Orbis Books, 1983). See also Orlando Costas, *Christ outside the Gate: Mission beyond Christendom* (Maryknoll, N.Y.: Orbis Books, 1982).
6. To cite just one of many examples, see Luke 16:21, where Jesus tells the story about the rich man and the poor Lazarus.
7. The term refers to a heretic movement during the early Christian church. The

word derives from the Greek *dokein*, meaning to appear, to seem. For this group corporeality was conceived as evil; thus, they claimed that Jesus' humanity was only apparent.

8. There are 12 million deaths due to undernourishment each year and 2 billion people suffer vitamin and mineral deficiencies. For a more through examination of this issue, see Bertrand Delpeuch, *Seed and Surplus: An Illustrated Guide to the World Food System*, trans. from the French by Chantal Finney and Alistair Smith (London: CIIR/Farmers' Link, 1994).

9. Caleb Rosado, "The Church, the City, and the Compassionate Christ," *Apuntes* 2 (summer 1989): 31.

10. A good example of this position is the reception of remarks by two Latin American delegates at an international congress held in Philadelphia. When it came their turn to speak, the first one addressed the crowd of more than nine thousand, saying, "My country is very poor, please help us." The response was enthusiastic applause by the audience. After that, the second, Dom Helder Câmara, addressed the audience with the following words: "Latin America is very poor, please help us in criticizing your government's policy and the transnational corporations as well." His words received only courteous applause from those gathered. This took place at the 41st International Eucharistic Congress, August 1–8, 1976, held at the Philadelphia Civic Center. The story was told by Gustavo Gutiérrez in a conversation with students at the Catholic Theological Union, Chicago, on June 1, 1995.

11. Justo L. González, "In Remembrance of Me," in *Hidden Stories: the History of the Latino Church*, ed. Daniel Rodríguez and David Cortés (Decatur, Ga.: Asociación para la Educación Teológica Hispana, 1994), 164.

12. To bring the matter closer to home, we concur with Roberto W. Pazmiño when he argues that the recent invention of the cultural pluralism model exhibiting Anglo supremacism continues this trend of cultural domination characteristic of the times of Jesus. Its self-seeking interest, its patronizing attitude, and its very narrow agenda deny voice to some ethnic communities where supposedly there is room for the coexistence of other cultures. As a real alternative Pazmiño proposes a multicultural model with a multiethnic education dimension to achieve unity within diversity. For a further exploration of this subject, see Robert W. Pazmiño, *Latin American Journey: Insights for Christian Education in North America* (Lanham, Md.: University Press of America, 1992), 17.

13. This position cannot be used for excluding women from Jesus' ministry of preaching. According to Markus Barth, the apostle Paul's advice for married women to wear a decent dress and to cover their heads (1 Cor. 11:2–16) cannot be used for justifying the subjugation of women either. "In 1 Corinthians 11:2–16 Paul discusses the temptations of married women to use the congregation's worship as an opportunity to demonstrate emancipation. Their dress in the assemblies has made them look like certain unmarried ladies from harbor pubs and other love-temples in the city of Corinth. In analogy it would cause more than raised eyebrows if married female church members of all age groups attended European and North American worship services clad in bikinis and having removed their wedding rings." Markus Barth, *Rediscovering the*

Lord's Supper: Communion with Israel, with Christ, and among the Guests (Atlanta: John Knox Press, 1988), 63.

14. Justo L. González, *Mañana: Christian Theology from a Hispanic Perspective* (Nashville: Abingdon Press, 1990), 148.

15. Roberto L. Gómez, "Mestizo Spirituality: Motifs of Sacrifice, Transformation, Thanksgiving, and Family in Four Mexican-American Rituals," *Apuntes* 4 (winter 1991): 86.

16. Alberto Rembao, *Chihuahua de mis amores* (Mexico City: n.p., 1949), 234.

17. Edwin Sylvest, Jr., "Re-thinking the 'Discovery of the Americas': A Provisional Historico-Theological Reflection," *Apuntes* 1 (spring 1987): 12.

18. From the application of these categories a handful of doctrines were developed. The transubstantiationists (following Aquinas) held that the presence of Christ takes place at the level of the substance whereas the accidents remain untouched. The consubstantiationists (following Luther) believed that what occurs is a new composition of the elements. The transignification position (inspired by Calvin) was of the opinion that both substance and accidents remained the same but what mattered was the spiritual presence of Christ in the bread and wine. For the symbolic or consciousness position, based on an interpretation of Zwingli, the Table became a mere mnemonic tool. This kind of language, together with an endless list of external rites and a myriad of superstitions, became very popular. Yet in so doing, theologians got rid of the social praxis implied in the sacrament, keeping the core of the eucharistic message divorced from its social implications in the lives of the believers.

19. The practice of *compadrazgo* can be manipulated by certain sectors of society by eliminating the sense of solidarity and reciprocity characteristic of this relationship. For a more careful exploration of this topic, see Ana Gutiérrez, *Se necesita muchacha*, with an introduction by Elena Poniatowska (Mexico City: Fondo de Cultura Económica, 1983), 7–86.

20. For a study of the impact of these principles in the early Christian community and on its leaders, see Justo L. González, *Faith and Wealth: A History of Early Christian Ideas on the Origin, Significance, and Use of Money* (San Francisco: Harper & Row, 1990). In this study González argues that the notion of *koinonia* (the sharing of material goods) reached as far as Alexandria and lasted as late as 135 C.E. He also highlights the fact that the main purpose of the offering raised by believers was to promote equality, and he explores how private property rights were subordinated to the needs of the poor.

21. *The Book of Concord: The Confessions of the Evangelical Lutheran Church* (Philadelphia: Fortress Press, 1959), 431ff.

22. Tomás Gutiérrez Alea (writer and director), *La Ultima Cena*, English subtitles, 110 min. Havana, 1976. Videocassette distributed by New York Films. Grand Prize Chicago International Film Festival.

23. Ernesto Cardenal, *The Gospel in Solentiname*, vol. 1 (Maryknoll, N.Y.: Orbis Books, 1976), 152–54. See also Justo L. González and Catherine González, *The Liberating Pulpit* (Nashville: Abingdon Press, 1994), 60.

24. John Calvin, "Commentary on Psalm 104:15, *Ioannis Calvini Opera*, 32:91.

25. González, "In Remembrance of Me," 164.

26. See Orlando Costas, "Evangelism from the Periphery: The Universality of Galilee," *Apuntes* 4 (winter 1982): 79. For a theological understanding of the term *mañana*, see González, *Mañana*, 157–67.
27. González, *Mañana*, 161.
28. González, "The Apostles' Creed and the Sanctuary Movement," *Apuntes* 2 (spring 1986).
29. González, *Mañana*, 164.
30. Daisy Machado, "A Borderlands Perspective," in *Hidden Stories*, 63.
31. Grassi, *Broken Bread*, 81.
32. For a careful examination of this area, see Dermot A. Lane, *Christ at the Center: Selected Issues in Christology* (Mahwah, N.J.: Paulist Press, 1991), chap. 6, 130ff.
33. Pablo Neruda, *Antología fundamental*, Selección de Jorge Barros (Santiago, Chile: Fundación Pablo Neruda, 1988), 189.
34. Susanne Heine, *Women and Early Christianity: A Reappraisal* (Minneapolis: Augsburg, 1987), 2.
35. For an insightful examination of this topic, see Tissa Balasuriya, *The Eucharist and Human Liberation* (Maryknoll, N.Y.: Orbis Books, 1979).
36. Justo González, *Out of Every Tribe and Nation: Christian Thought at the Ethnic Round Table* (Nashville: Abingdon Press, 1992), 45.
37. Balasuriya, *Eucharist and Human Liberation*, 162.
38. Harold Recinos, "Militarism and the Poor," *Apuntes* 4 (winter 1987): 94.
39. Haag, *De la antigua*, 127.
40. Haag, 129.
41. Neruda, *Antología fundamental*, 192–93.

4

The Holy Spirit—Personalization and the Affirmation of Diversity

A Pentecostal Hispanic Perspective

Samuel Solivan

The Holy Spirit as a person relates to us as persons. As persons we relate to the Spirit from specific points of reference—gender, language, culture, and social class, to name a few of the aspects that inform our relation to the Spirit. In this chapter, the social, cultural, and linguistic reality of the Hispanic/Latino American perspective will serve as the matrix for formulating the issues as well as informing viable responses.

What is different when we reflect upon the issue of the depersonalization of the Spirit from this perspective? What is it that makes it a Hispanic perspective?

Several factors are fundamental ingredients in this Hispanic perspective. First, it is written from a Hispanic perspective, in my case the vantage point of a Hispanic American of Puerto Rican parentage. Second, a Hispanic perspective intentionally recognizes the Hispanic community as its place of engagement and reflection.[1] Third, it consciously seeks to maintain the Hispanic community as its interlocutor.[2] Fourth, in my case, it draws upon the social and economic reality of the Puerto Rican community in the United States and Puerto Rico as its point of reference.[3]

For most Hispanics, religion and faith are deep and personal commitments. They are commitments that require all our passion as well as our intellect. This union of passion and intellect reflects the conjunctive nature of Hispanic culture. We are a "both-and" people. We like to have our cake and eat it, too.

Coupled with our rich Catholic faith and Protestant experience, these basic aspects constitute that interpretive matrix called the Hispanic or Latino perspective.[4] Of course these traits in and of themselves are not necessarily unique to Hispanics. What is unique is the interplay and the historical context within which these characteristics interact and the bilingual and at times monolingual medium they employ.

In this chapter I address broadly the doctrine of the Holy Spirit, formally known as pneumatology, that is, the study of the person and work of the third person of the Trinity. Pneumatology is the study of the one sent by the Father and promised by the Son. This locus or subject historically has often been subsumed or overshadowed by Christology, ecclesiology, and soteriology. Yet any proper understanding and application of these other loci required a solid grounding in pneumatology.

I will examine the issue of the depersonalization of the Holy Spirit and the important role that the Holy Spirit plays in affirming and empowering diversity, noting the insights and implications for the Hispanic/Latino church and community.

Before I engage in this task, I must lay out some underlying assumptions, that inform my work. First is the assumption that the scriptures are the authoritative self-disclosure of God, and they set before us God's intent and purpose regarding the redemption of humanity and the earth. Second, Jesus Christ as incarnate and resurrected Lord and Savior serves as the norm against which all pneumatology is to be judged. Third, the Holy Spirit is that person present among and in us re-presenting Christ's will. Fourth, a Trinitarian paradigm is assumed within which God the Father, Christ the Son, and the Holy Spirit are interrelated. For my purposes here, attention will be given only to the Holy Spirit. In doing so I recognize the potential hazards of dislocating the Spirit from her Trinitarian relation.[5] Yet I argue that the opposite hazard has already occurred, that of subsuming the third person in the Trinity to the extent that she has lost her own identity, often being reduced to an influence or attribute of the first and second persons.

As recently as ten years ago many—especially in North American seminaries—considered the language of pneumatology to be a throwback to a time of religious superstition and scientific obscurantism. Times have changed. Recently one of my graduate students approached me about examining the connections between Christian notions of Spirituality and corporate spirituality. He was serving as a member of an executive planning team at the Lotus Corporation, exploring the meaning and content of the "Soul of Lotus."

From the church pew to the executive office the language of spirituality is becoming, if it is not already, commonplace, with expressions such as "get with the spirit," "team spirit," and "school spirit" in wide use. On the national political scene, we hear such expressions as the "spirit of the national electorate" or the "spirit of the nation (or party)." In theology we are acquainted with the expression *Zeitgeist*, or the "spirit of the times," and most know the French expression *esprit de corps*, or "the spirit of group honor."

Recently in Massachusetts the state invited tourists to catch the "spirit of Massachusetts." The Methodist church, not wanting to be outdone, promoted itself by encouraging its parishioners to "catch the spirit," as if it were a virus or a baseball. Spirituality and spirit language have again become fashionable.

Most North American seminary catalogues present a variety of course offerings dealing with one or another sort of spirituality. Recently I was invited to attend a course on the "spirituality of healing." The spirit being invoked was that spirit present in the energy of crystals placed on and round about the body of a student needing healing. At the World Council of Churches General Assembly in Canberra, Australia, much attention was given to the theme "Come Holy Spirit, renew the whole creation." Several denominations, in keeping with this theme, prepared denominational study guides to help local congregations explore this important aspect of Christian faith.

One of the keynote speakers of the Canberra WCC Assembly spoke of the "spirit of Tiananmen Square" and the "spirit of the Amazon," among other spirits. Amid this "spiritual" smorgasbord we are faced with a variety of questions related to the Christian understanding of spirit and spiritual. The competing voices all claiming in some fashion or other to be "the Spirit" or "a spirit" of God challenge the Christian community to discern which if any of these claimants is the Holy Spirit spoken of and revealed in the scriptures.

This fascination with the "spirit" should not surprise us. To a great extent it reflects humankind's quest after wholeness congruent with that innate spirituality given us by God as an extension of himself in the *imago Dei*. We have been created in God's likeness and image, spiritual beings. Yet are all these voices, or what Christopher Morse calls "claimants" of the "Spirit" or the "Holy Spirit," spoken of and promised to us as the paraclete?[6] Competing claimants, authorities, powers, or influences are not something new. Old Testament prophets claimed to speak on God's behalf, just as the prophets of Baal claimed to speak on behalf of god, a pagan god. The people were cautioned to question and test the prophets because some prophets were in fact profit-making prophets and represented their own self-interest. The prophet, we were told, was known when what he prophesied came true. Fulfillment was to be the standard against which the claim was to be judged true or false.

In the New Testament we find a similar rubric. The writer of the First Epistle of John cautions us "not to believe every spirit" (1 John 4:1). We are told to test the spirits to see if they be of God. Our present-day appeal to the "spirit" requires us to differentiate between that Spirit of God revealed as "Ruach Adonai," Spirit of the Lord, and other, false spirits that are in fact anti-Christ. Like the early church, we are confronted today with competing authorities and powers that seek our loyalty. We, like them, are called to distinguish between those powers and influences that give life and those that take it. This discernment must consider not only those claimants that are obviously false but also those that we often assume are true because they are found among us or seem to be in harmony with our present understandings and practices because they lend themselves to our agendas of personal influence and/or power.

The Spirit:
Power, Influence, Energy, or Person?

Thomas Oden has noted that

> the depersonalization of God the Spirit has occurred in the period of philosophical idealism. Hegel reduced the Spirit to a logic of history. Tillich reduced the Spirit to an existential category of being itself. Process theology reduced the Spirit to creative energy. Much liberation theology reduced the Spirit to political praxis. Each reduction is tempted by unconstrained application of a mistaken impersonal analogy to the person of the Spirit.[7]

The depersonalization of the Spirit is also evident in ways the Spirit is referred to in Bible study groups and seminary classes. Neuter appeals to the Spirit as a force, energy, or influence reflect this depersonalization of the third person of the Trinity. Rarely is the Spirit understood or addressed as a person, contrary to 1,500 years of Christian tradition and biblical practice.[8]

The personalization of the Holy Spirit is important to Hispanic American pneumatology because the relationship of the Spirit to persons, in this case Latinas and Latinos who daily experience treatment as nonpersons, can provide a transformative model of personhood and self-esteem. Hispanics are constantly at the mercy of powers, forces, and influences that serve to further dehumanize and objectify them. The depersonalization of the Holy Spirit serves the interest of those who would employ a divine image to further their own desires for control, those who seek to domesticate the divine, the ultimate expression of idolatry. The depersonalization of the Holy Spirit is counter to the *imago Dei* given to all human creation through the agency of the Spirit. A depersonalized spirit reflects the depersonalization of God as Spirit. God as Spirit is life, and as such human life is subject and not object. The Holy Spirit in his person reflects the personality of the Godhead.[9] The Trinity reflects this communion of persons, not of influences or energies.

The Holy Spirit as the one sent from the Father and promised by the Son re-presents the wholeness of Christ in relation to us. John's use of "another advocate" (*allon parakleton*) in John 14:15 rather than "other" (*heteron*) but meaning "different from himself" is most telling. Christ did not replace his personal presence with some force, influence, or energy. The use of *allon* is indicative of the importance of sameness in regard to person as well as authority and dignity. The depersonalization of the third person of the Trinity introduces a radical shift in the nature of the relationship between us, the receptors of the Spirit, and the Spirit herself. It is no longer a relationship of persons or of subjects. The reception of the Spirit is reduced to an impersonal relation between subject and object.

The importance placed on our human *persona* is so significant to the nature and content of redemption that the incarnation of Christ as reflected in John 1:14 and Philippians 2:6–10 bear witness to Jesus the Christ having taken upon himself actual flesh and personality. If Christ is the norm against which we are to understand and define the Holy Spirit and, as such, the Spirit is the one who reveals Christ to us, the depersonalization of the Spirit fundamentally contradicts what we know to be revealed in Christ. A nonpersonal influence or force is incapable of sharing or revealing what is personal.

Not only does our present experience of nonpersonhood and marginalization require a relationship with the person of the Holy Spirit, but our condition as sinners (incomplete and fractured selves) requires the person of the Holy Spirit as healer of our brokenness. The person of the Holy Spirit is the one promised to us as the rectifier of life. As the rectifier of life, "the Holy Spirit is confessed as sanctifier or giver of holiness and wholeness.[10]

It is the person and work of the Spirit that enables human and social transformation. The scriptures, the tradition of the church, and the present work of the Spirit among us today all bear witness to the Spirit's personhood:

> Like a person, the Spirit can be resisted (Acts 7:51), avoided, or responsively answered (Acts 10:19–21). Only a person can be vexed (Isa. 63:10) or grieved (Eph. 4:30). Only one with intelligence and the capacity for communication can speak from heart to heart. These are the qualities of personhood. Only a person can teach, talk, reveal his will to other persons, become angry (Isa. 63:10). As persons speak and communicate, so does the Holy Spirit speak in Scripture to the faithful (Mark 13:11; Acts 8:29; 21:11; 1 Tim. 4:1; Rev. 2:7) to disclose his will and listen responsively to creatures.[11]

We also need to distinguish between the Spirit as person and the attribute of spirituality. There are as many spiritualities as there are spirits. Yet not all expressions of spirituality are Christian. The person of the Holy Spirit is more than a divine attribute of spirituality. Care should be taken not to reduce the Holy Spirit to a characteristic of God. As noted by the church father Basil:

The Spirit is a distinctive divine person who possesses these characteristics and qualities ascribed as divine attributes. The Holy Spirit is not merely a quality or emanation of God, but rather a distinct person within the God-head.[12]

Nothing less than full personhood of the Spirit is sufficient to reflect the testimonies of the scriptures and the needs of the Hispanic community and the world. The Holy Spirit as gift of God and the bearer of gifts requires that we correct the present tendency toward pneumatological docetism. The Holy Spirit is given to us collectively as the body of Christ and fills us with his presence and power. It is in both the personal and the collective aspects of the Spirit that we come to know and experience the fullness of his person as gift, gift bearer, and rectifier.[13]

The reclamation and reformation of Hispanic self-esteem and historical purpose remains unserved by a depersonalized spirit. The restoration of our full humanity as children of God and beloved of Christ is made possible through the transforming power and presence of the third person of the Trinity, who is the bearer of the gifts of wholeness, faith, hope, and love. No lesser being is able to overcome the forces and powers of the evil one. No other has been given to us as the *arrabon*, the down payment or deposit on our liberated future.[14] It is the presence of the Holy Spirit as we are possessed of her that enables us to exclaim as did the apostle Paul, "Greater is he who is in thee than he that is in the world."

It is the person of the Holy Spirit given to the church and present in believers who makes possible and necessary the cultural, ethnic, and linguistic diversity of the body of Christ. A depersonalized spirit, influence, or power has little need for personal differentiation. Objects have no need for subjective particularity. Rather, subjects in relation to other subjects have the need for diffentiation.

The Holy Spirit and Cultural Diversity

A Traditional Pentecostal
Reading of Acts 2

Throughout the history of the Christian church the outpouring of the Holy Spirit on the day of Pentecost has played an important and formative role in not only defining the mission of the church in its outreach to the nations but also introducing a counter paradigm to those social constructions which functioned to separate diverse types of people and communities from one another on the bases of race, gender, language, and economic status.

For both Jew and Gentile Christians the Pentecost event introduced a new set of possibilities and expectations for the formation of a new community: a community that would reflect the nature and content of the kingdom of God among us and the global reconciliation between peoples separated from one another since the time of the Fall (see Genesis 11).

This new alignment of relationships was made not only possible but necessary by the outpouring of the Spirit on the 120 people in the upper room and on others present on the day of Pentecost, and later as those empowered by the Spirit shared the gospel around the world.

Pentecostal historians, theologians, preachers, and teachers have traditionally emphasized the miraculous sign of the Spirit's outpouring by highlighting speaking in tongues as a sign or evidence of the Spirit's baptism. In Acts 2:3–13 we read:

> Divided tongues, as of fire, appeared among them, and a tongue rested on each of them. All of them were filled with the Holy Spirit and began to speak in other languages, as the Spirit gave them ability.
>
> Now there were devout Jews from every nation under heaven living in Jerusalem. And at this sound the crowd gathered and was bewildered, because each one heard them speaking in the native language of each. Amazed and astonished, they asked, "Are not all these who are speaking Galileans? And how is it that we hear, each of us, in our own native language? Parthians, Medes, Elamites, and residents of Mesopotamia, Judea and Cappadocia, Pontus and Asia, Phrygia and Pamphylia, Egypt and the parts of Libya belonging to Cyrene, and visitors from Rome, both Jews and proselytes, Cretans and Arabs—in our own languages we hear them speaking about God's deeds of power." All were amazed and perplexed, saying to one another, "What does this mean?" But others sneered and said, "They are filled with new wine." (NRSV)

Tongues of fire, speaking in other languages, speaking as they were led by the Spirit of the mighty acts of God are pictures of the Pentecost event. Those foreigners present were amazed, dazzled, perplexed, confused. They asked themselves, "What does all this mean? A rereading of the question "What does this mean?" leads us to a different set of questions about what they are saying. The text indicates that they understood what they were saying but did not know what it meant. Clearly, meaning or meaningfulness is wedded to persons and not to an impersonal ability for linguistic gymnastics. This distinction was made clear to me while I was doing doctoral studies at Union Seminary in New York. In a class he taught on liberation theology, Gustavo Gutiérrez, told me that he did not get along with Pentecostals, because, he said, Pentecostals spoke all the languages of the angels but did not speak the language of *el pueblo*, the people. I quickly assured him that that was not the case, at least not with me.

Traditionally Pentecostals have responded to this question of meaning by pointing to the Spirit's baptism as prophesied by the prophet Joel. The emphasis has been on the empowering presence of the Holy Spirit evidenced by speaking in tongues. As early as the Azusa revival's publication *Apostolic Faith* in 1906,[15] testimonies were recorded of persons believing that the tongues or language they received were for the purpose of evangelism and mission. Some went so far as to believe and expect that upon arrival at some foreign mission field, the Holy Spirit would give then the tongue, the language they would need in the country in order to preach the gospel. Many returned disappointed, unable to speak the language of their place of mission.

The meaning of the Pentecost event in such cases has been reduced to the Spirit enabling a person to speak in an unknown tongue, often unknown to both the speaker and the listener, and therefore needing the gift of interpretation, objectifying and reducing the work of the Spirit to an utterance of sounds.

Among Pentecostals, *power* for service and *boldness* for mission and evangelism continue to be the two principal interpretations of the Holy Baptism in Acts 2, even in the most recent Pentecostal systematic theology text.[16] For charismatics and so-called mainline churches, however, the outpouring of the Spirit on the day of Pentecost was an event of Christian initiation.[17]

I propose an examination of the Acts 2 passage from a different vantage point, one closer to that of the apostolic witnesses. This examination can provide helpful insights relevant to concerns for diversity both as understood and experienced in the past by the early church and today as we look for biblical and theological paradigms that address the need for greater diversity within the body of Christ.[18]

I believe that an ethnic or personalized but not private rereading of Acts 2 will provide different answers to the question "What meaneth this?"[19] This rereading will reveal a meaning that moves us beyond glossolalia as "spiritual empowerment" for service and toward an appreciation of glossolalia in its broader setting of cultural, ethnic, and linguistic affirmation of diversity. This meaning will raise up and echo the personal and collective implication of Pentecost consistent with the order of creation and the order of salvation. I further propose that this broader meaning of tongues was as present on the day of Pentecost as it was at Azusa Street in 1906 when, as Frank Bartleman observed, the "color line" was washed away in the blood.[20]

The remainder of this chapter will seek to tease out some of the implications and challenges raised for Pentecostals and charismatics in the United States today.

Jesus in the Gospels— ### Precursor to Diversity

A number of events in the gospels foreshadow what the Holy Spirit will lead the church to do as the church is empowered to fulfill the purpose of the reign of God. Some of these events deal with the issues of diversity and inclusivity. Among them is the story of the Syrophoenician woman (Mark 7:24–30), who seeks an act of mercy from Jesus though she was not a Jew. Jesus responds to her need. The Samaritan woman (John 4:7–30) is another well-known case. This Samaritan woman, a double minority, is evangelized by Jesus and soon becomes an evangelist to her community. Note that the disciples seemed to be somewhat scandalized by Jesus' speaking with a Samaritan, and to make matters worse, a woman.

Another precursor of the diversity and inclusivity to which the Spirit would lead the church is evident in Jesus' conversation with the centurion, as told in Matthew. Jesus is impressed with the faith of this Gentile, a faith unseen among the children of Israel, which leads Jesus to declare,

> Truly I tell you, in no one in Israel have I found such faith. I tell you, many will come from east and west and will eat with Abraham and Isaac and Jacob in the kingdom of heaven, while the heirs of the kingdom will be thrown into the outer darkness, where there will be weeping and gnashing of teeth. (Matt. 8:5–13, NRSV)

This reference to the east and the west speaks most clearly to the diversity and inclusivity of what Jesus called the kingdom of heaven. The foundation of God's divine redemptive plan was diversity, and inclusivity was and remains an essential aspect of God's saving grace. Israel is often reminded of this and at times chastised for ignoring it. Consider Jonah, for example. He is called to take a message to a Gentile city, a message of destruction. Yet Jonah knows God will be merciful. The city repents and God withdraws his judgment. This divine act of forgiveness annoys Jonah to the point that he wishes he were dead. He does not rejoice in the fact that these Gentiles have repented and come to know God's mercy. He would rather die than be identified with them. An entire biblical book is dedicated to making the point that God's mercy and love are inclusive. Can those who claim to be filled with the Holy Spirit, the Spirit of Christ, be any less inclusive? Can one filled with the Spirit weep like Jonah because good news has come to those who were aliens and sojourners, yet now by the grace of God are made co-heirs and fellow citizens of God's kingdom?

We do as Jonah did when we allow the values and structures of the world to define the diversity and inclusivity of the body of Christ. Jesus told his disciples before ascending to the Father that they would be witnesses— both in their homeland and to those who were of the house of Israel, and beyond. Not only would they be called and led to reach out to their own people, but the Holy Spirit would lead and empower them to break the boundaries that separated them from people unlike themselves. They would go to Samaria and even to the uttermost parts of the world as heralds of a diverse community of hope and love. For the Lord of the church came so that all might have life. He loved not some of the world but all of his creation and provided a means of redemption for them. The writer of Revelation echoes this expectation:

> After this I looked, and there was a great multitude that no one could count, from every nation, from all tribes and peoples and languages, standing before the throne and before the Lamb, robed in white, with palm branches in their hands. They cried out in a loud voice, saying, "Salvation belongs to our God who is seated on the throne, and to the Lamb!" And all the angels stood around the throne and around the elders and the four living creatures, and they fell on their faces before the throne and worshiped God. (Rev. 7:9–11, NRSV)

As we examine Jesus' words and deeds, we see that diversity and inclusivity are held side by side. It is not enough to care for your neighbor. True caring moves one to interact with and on behalf of those one loves. Whether in the good Samaritan story or the story of the Syrophoenician woman asking for mercy, the message is that diversity requires inclusion. The incarnation of Jesus witnessed to in John 1:14 is a fundamental paradigm for informing our attitude toward diversity. Even as Jesus identified with our human condition, we are to identify with others. Even as the incarnation required that divinity take on a foreign identity as flesh, that immortality vest itself in mortality and infinity limit itself within our human existence, we are called to venture into the world of the "other"—different, at times strange, yet so much like our own. As Jesus located himself amid the corruption of our sinfulness, we can do no less than locate ourselves alongside, in fellowship with, those who are different from us. Solidarity, *koinonia*, fellowship are essential aspects of unity. We cannot be one if we are not in fellowship with one another. John tells us that in the incarnation of Jesus he and others beheld the glory of God, full of grace and truth. The world around us needs to witness as John did the glory of God. What greater reflection of God's grace and truth than that he has called together that which had been separated. He has bonded into one that which was broken. Love expressed in unity amid diversity is the strongest evidence that we have been and are being filled with the Holy Spirit. Unity, oneness, without uniformity is the work of the Holy Spirit. Jesus expected his disciples to incarnate their faith. As with the disciples, the Holy Spirit calls us to be one, to be reconciled to one another and to God. Only the Spirit is capable of such a *metanoia*.

Both natural and revelation and special revelation disclose this divine intent of diversity and inclusion. Creation reveals an immense diversity amid harmony in the created order. Similarly inclusivity expressed through diversity is also evident in God's redemptive plan.

Diversity in the Order of Creation

We read in Acts 2:9–11 that during the Feast of Pentecost there were gathered in Jerusalem a host of diaspora Jews from different parts of the then-known world, representing the cultural and linguistic diversity of the Roman Empire and beyond. How thoughtful and instructive that on this, the feast of the ingathering of the wheat harvest, the day when the first fruits of the wheat harvest were offered to God, God would be preparing his own ingathering. At Pentecost, Jews from Palestine gather with their diaspora family to remember and give thanks for God's bounty. The Feast of Pentecost became a popular Jewish feast after the Babylonian exile. It was a time for North and South to gather and be one people. What better metaphor for diversity could one ask for than the Feast of Pentecost? What better offering could be presented than that of unity in diversity? Pentecost was a Jewish picture of what God desired for all the people, tribes, and nations of the world, that they might be one.

The Pentecost event was an inbreaking of the Holy Spirit, manifesting to the world that which God had proposed both in the order of creation and the order of salvation, unity amid diversity. Not a suspension of difference but the free and liberating inclusion of difference mediated by the Holy Spirit in love, hope, and peace. Pentecost echoed the diversity present since the moment of God's creative *dabar* (word) accompanied by the *ruach 'adonai* (Spirit of the Lord) separated the water from the land and brought into being all manner of life. The creation itself mirrors the most complex diversity known to us—ecosystems. These natural environments, diverse and seemingly unrelated, are actually an immense, interdependent, symbiotic diversity of creation, working in balance to sustain life as we know it. From the smallest microbe to the largest of plants and animals, all are interrelated and interdependent and provide a holistic ecosystem capable of sustaining life. This diversity and interdependency of creation manifest God's purpose not only for the vegetable, mineral, and animal kingdoms but also for creation. Diversity is not an accident of creation but a reflection of divine intent.

Diversity in the Order of Salvation

The order of salvation, that is, the purpose and content of God's salvific intent, also discloses a divine appropriation of diversity as an essential and intentional aspect of God's purpose. If salvation is God's plan for restoring humanity to its original relationship with God, diversity then plays an important role. Since the Fall, humans have sought to oppress, control, and belittle others. This need to be or feel superior to others is one of the most powerful characteristics of the fallen nature of humanity. Stewardship over creation has often meant power, control, domination over, for the purposes of feeding one's ego. It is an expression of humanity's quest to be godlike, but unlike the God revealed in scripture as loving and compassionate.

The scriptures bear witness to a compassionate God, full of mercy and love, a God who reconciles all of creation unto himself through his only begotten son Jesus the Christ empowered by the Holy Spirit (Luke 3:22; 4:1; 10:21). God's redemptive love encompasses all of creation's diversity and need. His will is that none be lost. This divine interest is evident in the inclusive nature of the salvation event in the exodus story.

The exodus story, in Exodus 12:38, presents us with the interesting Hebrew term *'ereb*, meaning mixed multitude. Luther translated it "rabble." Old Testament scholar John Bright describes *'ereb* as a group of slaves from other nations, perhaps even Egyptians. Bright goes on to comment that this "suffices to show that Israel, even in the wilderness, had picked up groups of miscellaneous origin, some of whom no doubt had been neither in Egypt nor Sinai but who had, one might say, become converts."[21] Later in the history of the settlement of the Promised Land others such as the Gibeonites of Joshua 9 and the people of Shechem and Tirzah were also incorporated into the tribe of Manasseh (Josh. 17:2f).

Bright goes on to observe that "the very nature of the Jewish community made a stringent separatism inevitable."[22] However, he notes, "a sense of world mission was never wholly lost in Israel. . . . Prophets of the restoration period, concerned as they were for the religious purity of the community, awaited the time when foreigners would flock to Zion."[23] This hope of God redeeming the nation is voiced beautifully by the prophet Zechariah:

> Sing and rejoice, O daughter Zion! For lo, I will come and dwell in your midst, says the LORD. Many nations shall join themselves to the LORD on that day, and shall be my people; and I will dwell in your midst. And you shall know that the LORD of hosts has sent me to you. (Zech. 2:10–11, NRSV)

The fulfillment of the prophet's hope is realized in the exclamation of Simeon, who we are told was inspired by the Spirit as he went into the temple the day Jesus was brought to be presented by his parents. Seeing them, he takes Jesus in his arms and says:

> Lord, now lettest thou thy servant depart in peace, according to thy word; for mine eyes have seen thy salvation which thou hast prepared in the presence of all peoples, a light for revelation to the Gentiles, and for glory to thy people Israel. (Luke 2:29–32)

God's design for the salvation of "whosoever calls upon the name of the Lord" reached its most explicit expression in the incarnation of Jesus the Christ, son of God. John spoke of him as the Lamb of God who takes away the sin of the world (John 1:29). The writer of Revelation states that he "saw another angel flying in midair, with an eternal gospel to tell to the inhabitants of the earth, to every race and tribe and language and people" (Rev. 14:6).

From Genesis through the book of Revelation it has been God's redemptive intent to draw all unto him. Diversity and inclusivity are a sign of the reign of God and the presence of the Holy Spirit among his people. Pentecost was another sign of the inbreaking reign of God. The outpouring of the Spirit was and continues to be a precondition for the possibility of diversity in the church today. Neglect of this aspect of the Holy Spirit's outpouring on the Day of Pentecost has contributed to an understanding of the Spirit's fullness that does not require that we love one another. Oversight of this aspect of the Spirit's ministry among us has led to racism, sexism, and bigotry by those who claim to love Christ and be filled with the Spirit. The fullness of the Spirit's presence and power will be incomplete at best or absent as long as we continue to ignore or devalue the importance of the place of diversity expressed through our culture, language, ethnicity, and gender. As long as the diversity God has intended and the Spirit has empowered is disallowed intentionally or unintentionally, we all fall short of the Holy Spirit's fullness we claim to have or at least seek. The tongues spoken of on the day of Pentecost were not just heavenly tongues. They were languages of a given people. The Spirit proposed to make himself known to all those present in Jerusalem. Rather than have the crowd present learn a single language in order to hear and understand the gospel, the Spirit empowered the 120 to speak the languages of those gathered.

In this, the Spirit introduced an important principle to the newly born church—the importance of language and culture. The good news was that Christ has reconciled us to himself and to one another. No longer should cultural differences and languages serve as barriers to fellowship. The Holy Spirit did not suspend God's cultural gifts; rather, he empowered us to use them wisely and lovingly for the good of all people. Who we are in our diversity is an expression of God's graciousness. Any claim that one culture or racial group is superior to another is a direct assault on the justice and grace of God. We were all created equal and good, for the glory of God.

History has taught us that much more than theological assent, creedal formulation, or even church councils will be required to incarnate Christ's will that we be one. The Holy Spirit has been given to the church to make what Christ desires possible among us. Yet it is not automatic. Loving Christ does not automatically, by pneumatological or doctrinal fiat, bring about communion among the diversity of the saints. The Holy Spirit works in us by empowering us to overcome our sinful tendencies to lord it over others or allow others to inappropriately lord it over us.

The important roles that diversity, race, and ethnicity had in the early church are significant and informative for us. From the days of the disciples walking with Jesus through the unfolding story of the acts of the Holy Spirit in the book of Acts and the Pauline epistles, the issue of diversity and inclusivity has played an important role in the self-understanding of the church as a reflection of the reign of God.

In Acts the church continued to struggle with the implication of living in the power and under the direction of the Holy Spirit. To claim to be filled with the Spirit then and no less today is to claim to live in harmony with the reign of God. To claim to be Spirit-filled is to assume the responsibility of being Spirit-led. To be led by the Spirit is no easy task; it is a call, a vocation to incarnate the kingdom of God, to incarnate in our daily lives, collectively and individually, the ethic of love that directs us to love the unlovely, to care for the stranger and the sojourner, and to extend hospitality to the foreigner and the sinner.

To walk in the Spirit is to be open to the gift of grace present in all for whom Christ died. It is to recognize that all people, races, tribes, and nations are God's creation and as such they are expressions of God's graciousness. To separate what God has called to be one is the work of the Antichrist. Let us heed James's words of exhortation:

> My brothers and sisters, do you with your acts of favoritism really believe in our glorious Lord Jesus Christ? For if a person with gold rings and in fine clothes comes into your assembly, and if a poor person in dirty clothes also comes in, and if you take notice of the one wearing the fine clothes and say, "Have a seat here, please," while to the one who is poor you say, "Stand there," or, "Sit at my feet," have you not made distinctions among yourselves, and become judges with evil thoughts? Listen, my beloved brothers and sisters. Has not God chosen the poor in the world to be rich in faith and to be heirs of the kingdom that he has promised to those who love him? But you have dishonored the poor. Is it not the rich who oppress you? Is it not they who drag you into court? Is it not they who blaspheme the excellent name that was invoked over you?
>
> You do well if you really fulfill the royal law according to the scripture, "You shall love your neighbor as yourself." (James 2:1–8, NRSV)

Conclusion

Our identity as a people, as Hispanics, as Latina and Latino Americans, is made possible and further empowered by the transforming and liberating work of the Holy Spirit. The Spirit as the giver of faith, hope, and love makes it possible for us not only to overcome the oppressive forces that seek to dehumanize us; the Spirit makes it possible for us to liberate our oppressors because we can overcome the sinful tendency to oppress others.

The personhood of the Holy Spirit is intricately bound with our own personhood. The personhood of the Spirit is also tied to the dignity and worth of all people. The personhood of the Spirit promised and given us is the guarantee (*arrabon*) that the present depersonalization of oppressed people will be overcome by the reign of God, who seeks to restore the full personhood given and intended.

> As presence, the coming vindication and glory of Jesus Christ is not pie in the sky by and by but is now given in the Spirit as a living foretaste and shown to be proving itself true. As a coming glory that is still coming due, this presence of the Spirit allows for no sacralized stasis of the present order, no closing of accounts as the deification of any status quo.[24]

NOTES

1. The Hispanic Pentecostal Church serves as the specific Christian community out of which I do theology. See Eldin Villafañe, *The Liberating Spirit: Toward a Hispanic Pentecostal Social Ethic* (Grand Rapids: Wm. B. Eerdmans Publishing Co., 1992), for an excellent social ethical study of Hispanic Pentecostalism.
2. For further study, see Justo L. González, *Mañana: Christian Theology from a Hispanic Perspective* (Nashville: Abingdon Press, 1990); and Justo L. González, ed., *Voces: Voices from the Hispanic Church* (Nashville: Abingdon Press, 1992).
3. Joseph P. Fitzpatrick, *Puerto Rican Americans: The Meaning of Migration to the Mainland* (Englewood Cliffs, N.J.: Prentice-Hall, 1971).
4. Elizondo has called this perspective *Mestizaje*. Virgilo Elizondo, *Galilean Journey: The Mexican-American Promise* (Maryknoll, N.Y.: Orbis Books, 1983).
5. Throughout this chapter I interchangeably use feminine and masculine pronouns when speaking of the Holy Spirit. The reason for this lies in the fact that the Hebrew term for spirit (*ruach*) is feminine and the Greek term used for spirit (*pneuma*) is neuter. The masculine use of spirit arises from the Latin Vulgate translation of the scriptures where *spiritus* is masculine.
6. The term *claimants* is used by Christopher Morse in his chapter "The Holy Spirit, Giver of Life" in *Not Every Spirit: A Dogmatics of Christian Disbelief* (Valley Forge, Pa.: Trinity Press International, 1994), 189.
7. Thomas C. Oden, *Life in the Spirit: Systematic Theology*, Vol. 3 (San Francisco: Harper Collins, 1992), 20.
8. For the first three centuries of the Christian era there was no consensus regarding the doctrine of the Holy Spirit. It was not until the Council of Constantinople in 381 that the church formulated its pneumatology.
9. Ibid.
10. Morse, *Not Every Spirit*, 189.
11. Oden, *Life in the Spirit*, 20.
12. Basil, *On the Spirit*, 1:21–23, Nicene and Post-Nicene Fathers, series 2, vol. VII, 33–35, as cited in Oden, *Life in the Spirit*, 21.
13. Oden, *Life in the Spirit*, 19.

14. Morse, *Not Every Spirit*, 190.

15. *Apostolic Faith* was a congregational newspaper published between 1906 and 1909 by the Apostolic Faith congregation at Azusa Street, Los Angeles, where the great Pentecostal revival of 1906 occurred.

16. See Stanley M. Horton, ed., *Systematic Theology: A Pentecostal Perspective* (Springfield, Mo.: Logion Press, 1994).

17. James D. G. Dunn, *Baptism in the Holy Spirit* (London: SCM Press, 1970).

18. This approach builds upon and assumes the work of James Dunn, Howard Irving, Dale Brunner, and others who have interpreted the baptism of the Holy Spirit of Acts 2 as an initiation.

19. By personal rereading I mean a particular rather than universal perspective on the text. This personal rereading allows for a serious integration of gender, culture, language, and social class implications of the text for the present interpretive task. Personal is not to be taken to mean private; the personal retains a communal aspect within which culture, language, gender, and social class function and are defined.

20. Frank Bartleman, *How Pentecost Came to Los Angeles* (Los Angeles: F. Bartleman, 1925), 54.

21. John Bright, *A History of Israel*, 2d ed. (Philadelphia: Westminster Press, 1975), 131.

22. Ibid., 446.

23. Ibid., 447.

24. Morse, *Not Every Spirit*, 190.

5

The Bible

A Hispanic Perspective

Pablo A. Jiménez

The Bible occupies a key place in Latino Protestantism. In most Hispanic Protestant congregations, parishioners are avid readers of the biblical text. They have utmost respect for scripture, expecting both ministers and lay leaders to use biblical texts as ground for all teachings, arguments, and sermons. New members of the congregation—both the newly converted and the siblings of older members—acquire an attitude of confidence and devotion toward the Bible, which is a source of security, promise, and blessing.[1]

Use of the Bible in the Latino Church

As with most theological concepts, the Hispanic understanding of scripture has been largely influenced by European theologies. To understand the use of the Bible in the Latino church, first consider some traits of this inherited approach to scriptural authority.[2]

First of all, most Hispanics see the Bible as a supernatural book and thus receive it with profound respect. This understanding of the Bible has two sources. The first source was Latin American Catholicism before Vatican Council II, which discouraged parishioners from reading the Bible, highlighting both the sacredness and the complexity of the text. This wrapped scripture with a shroud of mystery. The second source was the missionaries who were instrumental in the development of Protestantism in Latin America and the Caribbean. The majority of these missionaries stressed the supernatural character of the Bible. They did this for two reasons. First, most missionaries were either conservative or evangelical (mainstream Protestantism had a rather limited participation in the missionary movement south of the border). They believed that the Bible is authoritative by virtue of its miraculous origin: divine inspiration. Second, in contrast to other fields of mission, Latin America was a Catholic continent. In such a setting, the infallibility of scripture became a battering ram against the Roman Catholic doctrine of papal infallibility.[3]

At this point we must recognize that such emphasis on the supernatural character of scripture is the source of some excesses. For example, in some Latino homes there will always be an opened Bible—usually open to Psalm 23—as a means of protection against evil. Moreover, in some congregations, the Bible is used for healing purposes, such as the touching of an ill person's body with the Bible.[4]

Second, most Hispanic Protestants see the Bible as a historical source. Conservative and Pentecostal Hispanics tend to affirm that the Bible is historically accurate, explaining away difficult passages by the use of evangelical apologetics. Mainline Hispanic ministers, particularly those who have attended seminary, use historico-critical exegesis to study scripture. Therefore, Latino and Latina ministers in general highlight the relevance of history for understanding the Bible. Once again, such emphasis on "what really happened" may obscure the message of the text, especially if the preacher focuses too much on the facts behind the text and disregards its meaning.

Third, the Bible is central to Hispanic Protestant devotional piety. Most Latino congregations stress the importance of the daily devotional use of scripture. For this reason, most Hispanic Protestants have an ample—if somewhat uncritical—knowledge of the biblical text. This situation presents a challenge for Latino and Latina ministers. It requires that Hispanic ministers—both ordained and licensed—must know the Bible well and must develop good exegetical skills. Otherwise, they may be questioned and confronted by church members with more knowledge of the scripture than the minister has.

Fourth, most Hispanic Protestants have a privatized and individualistic understanding of the Bible. This is not surprising, given that modernity has fostered such an understanding of religion in general and scripture in particular. This approach is based on four assumptions.[5] The first is *interiorization*, the assertion that the aim of the biblical message is to facilitate a personal relationship between the "heart and soul" of the individual with God. The second assumption is *otherworldliness*, the claim that the gospel does not affect the societal and political structures of this world, because it belongs to a totally different one. The first two assumptions foster the third one, an *individualistic ethic* that proclaims universal moral values and attitudes for the individual, and redemption from personal sin, disregarding the social implications of the gospel. The fourth assumption is a *legalistic reading* of the Bible in which faith becomes intellectual assent to cosmic norms rather than being a way of life.

In addition to this inherited approach, the Latino Protestant community is developing an indigenous approach to the study of the Bible, rooted in characteristic traits of the Hispanic situation and culture. First of all, Hispanic hermeneutics are influenced by the social location, by the reality that the Latino community experiences daily in this nation. Let me enumerate briefly some aspects of that reality. Most Hispanics live in poverty. The majority of the Latino people provide cheap labor and do blue-collar work, falling into the category of "the working poor." Another aspect of the Hispanic social location is their status as immigrants. Approximately two-thirds of the Hispanics who live in the United States are either immigrants or descendants of immigrants. This has fostered a stereotype in American culture that equates Latinos and Latinas with undocumented workers, even though a third of the Hispanics who live in the United States are descendants of people who became American citizens when the territories in which they lived were either bought or conquered by the United States in expansionist wars.[6] This leads us to the third social reality, the struggle against racism and discrimination. Latino people face the criticism of those who resent their continued use of the Spanish language—in contrast with the immigrants who lost proficiency in their vernacular tongue—and their fidelity to their cultural roots.

Therefore, Hispanics read the Bible from a situation of poverty, alienation, and discrimination. As Latin American liberation theology has demonstrated, this means that Latinos and Latinas have an epistemological privilege in reading the Bible, given that the God who is revealed in scripture has taken a clear option for the poor.[7] When Hispanics read the Bible, they bring to the study of the text their own experiences of poverty, pilgrimage, exile, alienation, hunger, survival, endurance, illness, and discrimination, as well as the hope for a brighter future. They also bring the characteristic traits of their culture:[8] an emphasis on values such as honor, passion, heart (heroism), dignity, and respect; a lifestyle based on a network of personal relationships; the "paradox of the soul," defined as idealism and realism intimately entwined; a high regard for the community, seeing participation in the collectivity as the basis of human existence; the use of music, poetry, and literature to transmit values; a commitment to family, emphasizing family relations over individual ones; and a shared feeling of ethnicity, symbolized by terms such as *la raza* (the race, lineage) and *pueblo* (people) as powerful cultural and political self-referent terms.

From this vantage point, Hispanics find important points of contact between their experience and the stories narrated in the Bible. Even those Hispanics who read the Bible uncritically can relate to Israel's exodus, Abraham's pilgrimage, and the suffering of Agar (Hagar). Latinos and Latinas have an exceptional understanding of the situation of the poor, the marginalized, and the sick who reach to Jesus Christ in the biblical story.

Second, Hispanics have a rich mystical and spiritual tradition that impacts their hermeneutics. On the one hand, that tradition is rooted in Spanish Catholicism. Culturally, Hispanics are the heirs of San Juan de la Cruz, Santa Teresa de Jesús, Fray Luis de León, and other Spanish mystics.

On the other hand, popular religiosity plays an important role in Latino culture. All Latin American nations have lively popular religious practices, most of them ensuing from the blend of Amerindian and African traditions with Spanish Catholic practices.

In the Hispanic Protestant community, this emphasis on mysticism and spirituality translates into an emphasis on the centrality of the Holy Spirit in the theological endeavor. Latinos and Latinas are aware that without the activity of the Holy Spirit the hermeneutical chain that connects us with the mystery of divine salvation is broken. Without the Holy Spirit the Bible is a mere collection of ancient books, not the canon of the Holy Scriptures.[9] For this reason, Hispanic ministers tend to emphasize the importance of the Holy Spirit for the life of the church in general and for hermeneutics in particular, even those ministers whose denominations traditionally do not have such an emphasis.

Third, Hispanics prefer narrative approaches to the study and the exposition of scripture.[10] This preference is rooted in Spanish and Latin American literary traditions, not in the recent scholarly revival of narrative theology and inductive homiletical techniques. The Spanish language has a rich literature. Most Hispanics have at least a popular knowledge of this literature. For example, even those who are not well read are likely to have heard about literary characters such as Don Quijote, Sancho Panza, El Lazarillo de Tormes, Doña Bárbara, and Don Juan Tenorio. For this reason, even those ministers who lack formal theological training usually base their sermons on biblical stories, use stories as illustrations of their sermons, and, instinctively, use inductive approaches to both the study and the exposition of scripture.

The Use of the Bible
in Hispanic Theology

Hispanic theology questions whether the theology that we have received is relevant to the needs of the Latino people. It also questions the privatistic faith that is preached from most pulpits in the United States. Thus, it emphasizes the development of a theological reflection done from the perspective of the oppressed Hispanic community.[11]

One of the key theological areas under consideration is a new approach to hermeneutics.[12] Major facets of this approach are described in the sections that follow.

Marginalization as an Entry Point

Latino theology ponders the social situation of the Latino people in the United States. The experiences of marginalization, oppression, and discrimination endured by the Latino people serve as the point of entry to the liberating power of the Bible.[13] The particular social location of the Latino people makes possible a liberating dialogue with scripture. A Hispanic person who reads the Bible finds a message written by and for the marginalized and the oppressed. This grants Latinos and Latinas unique access to the "core" of the biblical message.

The Bible as a Liberating Text

Hispanic theology recognizes the centrality of the Bible in Latino theological discourse. However, it sees the Bible as a liberating text. That is, it affirms that the message of scripture is in and of itself liberating and that "the life and struggles of the Hispanic American community, howsoever defined, have been anticipated in the life and struggles of the people of God in the Bible."[14]

This new understanding of the Bible presents a sharp contrast with traditional privatized and individualistic readings. Furthermore, it questions whether the manner in which the scripture has been traditionally interpreted by the powerful is accurate.[15] This doubt arises out of what is called "ideological suspicion," that is, the suspicion that important aspects of the biblical message have been overlooked or distorted for ideological reasons.[16] Although those in power may have deliberately set out to interpret the Bible in an oppressive way, the truth is usually more subtle than that: "What actually takes place is an unconscious process through which values, goals, and interests of those in power are read into Scripture."[17]

A Correlation
between Social Locations

Given this social analysis and the understanding that the Bible is a liberating text, Hispanic theologians proceed to read the Bible seeking points of contact between the social location of the Latino people and the Bible. Once they find such points of contact, Hispanic theologians establish a "correspondence of relationships"[18] between the social location of the Latino community and the social location of the Bible. New Testament scholar Fernando Segovia describes this process as follows:

> The theological visions of these . . . Hispanic American theologians . . . [are] examples of a "correspondence of relationships," with a formal analogy drawn between the relationship of the Bible to its social context, howsoever conceived, and the relationship of the contemporary Christian community to its own social location.[19]

Clodovis Boff affirms that the model of "correspondence of relationships" goes farther and deeper than the model of "correspondence of terms" employed by the traditional historical criticism.[20] The latter seeks to establish the meaning of a biblical concept, the significance of narrative, or the implications of a historical event.[21] Once a conclusion is reached, the model calls the Christian community to *apply* these findings.[22] We can see good examples of this model in the many studies devoted to determine if Jesus was a pacifist or a Zealot.[23] The implications of these studies are obvious: If one can demonstrate that Jesus was a Zealot, the participation of Christians in the process of a revolution can be justified, but if it were possible to prove that Jesus was in fact an avowed pacifist, then "revolutionary Christianity" would be divested of any legitimate base.

The model of "correspondence of relationships" seeks to establish a correlation between the social relations that underlay and therefore shaped the biblical text and the social relations that underlie and shape our experience.[24] The correlation is not between the words of the text, nor even between experiences depicted in biblical narratives that may be similar to ours. The model of "correspondence of relationships"—in contrast to "correspondence of terms"—does not yield formulas to be copied or techniques to be applied. It is much more subtle in its approach to the Bible. This reading offers orientations, models, types, directives, and inspiration. The aim of such reading is to give us elements to be used as tools in the interpretation of both our current reality and the possibilities that the future will bring. That is, the purpose of this reading is to provide part of the criteria that will help us to move us along our "hermeneutic circle."

While I was researching this topic, I was invited to preach at the annual retreat of leaders of my denomination. The topic I was assigned seemed simple enough: our partnership in the gospel. Likewise, the message of Philippians 1:1–6 looked innocuous—that is, until I established a correlation between my social location as a Latino in an Anglo nation and Paul's social location as a Jew in the Roman Empire:

> As early as the crib we learn that there are two kinds of people: "us" and "them." "Us" people are good; "them" people are bad. "Us" people are right; "them" people are wrong. "Us" people do not enter in partnership with "them" people. I learned it; you learned it too.
>
> Paul, "a Hebrew born of Hebrews" (Phil. 3:5), learned this lethal lesson early in his life. He learned that the Jews were the "us" people and that the *"goyim"*—the non-Jews—were the "them" people. "Us" people do not enter in partnership with "them" people. This was the motto that steered his life. Then some of "us" (Jews) began to preach a gospel that included "them" (non-Jews) in a partnership with God. And Paul, guided by his exclusionary motto, began to persecute, terrorize, and even kill the traitors among "us." Yet the zealous young

Pharisee found—or may we say was found by (Gal. 4:9)—Jesus on the way to Damascus.

Therefore, what we find in Philippians is startling: A former "us" person testifying that he lives in partnership with those he formerly thought of as "them" people. A "subversive partnership" indeed.

The text does not offer a perfect parallel with the situation of the Latino people. Hispanics do not share the sense of election that characterizes the Jewish people in scripture. Yet the text gives us the opportunity to establish a correlation based on the practice of racism in society. Both the ancient Israelites and the contemporary Hispanics—as minority groups—face ethnic, cultural, and linguistic discrimination. Paul testifies that, through the gospel, he is now in a partnership that surmounts racism. Through the gospel, members of different ethnic groups are empowered to recognize the full humanity of the others, thus forging a new multicultural community.

A Key Metaphor

Hispanic theologians communicate the implications of this correlation through a key metaphor. This metaphor embodies their findings and thus it functions as a paradigmatic concept. In a way, it summarizes the whole process. Then the paradigm is used to exegete both the Bible and Hispanic reality.

Hispanic theologians have used metaphors to convey their insights. Let me discuss briefly some of the metaphors commonly employed in Hispanic theology.

The Galilean Principle

Hispanic theologians have used Bible stories about the region of Galilee to describe Hispanic reality. The points of contact between the Galilean experience—as depicted in the Bible—and Latino reality are evident. Galilee is a region that stands on the frontier between the territories of Israel, Lebanon, and Syria. In biblical times, the Jewish religious elite—especially those who lived in Jerusalem—despised the inhabitants of the region.[25] They considered Galileans to be "unclean" people who had contaminated themselves with foreign religious practices. Ethnically, Galileans were closer to Samaritans, who were considered mestizos by the elite. According to Virgilio Elizondo,

> At the time of Jesus, Galilee was peopled by Phoenicians, Syrians, Arabs, Greeks, Orientals, and Jews. In this mixed, commerce-oriented society, some Jews had allowed their Jewish exclusivism to weaken, but others became more militantly exclusivist. Some of the "goyim" (non-Jews) converted to Judaism

and intermarried with Jews. Some religious ideas of other groups were also assimilated, as is evident in the case of the Essenes. A natural, ongoing biological and cultural "*mestizaje*" was taking place.[26]

Similarly, Hispanics live at the margin of the great centers of power. In the same way that Galileans were looked down upon by Jewish leaders, Latinos and Latinas are despised by some Americans of Anglo-European descent. Hispanics know firsthand what it means to be mestizo, mulatto, and bicultural. We know the pain of being rejected both in the States and in the homelands of our ancestors. Hispanics know what it means to be— permanently—"the others."[27] In summary, Latinos and Latinas share the experience of oppression and marginality that characterizes Galileans in the scripture.

Several Hispanic theologians have employed the Galilean principle in their theological writings. The most renowned is Virgilio Elizondo, a Catholic Mexican American who was the first theologian dedicated to the development of a Latino theology. Elizondo developed both the Galilean principle and the metaphor of *mestizaje*. On the basis of Elizondo's work, most Latino and Latina theologians see the concepts of "marginality" and *mestizaje* as hermeneutical keys in Hispanic theology.[28]

Another author who developed the image of Galilee in his theological thinking was the late Orlando E. Costas. Costas used Galilee as a key metaphor in several articles.[29] However, instead of using the concept of *mestizaje*, Costas preferred "periphery":

> If, as the various books of the New Testament teach, evangelization is addressed in the first place to the poor, the dispossessed, and the oppressed, and if they are the ones who are most able to understand the meaning of the Gospel (cf. Matt. 11:25), then it follows that Galilee, as a symbol of the *periphery*, should be understood as a universal in relation to the theology of evangelization. Thus, the particularity of the periphery should inform all and each evangelizing context.[30]

Reading the Bible in Spanish

Justo L. González has advanced the idea of reading the Bible in the vernacular, that is, "in Spanish." His proposal is based on the belief that Hispanics bring a particular cultural and sociopolitical perspective to the interpretation of the Bible, as well as to history and theology.[31] Therefore, reading the Bible "in Spanish" is the metaphor employed by González to advocate a reading from the particular perspective that Hispanics bring to the study table by virtue of their social location:

> But perhaps we ought to see another dimension in what happens when the Bible is read in the vernacular. It becomes the people's book, no longer under

the control of those who control society. When the people read the Bible, and read it from their own perspective rather than from the perspective of the powerful, the Bible becomes a mighty political book. This is what I mean by "reading the Bible in Spanish": a reading that includes the realization that the Bible is a political book; a reading in the "vernacular," not only in the cultural, linguistic sense but also in the sociopolitical sense.[32]

For González, this reading "in Spanish" demands a particular reading strategy. This strategy—or "grammar" as he calls it—consists of four main rules.[33] First, to read the Bible "in Spanish" the interpreter must address sociopolitical concerns. He or she must understand that the Bible is a "political book"—because it addresses the issue of the use and abuse of power and the interplay between power and powerlessness—and, thus, he or she must ask "the political question."[34] To read the Bible "in Spanish" it is necessary to read it "from the margins," that is, as a member of a minority group that has little or no access to the power structures of society. He argues,

> When we approach a text, we must ask first not the "spiritual" questions or the "doctrinal" questions—the Bible is not primarily a book about "spiritual" reality, except in its own sense, nor it is a book about doctrines—but the political questions: Who in this text is in power? Who is the powerless? What is the nature of their relationship? Whose side does God take? In this approach to Scripture lies the beginning of a Hispanic-American theology, as well as the heart of the new reformation of the twentieth century.[35]

To those who object to such political readings, González replies that it is impossible to interpret the Bible in an apolitical fashion. Applying the criterion of "ideological suspicion," González expresses reservations about readings by interpreters who claim that their approaches have no political overtones or consequences. Furthermore, González asserts that the "apolitical" understanding of Christianity is very political indeed, given that it is intended to support the agenda of the status quo.[36]

The second "rule of grammar" stresses the public character of scripture. González reminds us that only a small portion of scripture was originally written to be read in private.[37] This is his way of affirming the communal orientation of scripture. A reading "in Spanish" must see the Bible addressing the community of faith; even when we read scripture in private, God is addressing all of us as a community of faith.

The third precept of González's "grammar" calls interpreters to attune their readings to what the poor find when they read the Bible. Such reading "must remember that the core principle of scriptural "grammar" is its availability to children, to the simple, to the poor."[38] Thus, whoever aspires to read the Bible "in Spanish" must provide opportunities for participation to those who are usually excluded from our Bible studies. We must hear what the "voiceless" find in the scripture and learn from them a new way of approaching the biblical message.

The fourth rule of this reading strategy calls us to read the Bible "in the vocative." This means "reading it with the clear awareness that we are not before a dead text, for the text that we address addresses us in return."[39] To read the Bible in the vocative is to recognize the difference between reading for information and reading for transformation, to acknowledge that both objectives are necessary; *and* to understand that the former is existentially subordinate to the latter.[40]

As in Elizondo's case, González's hermeneutical paradigm has inspired other Hispanic theologians, such as José D. Rodríguez[41] and Eduardo C. Fernández,[42] to advocate "reading the Bible in Spanish." Moreover, González's "rules of grammar" have become an important part of Hispanic hermeneutics.

Nonetheless, this is not the only metaphor employed by Gonzaález to describe the correlation between the social location of the Hispanic community and the Bible. He has also employed the Galilean principle, coupled with the idea of marginality. For example, the underlying concept of "marginality" is evident in the title of *Apuntes*, the theological journal of Hispanic theology that he has edited since 1981. *Apuntes* is a Spanish word that means both "marginal notes" and "aimings." In both cases the term emphasizes peripheral movements; whoever is writing marginal notes or taking aim is not at the "center."[43]

The City and the Barrio

In his many writings, Harold Recinos explores the situation of the Latino communities in the large urban centers of the United States, especially of those Puerto Rican "barrios"—a word that means "neighborhood" but that has come to denote Latino ghettos and inner-city communities—in the Northeast. This social analysis is the basis of Recinos's "barrio theology," a theology of survival that seeks to make sense of the reality of oppression—restoring a sense of human dignity to the community—guided by a vision of a new world based on justice and equality.[44]

> Theology in the context of the Barrio must make it clear to the faith community that God's promise of a new heaven runs counter to the dehumanization and social invisibility that mark the existential experience of the ghetto; hence, an important dimension of the mission of the Latino church in the U.S. churches includes enabling people to discover their own power.[45]

In his book on globalization and urban ministries,[46] Recinos dedicates a full chapter to the biblical image of the city. Here he establishes a correlation between the social location of the Latino community and the Bible, calling the church to see the city as a sacred place, and to engage in the transformation of the barrios in the direction of the reign of God.[47] In this sense, both *barrio* and *city* become metaphors that embody Recinos's theology.

Other Metaphors

Justo L. González has identified a number of metaphors employed by Hispanic religious leaders.[48] In addition to *mestizaje* and marginality, González calls our attention to the use of concepts such as *mulatez* (the miscegenation of people of African descent with Amerindians and Spaniards), poverty, exile, alienness, and solidarity. As he demonstrates, these concepts are used by different theologians and preachers to convey their readings "in Spanish" of the biblical text.

Other Models

Although the methodology explained above is in common use among Hispanic theologians, it is not the only one employed in Latino religious thought. At least two other methodologies are worth mentioning. The first calls for the use of the Bible as a primary resource for symbolizing the Hispanic popular religiosity, thus engaging in a dialogue with Latino culture.[49] This methodology has been advanced by C. Gilbert Romero.[50]

An additional methodology has been advanced by exponents of *mujerista* theology (a Hispanic women's liberation theology), particularly Ada María Isasi-Díaz. Mujerista theology calls for using the Bible to promote the critical consciousness of Hispanic women,[51] using the principle of a canon within the canon.[52] Isasi-Díaz states: "Only those parts of the Bible which allow and enable a true liberative understanding of Hispanic women are accepted as revealed truth."[53] Although Isasi-Díaz's remarks about the use of the Bible by Latinas have generated much controversy,[54] she affirms the liberating character of scripture, calling Hispanic women to interpret the Bible in a way that enables and enhances their moral agency.[55]

Toward a Hermeneutics of Assent

In the summer of 1992, I attended a lecture by Fred B. Craddock at the Lutheran School of Theology at Chicago. After the lecture, one of the students asked him about his opinion on the hermeneutics of suspicion. After a brief pause, Dr. Craddock answered: "In the latter part of my life, I find myself moving from a hermeneutics of suspicion toward a hermeneutics of assent."

Since then I have given much thought to Dr. Craddock's words, coming to the conclusion that suspicion and obedience are two important points in a hermeneutical continuum. In the case of Hispanic theology, suspicion is an important part of the theological process. In order to promote the self-determination and the well-being of the Latino community, we must deconstruct those readings that legitimate oppression, racism, sexism, and discrimination. Nonetheless, we must remember that God has called us to "build upon the foundation of the apostles and prophets, with Christ Jesus himself as the cornerstone" (Eph. 2:20). The deconstruction of oppressive readings is only the first step toward the reconstruction of liberating ones.

Therefore, suspicion must lead to obedience. After all, the goal of Latino biblical interpretation is to discern and to heed God's will.

NOTES

1. Paul Collingson-Streng and Ismael de la Tejera, "Bible and Mission in Hispanic Congregation," in *Bible and Mission: Biblical Foundations and Working Models for Congregational Ministry*, ed. Wayne Stumme (Minneapolis: Augsburg, 1986), 132–33.
2. In this section we follow Daniel L. Migliore, *Faith Seeking Understanding: An Introduction to Christian Theology* (Grand Rapids: Wm. B. Eerdmans Publishing Co., 1991), 43–45.
3. On the issue of the infallibility of the Bible, see Carl E. Braaten, "The Gospel and the Crisis of Authority," *Dialog* 31:4 (autumn 1992): 305–6; and Carl E. Braaten et al., *Christian Dogmatics I* (Philadelphia: Fortress Press, 1984), 66–67.
4. Collingson-Streng and de la Tejera, "Bible and Mission," 133.
5. Elisabeth Schüssler Fiorenza, "The Bible, the Global Context and the Discipleship of Equals," in *Reconstructing Christian Theology*, ed. Rebecca S. Chopp and Mark Lewis Taylor (Minneapolis: Fortress Press, 1994), 82.
6. Spain ceded Florida to England in 1763. Texas was invaded in 1819. This invasion was followed by several migratory waves that ended up in the independence of Texas in 1836. After the Mexican-American War, Mexico surrendered more than three million square miles to the United States for $15 million. Puerto Rico came to be a territory of the United States when Spain lost the Spanish-American War in 1898.
7. See Clodovis Boff and George Pixley, *The Bible, the Church and the Poor* (Maryknoll, N.Y.: Orbis Books, 1989).
8. Eldin Villafañe, *The Liberating Spirit: Toward an Hispanic American Pentecostal Social Ethic* (Lanham, Md.: University Press of America, 1992), 1–24, passim.
9. Braaten, "The Gospel," 308.
10. Pablo A. Jiménez, ed. *Lumbrera a nuestro camino* (Miami: Editorial Caribe, 1994), 127–29.
11. José D. Rodríguez, "De 'apuntes' a 'esbozo': Diez años de reflexión," *Apuntes* 10:4 (winter 1990): 75.

12. Fernando F. Segovia has published two studies on Hispanic hermeneutics, "Hispanic American Theology and the Bible: Effective Weapon and Faithful Ally," in *We Are a People! Initiatives in Hispanic American Theology*, ed. Roberto S. Goizueta (Minneapolis: Fortress Press, 1992), 21–39; and "Reading the Bible as Hispanic Americans," in *The New Interpreter's Bible*, vol. 1, ed. Leander E. Keck et al. (Nashville: Abingdon Press, 1994), 167–73.

13. Segovia, "Hispanic," 47.

14. Ibid., 46.

15. Justo L. González and Catherine G. González, *Liberation Preaching: The Pulpit and the Oppressed* (Nashville: Abingdon Press, 1980), 15.

16. On "ideological suspicion," see Juan Luis Segundo, *The Liberation of Theology* (Maryknoll, N.Y.: Orbis Books, 1976), 7–9, passim.

17. González and González, *Liberation Preaching*, 13.

18. Clodovis Boff, *Teología de lo político: Sus mediaciones* (Salamanca: Ediciones Sígueme, 1980), 275.

19. Segovia, "Hispanic," 45–46.

20. Boff, *Teología*, 275.

21. Ibid., 267–71.

22. Ibid., 269.

23. Boff, *Teología*, 270. For an introduction to this discussion, see Oscar Cullmann, *Jesús y los revolucionarios de su tiempo* (Barcelona: Editorial Herder, 1980); and Martin Hengel, *Jesús y la violencia revolucionaria* (Salamanca: Ediciones Sígueme, 1973).

24. Boff, *Teología*, 278.

25. For a general introduction to the characteristics of Galilee, see K. W. Clark, s.v. "Galilee" in *The Interpreter's Dictionary of the Bible*, vol. 2, ed. George A. Buttrick et al. (Nashville: Abingdon Press, 1962), 344–47. On the racial tensions between Judeans and Galileans, see Geza Vermes, *Jesus the Jew: A Historian's Reading of the Gospels* (Philadelphia: Fortress Press, 1973), 19–41.

26. Virgilio Elizondo, *Galilean Journey: The Mexican-American Promise* (Maryknoll, N.Y.: Orbis Books, 1983), 51.

27. Fernando F. Segovia, "Two Places and No Place on Which to Stand: Mixture and Otherness in Hispanic American Theology," *Listening* 27:1 (winter 1992): 25.

28. Rodríguez, "De 'apuntes,'" 81.

29. For further information, see Orlando Costas, "Evangelism from the Periphery: A Galilean Model," *Apuntes* 2:3 (fall 1982): 51–59, and "Evangelism from the Periphery: The Universality of Galilee," *Apuntes* 2:4 (winter 1982): 75–84.

30. Orlando E. Costas, *Liberating News: A Theology of Contextual Evangelization* (Grand Rapids: Wm. B. Eerdmans Publishing Co., 1989), 61.

31. Justo L. González, *Mañana: Christian Theology from a Hispanic Perspective* (Nashville: Abingdon Press, 1990), 75.

32. Ibid., 84.

33. Ibid., 85.

34. González and González, *Liberation Preaching*, 69–74.

35. González, *Mañana*, 85.

36. Ibid., 84.

37. Ibid., 85.

38. Ibid.

39. Ibid., 86.

40. Jean-Pierre Ruiz, "Beginning to Read the Bible in Spanish: An Assessment," *Journal for Hispanic/Latino Studies* 1:2 (February 1994): 36.

41. José D. Rodríguez, "The Challenge of Hispanic Ministry: Reflections on John 4," *Currents in Theology and Mission* 18:6 (1991): 420–26.

42. Eduardo C. Fernández, "Reading the Bible in Spanish: U.S. Catholic Hispanic Theologians' Contribution to Systematic Theology," *Apuntes* 14:3 (fall 1994): 86–95.

43. Justo L. González, ed. *Voces: Voices from the Hispanic Church* (Nashville: Abingdon Press, 1992), 3.

44. Segovia, "Hispanic," 35.

45. Harold J. Recinos, "Mission: A Latino Pastoral Theology," *Apuntes* 12:3 (fall 1992):120.

46. Harold J. Recinos, *Jesus Weeps: Global Encounters on Our Doorstep* (Nashville: Abingdon Press, 1992).

47. Ibid., 53.

48. Justo L. González, *Santa Biblia: Reading the Bible through Hispanic Eyes* (Nashville: Abingdon Press, 1995).

49. C. Gilbert Romero, "On Choosing a Symbol System for a Hispanic Theology," *Apuntes* 1:4 (winter 1981): 16–20.

50. C. Gilbert Romero, *Hispanic Devotional Piety: Tracing the Biblical Roots* (Maryknoll, N.Y.: Orbis Books, 1991).

51. Ada María Isasi-Díaz, "The Bible and *Mujerista* Theology," in *Lift Every Voice: Constructing Christian Theologies from the Underside*, ed. Susan Brooks Thistlethwaite and Mary Potter Engel (San Francisco: HarperCollins 1990), 267.

52. Segovia, "Hispanic," 33.

53. Isasi-Díaz, "The Bible," 268.

54. In "The Bible and *Mujerista* Theology" Isasi-Díaz states: "The Bible per se is extremely peripheral to the lives of Hispanic women." In her book *En la Lucha/In the Struggle: Elaborating a Mujerista Theology* (Minneapolis: Fortress Press, 1993), 46–47, she restates her position. These comments have prompted a response by Loida Martell-Otero, in "Women Doing Theology: Una perspectiva Evangélica," *Apuntes* 14:3 (fall 1994): 67–85.

55. Ada María Isasi-Díaz, "'By the Rivers of Babylon': Exile as a Way of Life," in *Reading from This Place*, vol. 1: *Social Location and Biblical Interpretation in the United States*, ed. Fernando F. Segovia and Mary Ann Tolbert (Minneapolis: Fortress Press, 1995), 154.

6

In Quest of a Protestant Hispanic Ecclesiology

Justo L. González

Do we have an ecclesiology? As I began to reflect on this question, my first thought was that as Protestant Latinos and Latinas we have inherited a theology in which ecclesiology plays a very secondary role. This can be explained by a number of factors.

First, the Protestantism that was brought to us, both in Latin America and in much of the United States, was a Protestantism that centered on personal salvation—as was most of the nineteenth-century Protestantism that fostered the missionary movement. What was important was one's own individual faith, rather than the faith of the community. As a matter of fact, there was much emphasis on the impossibility of being saved on the basis of the faith of the community. You had to be born again individually, no matter for how long or how deeply you had belonged to a church. This led to much preaching that, while taking place within the context of a church, was, however, deeply anti-church. The essence of this anti-church message was something like, "Do not think that because you belong to the church you will be saved. It is not a matter of belonging to the church. It is a matter of personal faith, of accepting Jesus as your Lord and Savior, of being born again." Within that theological framework, the church is at best a vehicle for the preaching of the gospel, and a source of support and assurance for those who have been born anew, and at worst it is an obstacle to salvation, a mirage that prevents us from attaining saving faith.[1]

Second, when transplanted into a predominantly Roman Catholic environment, that individualistic form of Protestantism became even more anti-church. Protestant preachers made much headway by pointing out the contradictions they saw between the Bible and the actual life and teachings of the Roman Catholic Church. Roman Catholic dogma, they said, was "of men [*sic*]," whereas the doctrine they preached was "of God." What "the church" had done through the centuries was to bring much human tradition into its life, thus corrupting the original gospel of Jesus Christ.[2]

Third, at a time when intellectual, economic, and political liberalism was on the upswing, Protestant preachers found it quite helpful to emphasize the authority of the individual to examine the Bible, and to deny and even ridicule the notion that the community of faith had any authority on matters of faith and doctrine, except in those cases in which it could clearly convince the individual believer that this was indeed what the Bible said. The picture of Luther at Leipzig, claiming that a single Christian with the Bible has more authority than all the popes, bishops, and councils without it, became the favorite icon of many a Protestant preacher and teacher. That this picture was taken out of context, and that Luther himself had a fairly high understanding of the church, was generally forgotten or ignored. The net result of this was to reinforce the notion that the church, rather than being necessary for salvation, quite often is an obstacle to it, and that the church has no authority except that which it derives from literally agreeing with scripture, or what authority the individual believer might deign to give it.[3]

Fourth, this sort of anti-church discourse was made easier and more acceptable to Roman Catholic Hispanics because in those days before Vatican II most people understood "the church" to be composed of the hierarchy. When good Catholic Hispanics said, even as late as the early 1960s, that "the church" teaches this or that, they did not include themselves in "the church," which they saw as some amorphous body cutting across time and geography, telling them what to believe and to do. Thus, although such good Catholics did accept the authority of the church, they did not feel themselves included in it. That authority was completely extrinsic. For many such good Catholics, to attack "the church" was not to attack them, nor even to attack their faith. They were not really part of "the church," even though they believed most of its teachings. Most were used to practicing various forms of popular religiosities which, while not condemned by the church, also were not sanctioned by it. In conclusion, they were already quite accustomed to a life of faith in which the church played only a secondary role—as many would say, "Soy católico, pero no creo en los curas" (I am a Catholic, but I don't believe in priests).[4]

Fifth, just as Vatican II was beginning to make its impact felt both in Latin America and among Latino Catholics in the United States, Protestantism broke forth in unprecedented growth in both of those contexts. Most of that growth was among Pentecostals, who still preached individual salvation and being born again, but whose emphasis on the gifts of the Spirit was often couched in terms that were antithetical to the authority of the community of faith. Just as earlier Protestants had affirmed an individual's right to interpret the Bible, no matter what the church said, Pentecostals tended to emphasize the freedom of the Spirit, even against the traditions and expectations of any church. Furthermore, since several of the earliest and most successful Pentecostal movements in Latin America had broken away from the more traditional Protestant churches, and in many of those churches there had been a process of trial and expulsion of Pentecostal leaders, there was reason to emphasize the possibility and even the likelihood that the church might err and go far astray, and to stress the freedom of the Spirit from all ecclesiastical constraints or precedents.

Finally, we must take into account the manner in which Latino churches have developed within the context of the United States. Hispanic congregations and individuals belonging to denominations whose membership is mostly white have generally remained at the margins of such denominations. On the average, their pastors have received less theological education than pastors of the dominant culture,[5] and their laity—most of whom are relatively poor—have not been given the positions of responsibility of white laity. The result is that in those congregations very little is said of the church at large, of its wider program, or of its ecclesiology. One of the consequences of such margination is that even in local churches that belong to strongly connectional denominations, the functioning ecclesiology tends to be congregational.

This is even more so among independent or semi-independent churches, many of which have been founded by a charismatic leader who disagreed with the leadership in another church—or simply by a leader who felt called to pastoral ministry and preaching, and for whom there was no place in an existing congregation.

In short, most Latino and Latina Protestants do not give ecclesiology much thought. And when we do, our thoughts tend to run along individualistic lines. Thus, for instance, the most common statements about the church take for granted the priority of the faithful over the church. In this view, it is the believers who come together to form the church, and the function of the church is to nourish and support the faith of the believers, and to help them witness to the faith so that there can be more believers.

This priority of the individual believer over the church is manifested in the strange form that ecumenism—usually under another name—takes among Latino and Latina Protestants. The very word "ecumenical" is taboo among many—partly because they understand it as an effort to get them to abandon some of the essential tenets of the faith in the elusive quest for a minimum common denominator which, if ever found, would be so bland as to be meaningless. There is also the suspicion—although hardly ever voiced—that the more sophisticated and higher-class partners in such a dialogue will manage to maneuver the conversation to their advantage, and that the lower-class Latino and Latina Christians will be blindsided. (Their suspicion is not entirely unfounded, when one takes into account the fact

that most of the official ecumenical dialogue takes place among denominations whose membership is at least middle class, and which look down at the
types of Christianity that are most prevalent among Protestant Latinos and
Latinas.) Among most Hispanic Protestants, to belong to independent congregations, quite apart from generally recognized denominations, is not
considered a serious matter. The result of all of this is that among many
Latinas and Latinos it makes very little difference to what church one belongs, and all sorts of cooperative ventures are possible in the Latino community that would be quite difficult in the old-line white denominations.

A Missional and
Metaphorical Ecclesiology

Taking all of this into account, my first reaction to the assigned topic was
that as Latino and Latina Protestants we have more to learn from the more
traditional ecclesiologies than we have to contribute to them. After further
thought, however, I have come to the conclusion that we do have a significant contribution to make along these lines—although such a conclusion
does not deny that we also have much to learn.

The first point to note in this regard is that there is a parallelism between
the development of our ecclesiology as Latinas and Latinos and the course
of ecclesiological development in the history of Christian thought. As one
reads patristic and early medieval theology, one is struck by the lack of systematic reflection on the church and its nature. True, there is Cyprian's
brief treatise *On the Unity of the Church*, responding to a specific challenge
and understanding of that unity.[6] But in general, ecclesiology is subsumed
under Christology, soteriology, the doctrine on the sacraments, and eschatology. It is not until the late Middle Ages, in the work of such theologians
as Giles of Rome and John of Paris, that theologians begin to discuss ecclesiology as a separate theological subject per se. Even then, the treatises
of these and other theologians are responses to the debate of the time about
the authority of the ecclesiastical hierarchy vis-à-vis the civil.[7]

Given its origins, and the challenge of the Protestant Reformation very
soon thereafter, Roman Catholic ecclesiology remained mainly scholastic
for a long time. While there were many who wrote of the church as "the
mystical body" of Christ,[8] professional theologians as a whole wrote treatises in which they sought to define the church in abstract and "objective"
terms, relegating the biblical images of the church to illustrations or
metaphors for what supposedly could and should be more clearly and precisely in abstract philosophical vocabulary. As part of the same methodology, the questions most often asked were "What is the church?" and "Who
is in the church?" In other words, ecclesiology was mostly a matter of

definition, both in the sense of clarification (What is the church?) and in the sense of demarcation (Who is in the church?).

It was mostly as a result of Vatican II that Roman Catholic ecclesiology began speaking more in terms of mission (What is the church for? Whom is the church for?) and reverting to the biblical images, not so much as quaint metaphors for what could be said better in abstract language, but rather as ways of describing the church as it seeks to fulfill its mission.[9]

What we thus have in that development of ecclesiology is a process that goes from an early, almost unreflective stage, to a more systematic and abstract one, to a third stage that, while retaining the interest in the church as a theological subject, draws heavily on the images and perspectives of the very first period.

As I then look at the course of Latino Protestant ecclesiology, I see a parallel development. In the first period, there is virtually no ecclesiological reflection. Churches are born, not out of a conscious understanding of "church," but simply out of the existence of a community of believers who gather because of their faith. During the first generation(s), there is little discussion of what the church is or should be. Church simply happens. It is the outcome of the preaching of the gospel, even when that gospel has some strong anti-church emphases. Then, mostly as a response to Roman Catholic challenges on who and what is the true church, Latino and Latina Protestants begin to develop a more conscious ecclesiology—although in sermons and Sunday school materials rather than in theological treatises. Like the late medieval ecclesiologies, this Latino Protestant ecclesiology seeks to respond to those who attack the church—in this case, not its hierarchy, but rather its very right to be called a "church." It is at this time that Latino theological reflection begins drawing on the distinction between the "visible" and the "invisible" church,[10] and develops an incipient ecclesiology that tries to understand "church" apart from tradition and institution. Here, as in the late medieval and the post-Tridentine Roman Catholic Church, the dominant questions are "What is the church?" and "Who is the church?" Significantly, to this day that is what most Latino and Latina Protestants understand as the fundamental questions of ecclesiology.

Currently, however, there is a recovery of ecclesiology that goes in two directions: first, a return to the biblical images that nourished our understanding of the church in "pre-ecclesiological" times; and second, a greater emphasis on the missiological question, what and whom is the church *for*.

This is perhaps our greatest contribution to ecclesiology. Apart from those instances when we have allowed ourselves to be carried away by the heat of anti-Catholic polemics, our ecclesiological reflection is missional rather than definitional, and it is often couched in terms of biblical images to which we resonate for a number of reasons, but which can never be expressed in more abstract, technical terms.

As a way to illustrate what this means, I shall look at the four traditional "marks" or "signs" of the church. Significantly, except for "holy," very seldom in Hispanic Protestant circles does one hear the traditional marks of the church referred to. Actually, more often than not, especially in popular preaching, they are used as words that others—mistakenly—apply to the church. Thus, terms such as "catholic," "apostolic," and even "holy" and "one" are often used in pejorative ways, signifying misunderstandings of both church and gospel. Still, when one looks at the deeper meaning of each of these terms, one sees that it functions within the praxis, even though not often in the vocabulary, of the Latino Protestant church. One also sees that the way the marks of the church are usually signified is not by their more traditional terms—one, holy, catholic, and apostolic—but rather by metaphors that describe our experience of church.

In order to clarify what this might mean, I shall explore briefly each of the traditional four "marks," and relate them to some of the metaphors we use to refer to them. And, in order to signify and emphasize the missional foundation of our functioning ecclesiology, I shall treat them in reverse order from the more common usage: apostolic, catholic, holy, and one.

The Church Is Apostolic

In Latino Protestant circles, the term "apostolic" is most often used in a primitivistic sense. Thus, when a church calls itself "apostolic," what it most commonly means to claim is, not that it has an unbroken line of succession with the apostles, but that through its reading and application of the New Testament it has managed to leap back over the centuries, in order to conform to the doctrines and practices of apostolic times.[11]

Significantly, there is a point of coincidence between that understanding of apostolicity and the more traditional Roman Catholic understanding, for in both to be "apostolic" means to be connected with the apostles—in one case through apostolic succession,[12] and in the other through agreement in doctrine and practice.[13]

Yet the manner in which I use the term here is more etymological, so that to be "apostolic" means to be sent. We tend to think that what makes an "apostle" such is having seen Jesus—and we read Paul's arguments to the Corinthians about his apostleship in that light. But in fact what makes an apostle is having been *sent* by Jesus. In Galatians 2:8, for instance, Paul says that the same one who made Peter an apostle to the circumcised has also worked in Paul—presumably, in the context of the argument, making him an apostle too—by *sending* him to the Gentiles. In 2 Corinthians 12:12, where he is arguing for his apostleship, his main argument is that "the signs of a true apostle were performed among you." And in 1 Corinthians 9:2, he declares that his Corinthian converts are "the seal of my apostleship in the Lord." It is also in this sense that Roman Catholics use the term when they refer to a mission as an "apostolate."

If being "apostolic" means being sent, having a sense of mission, there is no doubt that the Latino Protestant church is apostolic in the highest degree. Part of this comes from the manner in which the gospel was presented to us, as an urgent message of salvation which people must hear or perish eternally, and in that sense we share our missional impulse with others whose Christianity has been shaped by the same emphasis. But in part also our missional emphasis, as Latinos and Latinas in the United States, has to do with our being a pilgrim people. We are a people with no land. Even those of us whose ancestors were in these lands generations ago are still made to feel as if this land is not our land. And those others who are more recent arrivals certainly feel that they have no permanent roots—often, that they will not be allowed to develop permanent roots.[14]

Thus the image of pilgrimage is crucial both to our religious heritage and to our social circumstance. As I visit Latino churches, I find that in the book of Exodus what most fascinates our people is not the crossing of the Red Sea but the pilgrimage in the wilderness. And what is of most interest in the later history of Israel is not the story of the reigns of David and Solomon but rather the exile and return. In both cases, the image of pilgrimage is central. Significantly, however, this is not a pilgrimage we undertake as individuals, like Bunyan's pilgrim. Rather, it is a pilgrimage on which we have been sent as a people, in solidarity with others who suffer from the same lack of roots and share the same longing and hope.

How does this relate to apostolicity? Obviously, it relates first of all in the sense of being sent, of going, of being on the march. An apostolic people cannot have roots that tie them too deeply to one place and setting. And we, who for a number of reasons are denied such roots, can easily relate to that often neglected aspect of apostolicity.

But then there is another dimension in which the image of pilgrimage relates to mission. In order to understand this, one has to have been part of one of the *romerías*, pilgrimages, that are so common in our cultural tradition. A *romería* is a combination of religious pilgrimage, community picnic, and open invitation to a festival. As the people march in *romería* toward a shrine, they stop along the way to invite others to join. A *romería* is not like an army on the march, with sharply defined and closed ranks. It is more like a snowball rolling down a mountain, gathering more and more snow as it gathers speed. People are invited to join, and they join in part because there is food at the end, but also because there is fun and companionship along the way—and, if the way is too long, there might even be some food to sustain you until you reach the object of pilgrimage.

It is thus that the Latino Protestant church often understands its pilgrimage. It is marching joyfully toward a promised future, but along the way it invites others to join the march to the fiesta, and even to have a little glimpse of the great fiesta while still along the way.[15]

There is much discussion—mostly on the part of outsiders—about why our churches grow as they do. There are many ways to assess the reasons for their obviously phenomenal growth. But one of the elements that outsiders often miss is that we are a people in pilgrimage, a people in *romería*, who suffer the pain of having been "sent" away from home (or having our home taken away from us), but who also savor the joy of being on a great, divinely ordered *romería*. When we invite others to come join us, we do not invite them to come sit with us in a safe and boring place; rather, we invite them to join us in the great pilgrimage of our common pain, hope, and feasting.

We may seldom refer to the church as "apostolic." Yet the manner in which our community lives the pilgrimage of faith makes it apostolic in a sense that goes far beyond a connection with the apostles, be it through an uninterrupted succession or by an unblemished orthodoxy.

The Church Is Catholic

This is not a word one hears too often in Protestant Hispanic circles— and when one hears it, it usually refers to "them" over against "us" true believers. Even in many "mainline churches"—a contradiction in terms, for in a society of margination it may well be impossible to be at the same time mainline and a church of Jesus Christ—where the creed is repeated every Sunday, the most common Spanish translations, instead of saying "the catholic church," say "la iglesia universal." In our common language, as in English, *católica* is the same as Roman Catholic, and is used either appreciatively or pejoratively depending on one's feelings toward that church.

Yet, as I have shown elsewhere in more detail,[16] in its etymology and original usage "catholic" is not the same as "universal," and in some instances may be its exact opposite. While we say that something is universal when it is equally valid everywhere, and shows little or no variation from place to place, the word "catholic"—etymologically, "according to the whole"—implies a unity in which variety is not only embraced but also considered necessary for the whole. For instance, the universal rule of a world empire could never be called "catholic." Thus, much of what we Latino and Latina Protestants do not like about the word "catholic" is that it is understood in the sense of "universal," and then the claim follows that there is a particular way of being Christian which is universally valid, and which by definition tends to exclude every other way, and to reject the contributions that such other ways may bring to the whole.

As Latino and Latina Protestants, we have experienced claims of universality on the part of the dominant culture as oppressive and dehumanizing. This experience was expressed quite bluntly by the late Orlando Costas, the dean of Latino Evangelical theologians:

> The fact of the matter is that in North American Christendom the lost are not simply those who do not profess a personal faith in Jesus Christ, but especially those who are "outside" the domain of established religious institutions.
>
> In a real sense, the old maxim of the church fathers, "outside the church, there is no salvation," is applicable today to everyone who is not directly or indirectly, practically or formally part of the North American ecclesiastical compound. To be sure, the latter is as complex as it is sophisticated; it has invisible walls and a hidden gate. It is pluriformal and goes by different names. It can be a socioreligious network, denomination, or spiritual community. It can be labelled mainstream Christianity or established evangelicalism, United Presbyterian or Roman Catholic, American or Southern Baptist, United Methodist or United Church of Christ, Episcopalian or Assembly of God, Brethren or Schwenkfelder. Its form and identity notwithstanding, it is evidenced in the past history and present situation of North American society.[17]

What Costas meant is that the Christianity of the dominant culture, precisely because it is dominant, can easily make the claim of universality, and thus crush others into fitting its own mold, or leave them with no option but that of being called heretical.

But we know that the church is not, and should never be, universal.[18] It is not universal, not because of some lack of geographical expansion, or because some do not accept its authority. It is not universal by its very nature, precisely because it is catholic! It is not universal because it must bring and accept into its fold many people from many tribes, languages, and nations, and accept them in such a way that they each and all contribute to the whole.

Probably the image most often used in Latino Protestant churches to make this point is that of the body of Christ. Here again one notes a contrast with one of the most prevalent usages of that image in the dominant community. In the dominant community, the image of the body of Christ is often used in terms of instrumentality, as in the assertion that "Christ has no hands but your hands." In the Latino community, such an assertion is unthinkable. First of all, if Christ has no hands but ours, then Christ is weak and helpless—for we are generally helpless in a society of landlords and moneylenders, corrupt politicians and racist standards. We have little use for a Christ who has no hands but our hands. We worship a Christ whose hand upholds the universe, and whose justice shall overcome, no matter what our hands and our feet do or do not do.

Then, in the dominant community the image of the body of Christ is often used to stress the variety in the church. That comes closer to the way it is used in our Latino communities, for it makes it clear that all of us, no matter of what color, language, or social status, can be part of this body, and that our diversity is not something to be spurned, for we all have a place in the body.

Yet, while that point is certainly true, there is a further dimension in the image of the church as the body of Christ that comes closer to expressing true "catholicity" and that theology done from the perspective of the center often misses. The image of the body of Christ does not imply only that the various members are different, and that they each have a place. The image of the church as the body of Christ implies also and foremost that the body *needs* each of its varied members. From the Hispanic point of view, that is clearly what Paul means when he says, for instance, that if the whole body were an eye there would be no hearing (1 Cor. 12:17). This implies, not only that there is a place for the ear and a place for the eye, but also that, if the body is to be whole, it has to have eyes as well as ears, for each contributes something different, and that something different is needed by the entire body.

The church is "catholic" just as the body is catholic: by having many members, all different, but all making a necessary contribution to the whole, so that if one member is missing the entire body suffers. In short, from a Latino point of view, variety is not only acceptable and good; it is necessary.[19]

The Church Is Holy

It is probably at this point that the dependence of Latino Protestant churches on those who brought us the message of the gospel is most significant and tragic. For many of us, this means that the church must keep its holiness by expelling from its midst all the unholy—which, obviously, if carried to its ultimate consequences would leave no one in the church. The emphasis on moral holiness that lies behind this understanding is part of the legacy of Latino churches from the original missionaries who came to us, and quite often seems to rob the joy of our apostolic *romería*, for we seem to be stopping at every turn to determine who is worthy to join us, and who is not.

This has been reinforced by our social milieu. Most of the members of our churches come from settings in which they have seen Christians of the dominant culture live and act as if their faith meant nothing to them. Quite often they have been oppressed or belittled by such Christians. They have seen the ease with which such Christians combine their faith with the cultural and social standards acceptable in the dominant culture. Then, in our own cultures of poverty, many have firsthand experience with the corrupting and debilitating power of vices and of broken moral standards. Therefore, when Latinas and Latinos join a church, very often they are looking for an alternative both to the corrupt lifestyles that are so common in our own culture, and to the equally corrupt but sanctified lifestyles we see in the dominant culture. As a result, they insist quite strongly on the highest standards of morality and holiness—often conceived in terms of abstaining from certain practices and vices.[20]

Thus, to proclaim in a Latino Protestant environment that the church must be holy runs the danger of turning the church into a guardian of morality, and a place where people are constantly judging each other. And this is a danger often reinforced by some of the images we use in this context—for instance, the church as the bride of Christ, on which we then pour all our preconceived notions of virginal purity and strict morality.

Given that situation, what some elements in the Latino Protestant community are emphasizing is the contrast between saying that the church "is" holy, and saying that it "should be" holy. When we hear the word "holiness," most people immediately think of "oughtness," of "should" or "must." By emphasizing the point that the church "is" holy, we are underscoring the givenness of that holiness, which does not depend on the holiness of particular members, and which therefore cannot be built up by expelling those who are unholy. The church is holy because it is the body of Christ, in spite of all its sin; because the Word it proclaims and holds in earthen vessels is holy; because it is called to share in God's holy reign.

In this case, then, what we have is a situation contrary to what we saw in the previous two marks of the church. In the case of apostolicity and catholicity, we had words that the Latino Protestant churches seldom apply to themselves, but which they in fact practice. In those cases we had to clarify the meaning of the words, in order to show that Latino churches are in fact apostolic and catholic. Here we have a word, "holy," that many Latino Protestant churches would at least like to apply to themselves. And yet, this too we must clarify, so that Latinos and Latinas will cease applying it to themselves in a narrow moralistic way. And yet here again, as in the case of apostolicity and catholicity, we see Latino Protestant churches living the mark of holiness in ways that they would not immediately identify as signs of holiness.

If the church is holy because of its connection with Christ, and because it points to God's coming holy reign, then there are many ways in which the Latino Protestant church shows its holiness. The Latino Protestant church is a place where people encounter the Holy; in that sense, it is holy. The Latino Protestant church is a place where people worship the Holy; in that sense, too, it is holy. The Latino Protestant church is a place where people meet each other as children of the Holy God, and therefore as holy; in that sense, too, the church is holy.

Above all, however, in the Latino church one finds a sense that we are a holy people, not so much because of what we do as because of whose we are. We insist on practicing personal and communal holiness, not because by so doing we somehow attain salvation, but because we know to whom we belong. The sense of belonging to God—or, as I shall explain in the next section, of being the family of God—is very strong in many of our Latino Protestant churches. We insist on not walking in the ways of wickedness because, as the psalmist put it, "If I had said, 'I will talk on in this way,' I would have been untrue to the circle of your children" (Ps. 73:15). Our insistence on holiness is not so much an effort to become something as it is an attempt to be true to the God and to the family to whom we belong.

Thus, what is needed here is a vast work of redefining the meaning of holiness among our people, so that we may rejoice in the holiness of the church, and seek to receive of its holiness, even while we are well aware that we are still far from the goal of personal holiness.

The Church Is One

Finally, the unity of the church is also something that Latina and Latino Protestants live, although seldom naming it as such. Indeed, for many in our communities the "unity" of the church would seem to be quite undesirable. This is partly a reaction to Roman Catholicism's common definition of unity as being subject to a particular authority, and its use of that definition to exclude Protestants from the unity of the church. It is also partly because some Hispanic individuals and congregations in mostly white denominations have perceived "unity" as stifling. Finally, it is partly because most individuals and churches that now speak of the "unity" of the church are so involved in middle-class and North Atlantic prejudices that they see no place in that one church for the lower-class, less-structured, and less-inhibited Christianity of ethnic minorities—especially ethnic minorities not sharing the values and worldview of the dominant culture.

Still, there is a sort of unity in Latino Protestantism. It is a unity that cannot be described in logical, hierarchical, or organizational terms, but it is nevertheless there.

Perhaps the best way to explain the nature of this unity is to look at another image of the church that is common among Latina and Latino Protestants, and which the dominant majority usually neglects or even rejects. That is the image of the church as the family of God.

In dealing with this image, we must begin by making it clear that what we mean by "family" in the Latino tradition is different from what is meant by those who today in this country speak of "family values." To them, a "family" is a tightly knit and easily definable social unit, usually living under the same roof, and composed of parents and children. Thus, it is not uncommon to hear someone speak of "the families in our church." For us, on the contrary, when we speak of "family" we mean a much wider group of people, of uncertain and ever-expandable limits, that includes parents as well as aunts and uncles, nephews and nieces, cousins to various degrees, relatives by marriage, relatives of relatives by marriage, relatives by baptism (godparents, for instance, and the relationship, unknown in the English-speaking world, of *compadres* and *comadres*[21]), and a host of other possibilities. Such extended families are also interwoven, so that it is virtually impossible to belong to only one family. If you have two parents, you probably already belong to at least two such families. Then your aunt marries, and you are part of still another family. And so on.

What this means is that the main contrast between the nuclear and the extended family is not, as would seem at first glance, their respective sizes. The main contrast is that the nuclear family is by nature easily defined and closed, while the extended family is by nature undefinable, and open to such an extent that multiple membership for a person is more the rule than the exception. This contrast affects our values at many points, and is reflected, for instance, in the way the modern industrial society, built around the nuclear family, values privacy—a word for which there is no adequate translation into Spanish, except the anglicism *privacidad*. (Significantly, in Spanish *privado* means both private and deprived. In our culture, to be too private is a privation of life.)

At this point, it may be helpful to point out that in the Greco-Roman world of the first century there was a similar notion of "family" or "house." The house included not only the *paterfamilias* and his wife and children but also the women who had become part of the household by marriage, all other relatives under the authority of the *paterfamilias*, and even slaves. Such families were strictly hierarchical, with the *paterfamilias* having almost absolute authority over all those in his household.[22] Significantly, although more traditional exegetes have often missed this point, what the early church did was to take this structure and seek to limit its most authoritarian and dehumanizing aspects, speaking of a church that is "the household of God" (Eph. 2:19; 1 Tim. 3:15; 1 Peter 4:17), but in which masters are to remember that they have a Master, husbands are to remember that they are part of the Bride, and fathers are to remember that they have a Father (Eph. 5:21–6:9).[23]

For many Protestant Latinos and Latinas the church has become the extended family they cannot have in this society—if they or their parents are recent immigrants, because the rest of the family was left behind, and if they have lived here for generations, because the mobility of the modern industrial society has made extended families less viable. The vast psychological and material support system that has traditionally been a function of the extended family thus becomes a function of the church.[24]

Quite clearly, this understanding of the church as an extended family has much to do with the experience of marginalization, alienness, and exile, so common among Latinos and Latinas. The loss of community, and in particular the loss of the extended family, is one of the most painful aspects of life of Hispanics in the United States—particularly for recent immigrants. In many cases, the church provides an alternative community or a new extended family.[25]

What the dominant society calls "families" now becomes part of a real, extended family. In those "families," practices such as *el altar familiar*—a time and place set aside for Bible study and prayer—are designed to remind everyone of the larger family to which each belongs, and to strengthen that larger family. The education and disciplining of children is also the responsibility and the prerogative of all adults in the larger church family, and not just of the child's parents. That is why in Latino churches it is more common to hear talk of "the church family" than of "the families in the church."

Without understanding the essential difference between the nuclear and the extended family, this image of the church as a family can easily be misunderstood. Hence the resistance of many in the dominant culture when they hear such talk, for to them this means that the church becomes a closed community like the nuclear family, valuing its own privacy, and only seldom admitting new members. Likewise, from the perspective of the dominant society, to speak of church as "family" is intrinsically unecumenical and sectarian, for it leaves out any Christians outside the immediate family of the congregation.

That, however, is not what is meant by the church as "the family of God" within a cultural context in which the extended family is the norm. What is meant is several things, all of them important for our understanding of the unity of the church.

What is meant is first of all that there is a unity that, although sometimes stretched to its apparent limits, cannot be easily broken. Even when cousins argue, fight, and move away, they are still family. Accordingly, underlying the obvious sectarianism of much Latino Protestantism, there is still a sense of family—and therefore a sense of brokenness by division which the more sophisticated ecumenical movement has not even begun to explore. One might even argue that our churches are so riddled with strife and tension because we are acting in ways similar to an extended family, where there are always tensions, and these tensions cannot be solved by simply breaking away.

Second, the church as the extended family of God means that it is a community of sharing. In the Latino church there is often active solidarity in sharing to an extent that would surprise many in the dominant community.

It would be instructive to study Latino congregations, and see how many members declare that at some point in their lives, when they were unemployed or going through serious financial stress, other members helped them out—just as a relative is expected to help out another in an extended family. This sharing is not only of material goods but also of concerns and support. Thus, one should not be surprised, when attending a Latino church, to hear requests for prayer that involve airing problems and concerns that others would only discuss in the bosom of the family.

Third, the church as the extended family of God means that its limits are impossible to define. All who belong to God are part of this family. Some may be more distant cousins—even people whom I have difficulty understanding—but they are still part of the same family. This means that individuals and congregations must recognize each other as relatives, even though they differ in matters of practice, doctrine, or culture—a shocking fact for many from the dominant community who suddenly find themselves considered brothers or sisters of persons whom they were taught to discount. Also, since the limits are impossible to define, this means that this family of God stands ready to invite others into the family. Hence the ease with which Latino Protestant churches generally invite and accept new members.

Finally, the church as an extended family of God sometimes means that there can be genuine openness to the world and its various realities. Just as it is possible and even expected to belong to more than one extended family, so it is possible to belong to the family of God and still be involved in the various other "families" of society—for instance, in fields such as work, play, politics, culture, and so on. At other times, the church as the extended family of God falls into the trap of some extended families that try to demand exclusive loyalty of the members, forcing members to distance themselves from relatives in other families. In such cases, Latino Protestant churches try to absorb all their members' time, so as to preclude their relating in any active way with "the world." As in the case of extended families, this is obviously an unhealthy development—one that eventually tends to destroy the very family that demands such loyalty.

What all of this means, in summary, is that there is in the Latino Protestant community a sense that the church is one and must find ways to express and to live out that oneness; but that this sense of unity and the attempt to express it are quite different from what is expected by members of the dominant culture and its mainline churches.

The Order Is Important

As a final note, I return to my earlier decision to discuss the four traditional marks of the church in reverse order. That is important, because the

Latino Protestant church considers itself above all as an apostolic community—a community sent on a pilgrimage of faith and inviting others to join in the pilgrimage. Thus, rather than beginning with the unity of the church, it is best to begin with its mission, and from there move to its unity.

Returning, then, to the observations at the beginning of this chapter regarding the lack of an explicit ecclesiology in the Latino Protestant community, it may well be that this is an asset rather than a deficiency. Ecclesiology, when it is simply a matter of the church reflecting on its own nature, can easily fall into the trap of navel gazing. Indeed, there may be a negative correlation between a traditional ecclesiological consciousness and missional activity. It may be that to ask too intently, "What is the church?" tends to obscure the more fundamental ecclesiological question, "What is the church *for*?" If so, the very fact that the Latino Protestant church has done little by way of self-study and theological reflection on its own nature may well be a sign of obedience rather than of theological immaturity.

NOTES

1. Thus, for instance, Alberto Rembao, *Discurso a la nación evangélica* (Buenos Aires: La Aurora, 1949), 34: "Ya no se es salvo porque se pertenece a la iglesia; sino que se pertenece a la iglesia porque se es salvo." Although Rembao then makes a very strong case for the need of the church, such need is still seen as a function of individual faith and salvation.

2. A leading advocate of Protestant missions in Latin America declared quite bluntly that "Protestant missions in South America are justified because the Roman Catholic Church has not given the people Christianity." Robert E. Speer, *The Case for Missions in Latin America* (New York: Board of Foreign Missions of the Presbyterian Church in the U.S.A. [ca. 1912]), 5. And in 1927 an enlightened Protestant leader in Brazil felt compelled to argue that "the general attitude of Protestantism in this country which regards the Roman Catholic Church as not a Christian church at all is neither charitable nor justified." Salomão Ferraz, "Our Dominant Religion," in *As Protestant Latin America Sees It*, ed. Milton Stauffer (New York: Student Volunteer Movement for Foreign Missions, 1927), 81.

3. Commenting on this situation, Carmelo E. Alvarez says: "Es que la ideología liberal pondrá el énfasis en el ciudadano, el hombre burgués que en última instancia es la manifestación del ideal de libertad, el estado democrático, la sociedad burguesa. Por eso se enfatizará la idea del progreso económico, la empresa, la expansión, la acumulación, etc. El protestantismo contribuye en su expresión teológica a legitimar toda esta ideología. Es cierto que el protestantismo significó una alternativa de cambio, dinámico y potente, frente al catolicismo colonial." *El protestantismo latinoamericano entre la crisis y el desafío* (Mexico City: CUPSA, 1981), 24–25. Also Jean Pierre Bastian, *Breve historia*

del protestantismo en América Latina (Mexico City: CUPSA, 1986), 17: "Las nuevas clases dominantes (los liberales) . . . obstaculizaron el dominio antagónico de la Iglesia Católica Romana y propiciaron la penetración de nuevos credos religiosos disidentes que podían debilitar a la Iglesia sobre el terreno simbólico."

4. Speer declared that "Protestant missions are justified and demanded in Latin America by the character of the Roman Catholic priesthood" (*Case for Missions*, 5). A clear example of this Protestant view of the Roman Catholic hierarchy and its hold on the people is the manner in which the representative of the British and Foreign Bible Society in Buenos Aires referred to those who opposed his efforts to penetrate Bolivia, calling them an "anti-Christian sacerdocracy." Quoted in Daniel P. Monti, *Presencia del protestantismo en el Río de la Plata durante el siglo XIX* (Buenos Aires: La Aurora, 1969), 211.

5. For instance, during the academic year 1993–94, out of a total of 26,441 students enrolled in M.Div. (master of divinity) degree programs in schools accredited by the Association of Theological Schools (ATS), 706 were Hispanic. This is 2.67 percent of the total. At the Ph.D. level, out of a total of 3,093, 51 were Latinos or Latinas (1.65 percent). *Fact Book on Theological Education for the Academic Year 1993–94* (Pittsburgh: Association of Theological Schools, 1995), 75. At that point, there were more Hispanic Protestant churches in greater Los Angeles than Hispanic (Protestant and Catholic) students in all ATS schools!

6. One may read Cyprian's *De unitate ecclesiae* as responding on the one hand to the challenge of heretics who claimed that one did not have to be in communion with the church at large in order to be saved, and on the other hand to the strictly hierarchical and monarchical understanding of Pope Stephen of Rome. Against the one, he makes the famous statement that "one who does not have the Church as mother cannot have God as Father" (*De unit. eccl.*, 6). Against the other, he holds that there is no "bishop of bishops," and that "the episcopate is one, each part of which is held by each one for the whole" (*De unit. eccl.*, 5).

7. See Marie-Joseph Le Guillou, "Eclesiología," in *Sacramentum Mundi* (Barcelona: Herder, 1972), 2:424–31.

8. See above all the encyclical of Pius XII, *Mystici corporis*.

9. See, for instance, *Lumen Gentium*, where the church is spoken of as "a sheepfold," "the tillage of God," "the building of God," the "spotless spouse of the spotless Lamb," the "Body of Christ," and above all as "the people of God." In this regard, much of the groundwork had been laid by such French theologians as Yves Congar, who for years had been proposing and employing this manner of speaking of the church.

10. See, for instance, Alberto Rembao, *Discurso*, 23–24.

11. It is thus, for instance, that the Iglesia Apostólica de la Fe en Cristo Jesús employs the word. It is "Apostólica," not because it can claim an uninterrupted line of apostolic succession, but because it claims to believe, worship, and act just as the apostles did.

12. See Pius IX, *De unicitate Ecclesiae* (Sept. 16, 1864).

13. Significantly, in Tertullian's use of apostolic authority against heretics, both of these views are put forth. See *De praesc. haer.*, 20, 31.

14. See Roberto S. Goizueta, *Caminemos con Jesús: Toward a Hispanic/Latino Theology of Accompaniment* (Maryknoll, N.Y.: Orbis Books, 1995), 1–17; Justo L. González, *Mañana: Christian Theology from a Hispanic Perspective* (Nashville: Abingdon Press, 1990), 25–26, 41–42; Justo L. González, *Santa Biblia: The Bible through Hispanic Eyes* (Nashville: Abingdon Press, 1995), chap. 4.

15. For an example of a *romería*, adapted to a modern, urban, North American setting, see Goizueta, *Caminemos*, 32–37.

16. Justo L. González, *Out of Every Tribe and Nation: Christian Theology at the Ethnic Roundtable* (Nashville: Abingdon Press, 1992), 18–29.

17. Orlando Costas, *Christ outside the Gate: Mission beyond Christendom* (Maryknoll, N.Y.: Orbis Books, 1982), 190.

18. On the relationship between the universal and the particular, see González, *Mañana*, 51–53, and Goizueta, *Caminemos*, 151–62.

19. The new Spanish-language United Methodist hymnal, *Mil voces para celebrar*, will include a "Hispanic Creed" that declares: "Creemos en la Iglesia, . . . que es más fiel cuanto más se viste de colores; donde todos los colores pintan un mismo paisaje; donde todos los idiomas cantan una misma alabanza."

20. Although this is quite common in our contemporary Latino churches, it is not our exclusive problem. In fact, it has appeared again and again in the history of Christianity, particularly when a marginalized group has felt that those in power in the church were making too many concessions to the standards of society. In this regard, one remembers the schism of Hippolytus, Novatianism, Donatism, several of the movements of monastic reform in the Middle Ages, and some strands of Anabaptism at the time of the Reformation.

21. See Ada María Isasi-Díaz, *En la Lucha/In the Struggle: Elaborating a Mujerista Theology* (Minneapolis: Fortress Press, 1993), 26–27. Literally, *compadre* means co-father, and *comadre* means co-mother. Thus the father and godfather of a child are *compadres*, and the mother and godmother are *comadres*.

22. See John E. Stambaugh and David L. Balch, *The New Testament in Its Social Environment* (Philadelphia: Westminster Press, 1986), 123–24; Wayne A. Meeks, *The First Urban Christians: The Social World of the Apostle Paul* (New Haven, Conn.: Yale University Press, 1983), 75–77.

23. See Justo L. González and Catherine G. González, *The Liberating Pulpit* (Nashville: Abingdon Press, 1994), 87–92. A similar thesis is held in the still-unpublished essay by Frédéric de Coninck, "Dans le monde mais pas du monde: L'église, maison de Dieu, comme espace transitionnel."

24. This is so central that, in a study still to be published, Dr. Rubén Armendáriz asked a number of subjects to respond to the question, "Why are we a Hispanic church?" and a common answer was "Because we are family." On the Latino sense of identity as rooted in community, and not in the individual, see Goizueta, *Caminemos*, 47–76.

25. See, in this regard, Thomas F. O'Dea and Renato Poblete, "Anomie and the 'Quest for Community': The Formation of Sects among the Puerto Ricans of New York," *American Catholic Sociological Review* 21 (spring 1960): 18–36.

7

Doing Theology and the Anthropological Questions

David Maldonado, Jr.

Doing theology is a human activity. Not to be confused with divine revelation or made synonymous with the "work of the spirit," theology is simply a human attempt to reflect upon and to articulate religious faith in a sensible way. In so doing, it involves a critical examination of religious belief, experience, and community. It is not religious proclamation, witness, or instruction. This is not to suggest that these do not involve or assume a theology. Theology is indeed an important grounding for such human activity. The theological task is to reflect upon religious faith and to articulate our understanding of that faith and religious experience. It is human reflection on a human experience. As such it is a human activity.

Theology originates in and reflects the human experience. It grows out of the human experience of religious faith, the religious community, and the broader human context. However, religious experience and community are always particular. While the human family is global and universal, human reality is experienced in concrete localities and situations. This also applies to religious experience, including the Christian faith. Christianity has a global presence as a religious faith in a particular community. Christians are always found in specific and social locations. Theology, likewise, while a global activity, reflects the particulars of those engaged in doing theology. It articulates the Christian faith as practiced and experienced by individuals or groups in particular human contexts.

It is not surprising that a major task of theology, and especially traditional theological anthropology, has been to define what it means to be human. At least two major areas of examination have emerged in responding to this core question. The first question relates to the essence of the human being. Here the question is, What is the essential nature of the human being? The second relates to the human predicament or condition. This question is, What is the human situation? The former relates to human essence, while the second addresses the human condition and experience.

The first question focuses on defining the nature of the human being. What does it mean to be human? The Christian answer has been that humans are creatures of God created in God's image. However, what that means in particular has many varied explanations that lead to classic debates about the nature and essence of the human being. For example, much attention has been given to describing the human in terms of body, soul, and spirit. Much energy has been spent debating whether the human being is the first, second, or third of the above, and in what hierarchical order.

The second question in traditional theological anthropology wrestles with the realities of the human condition. How can human existence be understood? This question has led to the examination of human freedom, limitations, and sin. While human beings are free to think and to act, the human experience has involved sin. To what extent is the human free or not free to sin? Where is the point of responsibility? Is sinfulness an inevitable element in human nature?

The above questions are foundational in doing theology. They provide basic understandings of the nature of being human. However, an important assumption needs to be questioned—whether the basic unit of the human experience is that of the individual. This assumption leads to theological reflection in which the basic level of analysis and understanding have historically focused on the person. Human nature and human existence have traditionally been described in individualistic terms of the self. The human experience, religious faith, and the religious experience have also been described from an individualistic perspective. What it means to be human has been defined as being a self—an individual. As such, the human experience has been described as a finite individual, limited and ultimately standing alone before God in sin. Such an individualization of the human experience tends to define it in a narrow way that excludes significant factors such as community, culture, history, society, and the broader scope of the human community, which involves political, economic, and racial realities.

Therefore, doing theology calls for a grounding in a fuller understanding of the human situation. We must recognize the broader contextual foundations of the human experience. To ignore this broader human context is to deny the cultural and historical roots of religious experience and the significance of religious communities. Religious faith involves tradition and history—the passing of the faith to the next generation. Although it is appropriated by each new generation and by each individual, it is not developed anew by every generation and person. Rather, the Christian faith is passed from one generation to the next and experienced through varied communities of faith in new and different sociohistorical contexts. As such, religious faith has been an important part of culture and tradition.

This approach to doing theology calls attention to the social and communal nature of the human experience. It reminds us that the human being is a social being. To be fully human is to be in relationship, not in isolation. The story of creation suggests that such was the initial intent and subsequent reality. The historic covenants included relationship between God and humanity in terms of God and God's people. The human experience has involved existing in relationship and in community, belonging to a people and relating to God as a people. The sense of peoplehood, community, and relationship has been essential to the human experience, and especially to the religious experience within Judeo-Christian traditions. If this is the case, then religious experience needs to be understood not simply as an individualistic and isolated experience, but also one that is communal, social, and relational.

Thus the question is, What is the nature of the human experience and condition within which religious faith is known? What are those historical experiences and social conditions which define human existence in this particular place and time? How do these shape the worldview and religious experience of a people and define the theological task?

Anthropological Questions
from a Hispanic Perspective

Doing theology from a Hispanic perspective means doing theology from the perspective of the Hispanic context and experience. This calls for the crucial role of theological anthropology, which raises the question of how the Hispanic context is perceived and how the Christian faith is understood and experienced within that context. To be human within this particular human reality is to be Hispanic. Thus, the examination of what it means to be human calls for an examination of what it means to be Hispanic.

A Hispanic theological anthropology requires the examination of factors within the Hispanic context which go beyond the nature and existence of the individual. It calls for the examination of historical, social, and community realities, as well as economic, ethnic, racial, gender realities within which faith is known and religious life experienced. It raises the question of not only how these factors shape human life but also how they affect faith and theology. This is not to deny or devalue the importance of the individual and the unique experiences of each person, but rather to elevate the level of analysis to include communal and social realities. It is critically important to reflect on the conditions and experiences of Hispanics as a people, as diverse as the individual members might be.

To faithfully examine the Hispanic context and experience, it is essential to explore it through the perspectives of Hispanics themselves. While some might suggest that this approach is biased or self-serving, it is important to recall that religious faith flows from the human experience as known, perceived, and understood by its participants. In order to understand their faith theologically, it is equally important to understand their anthropology as experienced and interpreted by Hispanics themselves. This calls for an examination of how Hispanics define their human condition. It is from such a context that Hispanic theology flows and within which it finds articulation and validation.

Defining the
Hispanic Context and Experience

Defining and describing the Hispanic context, however, is not a simple task. Certainly, the context must be recognized as a diverse reality reflecting the many variants of Hispanicity. A definition of the contemporary Hispanic identity would reflect a diversity of national origins, ethnic identity, acculturation, socioeconomic status, gender, and especially religious traditions. There are as many national origins as there are Spanish-speaking Latin American countries, including Puerto Rico and the United States. Each provides a unique base of ethnic identity and cultural tradition. The diversity of socioeconomic status includes the extremely wealthy, the many who are poor and marginalized, and an emerging middle class. The Hispanic reality also reflects a broad range of acculturation to the host culture. There are newly arrived refugees, undocumented workers, and other immigrants, as well as those who have been in the United States for many generations.

Another important aspect of the Hispanic reality is its religious diversity, which incorporates long-standing Roman Catholic traditions, the historical influence of Protestant (mainline) churches, and the dynamic force of the emerging Pentecostal churches. A Hispanic presence is also found in religious traditions such as the Mormon church, the Seventh-Day Adventists, and the new nondenominational movements. Identification with these traditions is significant for many reasons. Most Catholics, for instance, have a strong sense of tradition and loyalty. For many, to be Hispanic is to be Catholic. Strong cultural traditions are closely connected with the Roman Catholic Church. For Protestants and other non-Catholics, there is significant identification with other religious traditions. Many have paid a price for maintaining such identities.

In spite of the diversities, a sense of mutual identification and understanding seems to be emerging among Hispanics across denominational and traditional lines; however, this differs from traditional forms of ecumenical dialogues and movements. Hispanic ecumenical dialogue and cooperative activities have not focused on doctrinal or liturgical issues. These have not been of urgent importance. Instead, the focus of Hispanic interdenominational activity has been on the shared experience of being Hispanic and being Hispanic Christians in particular. The discussion has involved what it means to be Hispanic in this particular place and time. Interestingly, this has led to a discussion of theological anthropology within the Hispanic context.

It is not surprising that the Hispanic theological agenda began with theological anthropology defined in its fuller understanding. The beginning theological task Hispanic theologians have chosen has been that of defining the Hispanic reality. A brief examination of three Hispanic theologians' work will illustrate how theological reflection within three major religious traditions (Catholic, Protestant, and Pentecostal) has led to broadly shared understandings of the Hispanic reality. While there may be variations in some areas, a sense of shared understanding seems to be clearly emerging in the definition of the Hispanic context and experience.

A Catholic Theological Anthropology:
Virgilio Elizondo

The best-known pioneer in Hispanic theology within the Catholic tradition is Virgilio Elizondo. A widely traveled and trained priest, Elizondo chose to begin his theological reflection from the deepest roots in his family, church, and community. His theology, as articulated in *Galilean Journey: The Mexican-American Promise*,[1] is strongly autobiographical, with deep roots in San Antonio and his Mexican American context. He makes his point of reference clear, as that of a Mexican American who is a product of Mexican immigrant parents, a San Antonio barrio, the Roman Catholic Church, and the Southwest. His theology is the outcome of a lifelong experience of working with and listening to Mexican Americans and sharing that experience himself.

Elizondo takes a sociohistorical approach to doing Hispanic theology. He begins with an examination of the historical experience of Mexican Americans, their cultural formation, and the social consequences of their history. Elizondo's historical anthropology explains Mexican Americans as being the product of two major conquests. The first was the Spanish-Catholic conquest and colonialization of Mexico and the second the Nordic-Protestant conquest of northern Mexico. In both cases, the conquests involved physical violence and sociocultural and religious consequences for those who were the victims of conquest.

The first conquest resulted in what Elizondo calls the "First Mestizaje." By *mestizaje* Elizondo means "the birth of a new people from two preexistent peoples."[2] This refers to a new people on the face of the earth—the biological blending of European and native populations. This is an important point for Elizondo, who suggests that although the Spaniards were as racist as the Anglos to the north, a major difference made Spanish-Indian *mestizaje* possible: the Spaniards were not racial purists.[3] Nonetheless, the Spanish conquest was also culturally violent, involving cultural and religious impositions upon the conquered natives.

The conquest to the north was the result of Manifest Destiny and the westward expansion of the Protestant Anglos. It was equally violent and oppressive. However, a major difference, according to Elizondo, was that the Anglos' racism included a purist ideology that was anti-Spanish and anti-Catholic. These were manifested in a persistent disdain toward the "papist, degenerate, and mixed-blooded" Mexicans.

Mestizaje produced not only a new people but also a sense of peoplehood. Ethnic identity is a basic characteristic of mestizo people. Ethnic identity becomes crucial and reflects identification and association with the collective; it reflects a sense of the whole as a shared experience. That experience is defined as one which, in addition to the historical identification as a conquered people, also includes the experience of rejection and marginality.

Such a historical anthropology forms the basis for Elizondo's historical hermeneutics. His interpretation of the Hispanic experience points to God's choice of the lowly, the marginalized, and the rejected to bring the new reign. Elizondo's Galilean principle—"what human beings reject, God chooses as his very own"—provides the theological interpretation of the special role and opportunities facing Hispanics. God knows their suffering and is with them, and also calls them as partners in confronting the social structures and the sinfulness of an oppressive world.

A Protestant Theological Anthropology:
Justo González

Probably the most prolific and influential Hispanic theologian within the Protestant tradition is Justo González. Trained as a church and theological historian in the classic Protestant tradition at Yale, González has emerged as the most articulate voice among Hispanic Protestants. His pioneering work, *Mañana: Christian Theology from a Hispanic Perspective*,[4] is autobiographical, especially in its opening sections. He begins the task of articulating a Hispanic theology by telling of his formative experiences in his native Cuba. González describes being a young Protestant man in a Catholic culture and a Hispanic in Anglo Protestant institutions. His point of reference is a broader Hispanic context encompassing Latin American and U.S. realities, with a special attention to Hispanic Protestants in particular.

Although González addresses the traditional debates regarding the question of what it means to be human, this does not appear to be central for his theology from a Hispanic perspective. According to González,

Hispanic theology is better understood as being rooted in the collective work of the whole. It is the product of the ongoing dialogue within the Hispanic community of faith. For him, theology, especially Hispanic theology, is not an individual task, but a communal enterprise. This is what González calls *Fuenteovejuna* theology—*todos a una* (all are one).[5]

In grounding Hispanic theology in the experience of the whole it becomes necessary to define the whole. Who are the Hispanics and what needs to be known about them in order to understand Hispanic theology? Again, this is the task of theological anthropology. It is not surprising that González defines Hispanics as "the people in exile." As an immigrant himself, González describes the experience of all Hispanics, whether newly arrived, second or third generation, or descendants of Spanish settlers, as people in exile. The refugee motif is an important element in this perspective and points to the sense of ambiguity which all Hispanics experience. This involves the mixed feelings of gratitude and anger: gratitude, especially among the many political and economic refugees, but also anger in that Hispanics live in a land defined as not theirs, in which doors are closed. To be a Hispanic in this land is to be a minority that is subject to injustice and marginalization.

As a Protestant, González explores a particular Hispanic perspective—the experience of U.S. Hispanics who are Protestants. Here, too, González reflects his broader Latin American perspective and traces the U.S. Hispanic Protestant experience to Latin American roots. These include the initial work of Anglo missionaries in Latin America, the impact of Protestant immigration to Latin America, and also problems with the Roman Catholic Church in Latin America. Latin American Protestants developed as a unique religious community and experienced a sense of ambiguity and alienation, a pietistic lifestyle, and economic mobility. Latin American Protestants also developed a critical perspective toward their immediate environment and an anti-Catholic attitude.

Latin American historical roots, however, do not limit today's possibilities in this country. While such roots form historical foundations, the experiences of Hispanic Protestants in the U.S. context now play a greater role in shaping the nature, life, and theology of Hispanic Protestants. The experiences of marginality and injustice, the civil rights movement, and dialogue with Roman Catholics have begun to give new direction to religious expression and theological reflection. González speaks of a "new ecumenism" in which historic tensions and gaps between Hispanic Protestants and Catholics have begun to crumble as Hispanics work together. They have been brought together by the common struggles of addressing the Hispanic reality.

Reading the Hispanic experience, especially that of the Hispanic Protestant, from this perspective suggests that it is Hispanic theological anthropology that defines what it means to be Hispanic and a Hispanic Protestant in particular. It means to be a pilgrim people on a journey toward the possible in which the spiritual is inseparable from the social, and in which there is a radically new understanding of God's kingdom. Hispanic Protestants are the *mañana* people—the people whose task is prophetic and whose hope is in the "power and the promise of none other than Almighty God."[6]

A Pentecostal Theological Anthropology: Eldin Villafañe

Among the most respected of current Hispanic Pentecostal theologians is Eldin Villafañe. A member of the theological faculty at the Center for Urban Ministerial Education of Gordon-Conwell Theological Seminary in Boston, Villafañe has attracted attention for his seminal work *The Liberating Spirit: Toward an Hispanic American Pentecostal Social Ethic.*[7] This is probably the most systematic articulation of a Hispanic theology from the Pentecostal perspective, and it provides a helpful insight into its anthropological foundations. While Elizondo wrote from the perspective of a Mexican American in the context of the Southwest, and González from his experience as a Cuban and the broad perspective of Latin America and the immigrant Hispanic, Villafañe's roots are in the Puerto Rican urban barrio, and he gives special attention to the experiences of Puerto Ricans in the Northeast.

Villafañe's construction of a social ethics for Hispanic Pentecostalism is solidly grounded in theological anthropology. His understanding of what it means to be Hispanic and Pentecostal in the United States is informed by a social understanding of the Hispanic reality. That reality is defined as the product of two types of factors and dynamics: cultural and sociodemographic. The first refers to cultural roots reflecting the three major strands that have contributed to the Hispanic heritage—the Spanish, African, and Amerindian. The blending of these cultural sources has produced a people who celebrate in fiesta and possess a broad sense of family. Other important aspects of the Hispanic character include passion, *personalismo*,[8] paradox of the soul, community, *romerías*, and musical élan. These cultural attributes combine to create a diverse people with a zest and spirit for life celebrated in community. As cultural factors these tend to be internal to the character of the people and thus shape Hispanic reality.

The second influence that shapes the Hispanic experience is a group of factors external to Hispanic culture and associated with social reality. These include poverty, immigration, political marginality, educational limitations, urban concentrations, and a general underclass status. These factors are usually reflected in the demographics of a lower socioeconomic profile.

In describing the Puerto Rican reality in particular, Villafañe points to the historic conquest of Puerto Rico and the subsequent neocolonialism, the economic forces of which contributed to the Puerto Rican cycle of migration and poverty. In essence, Villafañe defines the Hispanic reality as one in which a culturally rich people are subjected to urban poverty, marginality, and underclass status.

It is in such a human context that Pentecostalism has flourished. Villafañe describes how the social reality of the marginalized, impoverished, disenfranchised working classes in urban areas provided a fertile field for Pentecostalism. The social reality of Hispanics was even more oppressive, and Hispanic Pentecostalism can thus be understood as the church of an oppressed ethnic minority. To a large extent the church has provided important religious, cultural, and social functions necessary for the survival of a poor people.

However, the Hispanic Pentecostal church is more than a social agent; it is also a spiritual manifestation of God's power and presence. The church is present in the barrio and as such

> sacralizes the barrios, providing space and context for the gathering of God's people for intercession, prayer and strength. . . . The presence and location of these churches speaks theologically of: (1) a missional commitment to the poor; (2) an ecclesiological contextualization, in all dimensions, geographically, physically, etc.; (3) and an understanding of spirituality of the life of the church that need not be limited by the aesthetic quality of its church building and surroundings.[9]

The Hispanic Pentecostal church can be understood as the church of the spirit, and Hispanic spirituality itself in its authentic expressions reflects and is manifested in the core Hispanic cultural characteristics. For Villafañe, God's spirit is known and revealed in the people themselves, their culture, and their social reality.

Toward a Hispanic Theological Anthropology: Some Reflections

The discussion of theological anthropology from a Hispanic perspective has led us to a broader definition of the task. It is not limited to traditional debates about the nature of humanity at the individual level, but requires examining human existence in its broader and contextual realities. It calls for consideration of historical, cultural, and communal sources, as well as economic, political, and social forces that shape and define human existence. This is not to suggest a social determinism and to deny the significance of the person and self, but rather to call attention to the significance of the social context in which life is known and experienced. The individual is not understood in isolation, disconnected from the human and social environment, but rather as a social being in dynamic interrelationship with the human reality.

The brief review of the anthropology reflected in the works of selected leading Hispanic theologians provides insights in regard to how human existence is perceived from a Hispanic perspective. These works provide a glimpse of how the Hispanic reality is understood and interpreted from such a context. Five factors form a beginning list of what could be considered a Hispanic anthropology for doing Hispanic theology.

Ethnic Identity

An important characteristic of Hispanic theological anthropology is the centrality of ethnicity and ethnic identity. Elizondo, González, and Villafañe all made it a point to identify their own ethnicity as members of particular Hispanic ethnic populations and contextualized their observations and reflections within specific Hispanic ethnic settings. Although they are interested in addressing the broader experience of the larger Hispanic population, each found it important to be clear as to his own specific roots and to contextualize his personal observation within his own Hispanic identity. Thus, Elizondo made clear his ethnic identity as a Mexican American, González as a Cuban, and Villafañe as a Puerto Rican. Each spoke from his particular ethnic perspective, yet each endeavored to identify with and to address theological issues of other particular Hispanic groups and Hispanics as a whole. This is consistent with current sociological research that suggests that the primary ethnic identity among Hispanics is that of national origin, such as Mexican American, Puerto Rican, or Cuban. Panethnic identities such as "Hispanic" or "Latino" and "Latina" are secondary. However, panethnic identity becomes helpful and commonly used across ethnic lines when an experience or perspective is shared. Such seems to be the case within Hispanic theology. It is developed within specific Hispanic ethnic contexts, but as the various Hispanic populations perceive a common experience, their theologies begin to develop similar themes and directions.

The anthropological foundations of the emerging Hispanic theology point to the importance of ethnic identity among Hispanics, regardless of whether it is national origin or panethnic. Hispanics understand their personal identity as intimately connected to their ethnic identity. They seem to possess an ethnic self-identity. Their personal self-understanding is inseparable from their ethnicity. To be human is to be a Hispanic and to experience human life within the context of a particular Hispanic population. The significance of this is that identity is with the larger whole, whether it is of national origin or the broader Hispanic population. The realities of the whole are the realities of the individual. To possess an ethnic self-identity is not to give up personal identity or to devalue the person. In fact, among Hispanics, *personalismo* is an important social value. *Personalismo* refers to the importance of recognizing and valuing the person as an individual. Ethnic self-identity points to the importance of the whole ethnic context to the individual in terms of self-understanding. To understand the human experience and what it means to be a person within the Hispanic context calls for an understanding of the significance of ethnic identity and ethnic self-identity.

Ethnicity refers to a sense of peoplehood. Such a sense is developed through the perceived sharing of a history, culture, and sometimes racial commonalities. It refers to a sense of being or belonging to the same population. Ethnicity thus means being a people. There is a sense of mutual identity. For Hispanics this means that there is the perception of being a people. To be a people means to have and claim a history, to share and celebrate a culture, and to recognize and affirm a common humanity.

Historical Perspective

Hispanic theology calls for an anthropology in which human existence is understood within the context of human history. The human condition and social location of people are understood as being the result of the historical flow of events and processes that have social, economic, and political consequences for those involved. Key historical events and processes are identified and interpreted as important in understanding and defining the current human condition. For Hispanics, their sense of peoplehood incorporates a clear sense of a shared history. The review above suggests that Hispanics share a story in which conquest played a significant role in their birth as a people. This refers to the understanding that as Hispanics they are the human product of the historic conquest of native populations by the Spanish. The blending of Spanish, Amerindian, and African (in the Caribbean) has produced a mestizo and mulatto people. This is one example of how historical events such as the conquest play a prominent role in defining how Hispanics define themselves as a people.

A second and equally important historical force defining Hispanics is the colonialization of Latin America by the Spanish, French, and later the United States. Such colonialization created socioeconomic systems that resulted in numerous revolutions, population displacements, and migrations. Likewise, the conquest of the Southwest, where a Mexican population was already settled, resulted in imposed social, cultural, economic, and political systems which marginalized that Hispanic population.

The domestic and social history of the United States must also be included in the story. The pre–civil rights era, in which ethnic minority populations such as Hispanics were subjected to systematic policies and practices of exclusion and marginalization, must also be considered. Such experiences are critical historical experiences that have shaped and formed the Hispanic context and reality.

Doing anthropology from a Hispanic perspective involves viewing the Hispanic experience through historical lenses, and hearing and acknowledging the painful story of conquest, of their birth as a people, and of their struggles against oppressive social, economic, and political forces that have marginalized them as a people.

Cultural Roots

Hispanic anthropology has called attention to the significance of ethnicity and the sense of peoplehood among Hispanics. An important element of ethnicity is the sharing of culture or common cultural roots. Such is the case among the various Hispanic populations. These shared roots include Spanish, Native American, and in some cases African cultural roots. Key elements include a common language, religious antecedents, family values, and other cultural aspects of community. What needs to be recognized is the sense of ownership of culture and that Hispanic culture is important to the people. Culture is a source of pride and identity. It is to be celebrated and enjoyed to its fullest extent.

However, culture has also brought challenges to Hispanics. This is a population whose culture is different from the dominant population in this country, a situation that has led to discrimination, marginalization, and other negative attitudes and consequences. Being Hispanic and maintaining Hispanic culture has had painful consequences. Living in this country and having to compete for survival has also resulted in acculturation. This has emerged as a cultural issue. To what extent is acculturation desirable? How is religion related to acculturation, especially for Hispanic Protestants?

To do theological anthropology from a Hispanic perspective requires acknowledging the significance of culture for understanding the people known as Hispanic. It is a core element in their sense of ethnicity as a people. It is a formative force in their lives and communities. But it also calls for understanding their struggles to maintain their culture and the price they have paid for doing so.

Social Location and Oppression

The question of what it means to be Hispanic has been answered with a painful response. The history of Hispanic peoples reflects a series of conquests

and subsequent colonialization. Analyses of current social and economic conditions indicate that Hispanics are among the poorest segments of society in
the United States. Their socioeconomic profiles generally reflect low income, low educational attainment levels, poor housing, poor health, underemployment, and other indicators of marginalization. In addition to low
socioeconomic status is the issue of racism and cultural nativism. These suggest that Hispanic peoples and their cultures are somehow inferior and less
desirable, and therefore subject to racial and cultural oppression. Thus, in
doing theological anthropology from a Hispanic perspective, it is important
to recognize that this population has been subjected to oppressive forces
since its birth and that it continues to struggle with such social conditions.
To be Hispanic is to be among the poor and the oppressed.

Community

Hispanic life is experienced in community. While ethnic identity refers
to identification with the larger ethnic population, community refers
to living and knowing life as part of a particular living community.
Identification with that community is important but so is *being* part of the
community. The sense of belonging to and participating in a particular
Hispanic community is an essential component of being Hispanic. To be
Hispanic is to be in community with other Hispanics. The importance of
this anthropological concept for theology is that to be Hispanic and thus
to be human from a Hispanic perspective is defined, found, and affirmed
in community.

Conclusion

I propose that to do theological anthropology from a Hispanic perspective
calls for a broad definition of the task. The task of Hispanic theological
anthropology is to define what it means to be human within the broader
context of history, culture, community, and the social condition of the
Hispanic American mestizo/mulatto people. The level of analysis
and reflection is not limited to the individual or the self, but requires
the examination of forces and structures that are social in nature and
that provide the context within which life is known and experienced.
To be Hispanic is to experience life as a member of the American
mestizo/mulatto population, which understands its birth in the context
and outcome of conquest and which has experienced oppression and
colonialization throughout its history and continues today to identify
with the poor and the oppressed.

NOTES

1. Virgilio Elizondo, *Galilean Journey: The Mexican-American Promise* (Maryknoll, N.Y.: Orbis Books, 1983).
2. Virgilio Elizondo, *The Future Is Mestizo: Life When Cultures Meet* (Blooming-ton, Ind.: Meyer-Stone Books, 1988), 10.
3. Elizondo, *Galilean Journey*, 10.
4. Justo L. González, *Mañana: Christian Theology from a Hispanic Perspective* (Nashville: Abingdon Press, 1990).
5. Ibid., 28 (Fuenteovejuna is the name of a town).
6. Ibid., 167.
7. Eldin Villafañe, *The Liberating Spirit: Toward an Hispanic American Pentecostal Social Ethic* (Lanham, Md.: University Press of America, 1992).
8. *Personalismo* refers to acknowledging and valuing the individual as a person. It is an important factor shaping relationships.
9. Villafañe, *Liberating Spirit*, 127.

8

Sin: A Hispanic Perspective

David Traverzo Galarza

In this chapter I examine the problem of sin from within the Christian faith and tradition, especially from a Hispanic or Latino perspective. Given the constraints of space, I cannot pretend to develop a full-blown exposition of the subject. Instead, I will attempt to suggest a particular constructive approach with a special focus on a *Latino radical evangelical tradition*.

This chapter is organized in three major sections. First, I offer a basic working definition of sin. Then I review what some significant Christian thinkers, past and present, have contributed to an understanding of sin within the history of the church and Christian thought. I close with the paradigm of a *Latino radical evangelical* approach.

A Working Definition

In the Christian scriptures (both Old and New Testaments), a number of terms are used to refer to sin.[1] In both Hebrew and Greek, the word translated as "sin" has moral as well as religious meaning.[2] For instance, in both Hebrew and Greek, sin can mean moral and religious deviation, to miss the target, to take the wrong road, to fail, to miss the point. It can represent moral failure before God or neighbor or deviation from the good.[3]

In Hebrew, sin also denotes wandering or straying from the correct path. It could signify a deliberate perversion or conscious twisting. There is also a notion of willful breach of peace, of an alliance, or of a relationship. The opposite of righteousness, for example, is sin. With clear moral significance, sin can mean to treat violently.[4]

In Greek, to trespass is to sin.[5] Similar is the notion of deliberately violating morality. From a socioethical perspective, sin can be associated with immorality when referring to tax collectors or harlots. In a moral sense, sin is injustice to neighbor. It can signify both moral and religious depravity.

The consequence of sin is abnormal activity or an abnormal state of affairs. The results are both negative and disruptive.[6] Sin leads to separation from God and results in death.[7] Sin can be an individual act. It also affects all humanity and has a diabolical character. In the New Testament writings, the absolute victor over sin is Jesus the Christ.[8]

From a Hispanic perspective, the understanding of sin that many Latino and Latina Protestant/Evangelical/Pentecostal Christians have received as traditional more or less follows these lines of thinking. Clearly, within Latino Christian Protestant reality, there is a very *biblical, experiential,* and *universal* sense of the reality and power of sin in the world.

From childhood, we have been taught that as sinners, we are *all* alienated from an intimate communion with God and from clear comprehension of who God is (Rom. 3:23). As a result of sin, our disobedience, and our transgression of God's holy laws, we have been cast into a world engulfed and enslaved by misery, pain, suffering, sickness, death, and oppression. Universally, experientially, and in light of the biblical Word, we have *all* fallen short and have missed the mark. No one is exempt. Here there is total equality. *Everyone* is condemned by sin.

For Latinos who have experienced the ravages of sin through the turmoils of life, the Holy Scriptures testify as the Spirit does, that sin destroys, yet Jesus has come to give life and life in abundance (John 10:10). This we know in our hearts and minds.

Significant Christian Thinkers

In *Christian Thought Revisited,* Justo L. González has done a noteworthy job of reviewing some two thousand years of church history and Christian thought.[9] He suggests a threefold typology that serves to place the many dogmas, tendencies, crises, and thinkers into a workable and concise framework. The key to his analysis is how the diverse historical, geographical, cultural, and ideological leanings of three prominent Christian theological centers (Carthage, Alexandria, and Antioch) may account for the diverse thinking that has emerged in church history up to the present.

The significance of González's work for this book is that the doctrine of sin can be better understood by considering the three different inclinations of these Western centers in the history of Christian thought: *Type A:* Stoic—Tertullian model, *Type B:* Neoplatonic—Origen model, and *Type C:* Pastoral/Historical—Irenaeus model. We should keep in mind that while there is some evidence of thinking on the topic of sin during the premedieval period, it was not until Augustine that a well-developed doctrine of sin emerged. During the early centuries of Christianity the church did not have this concern at the center of its mission or intellectual activity. The Apostolic Fathers, the early Christian Apologists, the Greek Fathers, and others were busier clarifying issues related to the nature of Christ, redemption, the triune God, and the Christian biblical canon. Before the Edict of Milan in the early fourth century C.E., there was outright persecution, torture, and death to worry about.

González's work helps us to better appreciate how the three types of influences mentioned above worked themselves out in church history. For example, we can identify the Neoplatonic bent of Augustine's thought and how it impacted the development of Western Christian thought. González's typology understands that Augustine's thought *also* reflects both Tertullian (Type A: legalistic influences of sin as a debt to pay) and Origen (Type B: Neoplatonist views on history, evil, and the soul).[10] González also notes Irenaean (Type C) influence on how Augustine viewed the limits of human freedom and the power of sin to subject us to disobedience.[11]

We might summarize that Augustine, as "the great mentor of Western theology,"[12] with his more systematized doctrine of sin impacted Christian thought up to the Protestant Reformation period and beyond.[13] The coining of the phrase "original sin"[14] and the notions of sin as universal,[15] the utter corruption and depravity of humanity as a fallen people (*massa perditionis*), and sin as not merely an act but a state are all attributed to this master of Christian thought.

It was not until the thirteenth century C.E. and Thomas Aquinas that another major shift and lasting contribution to this doctrine was experienced. The contribution that we may note here was Aquinas's synthesis of a deeply Aristotelian view of sin, good, evil, and human nature and Augustine's foundational expositions on these same items, especially Augustine's Type A theology.[16] Sin, however, took on a more rationalist tendency than the deeply experiential dimension that greatly affected Augustine's understanding of sin in his *Confessions.*

In terms of the doctrine of sin and with the advent of the Protestant Reformation in Western European Christianity, both Martin Luther and John Calvin, to a great degree, followed the same lines as Augustine. The concepts of the universal and total depravity of humanity, our absolute bondage to sin, and sin as hereditary were all maintained by Luther and Calvin. González points out that although both these Reformers decreed salvation was by God's grace and not human merits, nevertheless, Luther's view of the state as a remedy or limit to sin, and Calvin's notion of Christ as a satisfaction for our sins place them *in these points* within more law-and-order Type A positions (the Tertullian model).

Today, however, in many of our more indigenous Pentecostal and Evangelical Bible institutes (a foundational theological training ground for both clergy and laity), it has been Louis Berkhof's *Systematic Theology*[17] and others like it that have served as a reference point for doctrinal clarification. A Hispanic perspective would be wise to acknowledge how ancient Christian thought continues to be expounded and claimed through the teachings of authors such as Berkhof, who, like Luther and Calvin, followed the material that was passed on by Augustine: sin as universal, hereditary, and reflecting a totally depraved human nature. At the core, sin is a state of being as well as acts and habits. Therefore, Berkhof wrote,

> As a result of the fall the father of the race could only pass on a depraved human nature to his offspring. From that unholy source sin flows on as an impure stream to all the generations of men, polluting everyone and everything with which it comes in contact.[18]

The results of sin are thus total depravity, loss of communion with God, and death.[19] According to Berkhof, sin is deliberate, active, and a positive transgression. It is the result of a free but evil choice by humanity.[20]

Latin American Contributions

Contrary to what some believe, the Christian thought of Gustavo Gutiérrez *does* contain a rather biblical and integral understanding of sin. In his classic text, *A Theology of Liberation*,[21] he advances a liberation approach that takes seriously history, politics, and salvation as God's way of working in the world. Within *one history* God liberates humankind, especially the poor, at three distinct yet interdependent levels: from structural or political oppression, for the human responsibility of freedom at a personal and historical plane, and *from sin* and alienation, which *is* the biblical meaning of the liberation.[22]

According to Gutiérrez, sin is both "a personal and social intrahistorical reality."[23] While it includes the individual or interior dimension, sin *also* has a social or structural reality. It is "the very source of social injustice and other forms of human oppression."[24] As the negation of love that disrupts our communion with God and neighbor, sin is the fundamental obstacle to the kingdom of God, Gutiérrez asserts.[25] In summary, he announces that

> sin is evident in oppressive structures, in the exploitation of humans by humans, in the domination and slavery of peoples, races, and social classes. Sin appears, therefore, as the fundamental alienation, the root of a situation of injustice and exploitation. It cannot be encountered in itself, but only in concrete instances, in particular alienations.[26]

Another Latin American thinker, Enrique Dussel, has noted that sin includes the domination of one person over another.[27] One person uses the other as a means. The other person then becomes an instrument of the first person. Alienation and destitution are the results of this relation of domination. Sin therefore represents a *negation of the other.*[28]

At a social level, institutions or systems that negate the other are also sinful.[29] The relationship of domination or negation that robs the poor of wealth represents robbery or dispossession.[30] Specifically, Dussel asserts that as people who are dominated, alienated, or negated, the poor are the fruit of sin.[31]

In terms of community ethics, Dussel claims that sin is a fundamental obstacle to community and thus to the reign of God on earth. This obstacle to community that prevents us from loving one another leads to death.[32] As Dussel suggests, a world that therefore represents a system of dominating social relationships (and all relationships are social as they interact with other social beings within social reality) is under what he names "the hegemony of evil." Such a world system exemplifies a "system of sin."[33]

From a Latino perspective, it should be noted that, as José Ignacio González-Faus has remarked: "One of the most characteristic contributions of Latin American theology to the theme of sin has been the notion of structural sin or structures of sin."[34] This contribution is also clearly and forcefully evident in the works of Elsa Tamez, a noted Central American biblicist, especially in *The Amnesty of Grace.*[35]

Tamez observes that sin has two dimensions. First, there are sinners and transgressors of God's law. We have all heard this and feel comfortable with this teaching. But second, we are not only sinners but *are sinned against.* We are victims of the forces that perpetuate bondage over our affairs in the world.[36] Therefore, as Tamez advocates, sin needs to be understood within the concrete, social, and historical reality of the *victims of sin,* especially the poor, who are killed by sin and by sinful oppressors.[37]

Also, contrary to popular belief in and outside the Christian church, Tamez asserts that the sins of the poor *do not equal* the sins of the rich. The poor are not only in a sinful and fallen condition but as she suggests, the power of the rich *also* falls on them. This is what the Rev. Raymond Rivera has termed the "double-barreled" situation of the poor. They are not only sinners but are sinned against by the rich and powerful.[38] For, Tamez notes,

> clearly, as the Bible asserts, all human beings are sinners. In practice, however, there is a paradox. The poor, whose sins cannot be compared to those of the powerful, are those who more consistently recognize their faults. Injustice becomes more obvious when it is committed against those who, with great frequency, remember that they are sinners. We know that sin cannot be reduced to social injustice, but in the present moment in Latin America, it is vital to make people see that any dehumanizing situation is an offense to God, and for that reason it is a manifestation of sin. The spiritualization of sin has often made it difficult to identify in concrete realities—an identification that is the precondition for fighting against sin.[39]

In a global, national, regional, or local system that may serve to dehumanize and to rob persons or communities of their sense of dignity and positive self-esteem, the sin of pride or self-aggrandizement does not mean the same thing for those who hold power as it means for those who are virtually powerless in the world. As Tamez declares, the insignificance and marginalization of the poor requires them to regain their sense of worth and not to be further stripped of it in the name of faith and self-renunciation.[40] In light of such an exposition, it may therefore be stated that, as Tamez writes,

> Sin is a system that threatens the life of many, a mechanism built by specific people by their practices of injustice guided by their greedy hearts. But in a given moment all people are slaves, and by not being masters of themselves, they have been dehumanized. Here the good intentions of individuals do not count, but only the effectiveness of the solidarity of all, in search for a new way of living, oriented by the firm conviction that the right to a life of dignity belongs to all.[41]

In order to address the question of "sin and salvation" in the context of Latin America, the late Orlando E. Costas approached the issue with the Bible in one hand and striking socioprophetic analysis in the other. In a paper titled "Sin and Salvation in an Oppressed Continent," which he presented at the Second Latin American Congress of Evangelization in Huampani, Peru, in 1979, Costas examined the Holy Scriptures and determined that sin constituted the following:

> disobedience to the lordship of God
>
> injustice and alienation
>
> unbelief and idolatry
>
> personal actions within a community context and social, collective guilt
>
> structural or institutional relationships

When he examined the context of Latin American reality, Costas also noted that Christianity had been corrupted by idolatry or oppressive structures that served to substitute for God.[42] Sin as "a destructive force that thwarts and deforms human life"[43] has also *formed and deformed* Latin American history. The conquest, colonization, and Christianization of the Americas was a process that manifested grave injustice, harvested severe alienation, and even established what Costas described as "a domesticating religious ideology, not the liberating gospel of Jesus Christ."[44] Costas submitted that Latin America "has been a continent born in and stratified by sin."[45] The Americas project by Spain thus represented what this Latino Evangelical author classified as the scene of one of the greatest rapes recorded in human history. This has included not only the genocide of millions of aborigines, but also the enslavement of Africans and their descendants, the exploitation of natural resources, the political and cultural domination of the emerging societies, and the continually increasing impoverishment of its people.[46]

The contradiction and ray of hope amid such a tragic history is that the gospel of Christ was proclaimed on what became a Christian continent, albeit one that fell into bondage to "structures that disregard life and perpetuate injustice."[47] The response of evangelization amid such a context prompted Costas to advance an integral salvation that could meet the problem of sin head-on. This would represent what he termed "a salvation that is concrete and global, present and future, personal, public, and cosmic."[48] Such an *integral* approach to the church's evangelization task acknowledged at the core that "the gospel is the efficacious power of God for salvation, and that it is the foretaste of the total transformation of history and the creation of new heavens and a new earth."[49] As Costas believed and articulated in his life, death, work, and thought, although sin has frustrated the work of God on earth, in Jesus the Christ, and in the power of the Spirit, we need not be ashamed of the gospel for it is God's power to challenge, convict, and change even the gravest sinful situations here on earth.

A Latino
Radical Evangelical Approach

In this last section I wish to submit an approach to better get at the problem of sin, from a Hispanic or Latino perspective. I suggest that a Latino radical evangelical paradigm may offer such a constructive model.

The Model

In my doctoral dissertation on the Latino radical social ethic in the work and thought of Orlando Costas, I attempted to review the writings of this missiologist, evangelist, theologian, writer, administrator, singer, baseball fanatic, and mentor to many Latinos and non-Latinos as well.[50] From within the discipline of social ethics, I examined his numerous writings and concluded that, yes, Costas did have a clearly articulated social ethical thought that developed during his years of writing and publication. It was developed intentionally and unapologetically as an evangelical liberationist approach for doing Christian ministry and theology. I termed this his "Latino radical evangelical social ethic."

Although he himself never used exactly these words, in his last, posthumously published work, *Liberating News: A Theology of Contextual Evange-*

lization,[51] Costas made it clear in the first chapter that he was writing from *a particular sociohistorical location and theological tradition.* The location Costas identified was that of Hispanic reality, along with that of other oppressed peoples from the North American racial-minority world and from Latin America. According to him, this social location was "an experiential vantage point" that stemmed from "the periphery of the Americas."[52] This was the *Latino* element of this approach.

He next identified the theological tradition for his reflection. This he called "the radical evangelical tradition." Listing sources from Bartolomé de Las Casas to Anabaptist evangelical ethics, the Second Great Awakening, and the Holiness and African American religious movements, Costas attempted to interconnect his contextual evangelization task with historic sources for doing theology and ministry "from the underside of history."[53] Such a radical evangelical approach would be marked by an integral, praxis-oriented and -grounded, preferential option modality for the church to fulfill its mission in light of a liberating gospel that announces good news to, by, with, and for the poor. This is the gospel that Jesus proclaimed and incarnated in his life and ministry on earth.

A Latino radical evangelical approach for attempting to better understand sin, from a Hispanic perspective, suggests that these three elements should be present and developed. Let me suggest a few directions that such a constructive model might take.

An Integral or Holistic Thrust

An integral or holistic approach to sin, from a Latino perspective, attempts to emphasize that sin involves not just personal or academic questions to consider (as important as they may be) but that sin is a reality, a force that delivers death and destruction to countless numbers of persons and communities daily. The social, institutional, structural, systemic as well as personal dimensions of sin require our attention and priorities. If it is integral, then the dimensions of individual *and* corporate, of social *and* religious, of academic *and* practical are all part of the mix. No one piece, emphasis, or dimension has a monopoly on our attention and response.

Costas's Latino radical evangelical approach to Christian theology, mission, and faith was framed within such a *totality.* The gospel, the church's mission, and a person's Christian identity are all part of a whole that intersected religious, social, political, cultural, and personal spheres of life. For Costas, this was a dynamic view that challenged more conventional ways of thinking.[54]

More specifically, we may want to make explicit the connections between an individual's ideological formation in a consumer-oriented, violence-ridden, egoistic society and how that individual *personally* helps to perpetuate sinful structures, systems, and institutions such as the military-industrial complex or a white, male-dominated social class system. We might ask ourselves, How does my personal lifestyle bless, challenge, or change the sinful realities that surround me in and outside church circles?

For example, as a poor or upwardly mobile Latino person who is a sinner, how are my decisions to vote for a mediocre candidate or to abstain from voting, to pay taxes or lie to the IRS, to purchase pirated videotapes or stolen Nikes or a hot VCR, related to the reign of sinful situations in my life and neighborhood? Where and what are the connections between the personal and the more institutional dimensions of sin in my personal and social world? Do I see the connections or do I miss the point (one of the initial definitions of sin)?

A Praxis Base and Orientation

The holistic thrust described above is related directly to praxis. Costas's approach to a contextual evangelization, for example, stemmed from his experience as a Puerto Rican/Latino Christian who had suffered displacement, racism, marginalization, and dehumanization as he moved from Puerto Rico to the Bronx to Bridgeport to Bob Jones Academy to Nyack College to Puerto Rico to Milwaukee to Costa Rica to Philadelphia, and finally to Andover Newton Theological School as academic dean and missiology professor. Even if certain things "got better," he chose to identify and orient his work toward what he called the "Galilean periphery." This meant engagement with the world so that the gospel of Jesus the Christ might effect a change in the lives of those who cried and suffered, yet had no real voice to advocate their interests.

In the life of Orlando Costas, sin was not merely an idea or academic problem to contemplate. Dealing with sin meant dealing with the abhorrent conditions of millions of U.S. Latinos who experience morally and spiritually devastating economic impoverishment, political paralysis, appalling educational dropout rates, or inferior housing and employment situations. From a Latino radical evangelical approach, praxis requires that the church's mission serve to incarnate hope amid the despair in our barrios and in our local churches as well. Sin as a radical ailment with deadly consequences requires a *radical* or fundamental solution.

From a Latino radical evangelical perspective, the liberating gospel of Jesus the Christ announces that indeed God *is* doing a new thing in our midst. Can we not perceive it? Such a witness calls for the very power of the risen Christ to take those by the hand who are paralyzed by fear and negative self-worth, and in bondage to a spirit of self-destruction, and for us to raise them up in the name of Jesus of Nazareth. Such spirit-filled mission engagement requires the building of new institutions, of independent or at least interdependent economic bases, and a leadership program that will identify, recruit, orient, train, empower, and support new generations of Latinas and Latinos for the task ahead. From such a perspective, if indeed we are grounded in and led by Christ, sin *does not* have the last word. Through a victorious Christ and the spirit of power, the triune God does pronounce signs of God's reign in our midst today. Praxis means change that includes both action and reflection. New ways of thinking and of mission are implied.

From the Underside of History

In order to develop a Latino radical evangelical approach for understanding sin, from a Hispanic perspective, a fundamental commitment to the poor is needed. Costas submitted that such a commitment was based upon the very model of Jesus—his Galilean ministry. Such an approach suggests that Jesus not only was found working among the outcasts of society but was born in a stable and was crucified outside the gates of Jerusalem, the holy city. If we wish to be faithful to the church's mission today, where may we find Christ in our world?

Costas affirmed that it is precisely at the fringes of power and prestige that God is at work to bring about a new agenda from "within the entrails of the beast" (José Martí). What was rejected and ridiculed has now stepped into the limelight of God's liberating project. The liberating news is that from within the harsh reality of sin and injustice God's reign of peace with justice has overturned the tables of social misery and human deprivation.

Costas's Latino radical evangelical approach offers U.S. Latino communities and others today a way for engaging the Christian church and other institutions of society in a historical project of transformation. According to Costas, the litmus test of Christian theology, of personal faith, and of the church's mission is efficacious service in the world.[55] This is a diaconal calling that stems from a living and loving encounter with Christ.

Costas's model for mission engagement and theological discourse invites us into the world of the disenfranchised. A Latino radical evangelical approach challenges us to reconsider the spurious assumptions that hinder effective ministry in our respective neighborhoods and barrios. Costas's model also suggests a reworking of the priorities, assumptions, and designs of our Christian projects. As we battle against sin, death, and oppression in the world through the power of God's spirit, let us prepare for and experience conversion toward the world of the oppressed. This is not only where we will find Christ but where Christ wants to find us. We may therefore expect and affirm with Costas:

At the periphery, in Galilee, one encounters the risen Lord, enlarging and deepening one's limited vision of human reality, challenging one's presuppositions, renewing one's mind, liberating one's life for service as a channel of grace in the "Galilees of the nations"—the shanties and ghettoes, the marginal provinces and forgotten nuclei of the world.[56]

From a Latino perspective, an understanding of sin also includes the battle against it and all its manifestations. Today there is emerging a new generation of Latinos and Latinas engaging mission from the vantage point of the downtrodden. For example, a Latino academic and ecumenical association such as La Comunidad of Hispanic Scholars of Theology and Religion, a national Latino Protestant group such as the Asociatión para la Educación Teológica Hispana (AETH), and a more local indigenous-based para-ecclesial agency such as the Latino Pastoral Action Center (LPAC), all represent new directions for engaging mission from a holistic, praxis-oriented approach from "the underside of history," namely the world of disenfranchised Latino reality.

Out of such bodies, there are new signs of evangelical thought with prophetic edges. There is articulation of structural concerns that do not deny the personal dimensions of suffering. There are theological educators who regard social change and personal encounter with Christ as integral ingredients of the church's task.

In the final analysis, the reality of sin threatens and engulfs us, but the even greater presence and promise of God to break the bonds of oppression in our personal and collective lives is also with us.

> What then shall we say to this? If God is for us, who is against us? . . . Who shall separate us from the love of Christ? Shall tribulation, or distress, or persecution, or famine, or nakedness, or peril, or sword? . . . No, in all these things we are more than conquerors through him who loved us. For I am sure that neither death, nor life, nor angels, nor principalities, nor things present, nor things to come, nor powers, nor height, nor depth, nor anything else in all creation, will be able to separate us from the love of God in Christ Jesus our Lord. (Rom. 8:31, 35, 37–39)

From a Hispanic or Latino perspective, the promise and presence of God in Christ will allow the church and its mission to proclaim a risen Christ who has challenged and defeated sin, death, and oppression in the world (Col. 2:15). This is the gospel that we have been taught to live and believe. What remains is to incarnate the signs of God's reign as we break down the walls of sin in our midst and restore life and dignity to the oppressed. This is a missional task that demands the power to challenge and to change: "For the kingdom of God does not consist in talk but in power" (1 Cor. 4:20).

NOTES

1. In this section I use the *New Bible Dictionary* (*NBD*), 2d ed., s.v. "Sin," by J. Murray, 1116–20, passim; and the *Theological Dictionary of the New Testament* (*TDNT*), s.v. "*hamartía*," by Gottfried Quell, Georg Bertram, Gustav Stählin, and Walter Grundmann, vol. 1, 267–316, passim.
2. *NBD*, 1117. See also the *Interpreter's Dictionary of the Bible* (*IDB*), s.v. "Sin, sinners," by Simon J. de Vries, 361–76, passim.
3. *IDB*, 361.
4. Ibid., 362.
5. Ibid., 371; and Robert Young, *Young's Analytical Concordance to the Bible* (Nashville: Thomas Nelson Publishers, 1982), 891.
6. *TDNT*, 279.
7. Ibid., 292.
8. Ibid., 295, 309, 307, and 303.
9. Justo L. González, *Christian Thought Revisited* (Nashville: Abingdon Press, 1989).
10. Ibid., 101–18.
11. Ibid., 105–6.
12. Ibid., 109.
13. José Antonio Sayes, *Antropología del hombre caído: El pecado original* (Madrid: Biblioteca de Autores Cristianos, 1991), 115.
14. Ibid.; Reginald S. Moxon, *The Doctrine of Sin* (London: George Allen & Unwin, 1922), 88.
15. Moxon, *Doctrine of Sin*, 89.
16. Sayes, *Antropología*, 150–51, 160; and González, *Christian Thought*, 122.
17. Louis Berkhof, *Systematic Theology* (Grand Rapids: Wm. B. Eerdmans Publishing Co., 1941).
18. Ibid., 221.
19. Ibid., 221, 225, 226.
20. Ibid., 231.
21. Gustavo Gutiérrez, *A Theology of Liberation: History, Politics, and Salvation* (Maryknoll, N.Y.: Orbis Books, 1988).
22. Ibid., 24–25, 102–3.
23. Ibid., 85.
24. Ibid., xxxviii.
25. Ibid., 103.
26. Ibid.
27. Enrique Dussel, *Ethics and Community* (Maryknoll, N.Y.: Orbis Books, 1988).
28. Ibid., 18.
29. Ibid., 19–20.
30. Ibid., 23.
31. Ibid., 22.
32. Ibid., 26.
33. Ibid., 31.
34. Ignacio Ellacurría and Jon Sobrino, eds., *Mysterium Liberationis: Fundamental Concepts of Liberation Theology* (Maryknoll, N.Y.: Orbis Books, 1993), 536.

35. Elsa Tamez, *The Amnesty of Grace: Justification by Faith from a Latin American Perspective* (Nashville: Abingdon Press, 1993).
36. Ibid., 14.
37. Ibid., 20–21.
38. Raymond Rivera, "The Ethics of a Kingdom Lifestyle: A Challenge to the Status Quo," lecture at Dover Plains, N.Y., June 3, 1995.
39. Tamez, *Amnesty*, 21.
40. Ibid., 42–43.
41. Ibid., 43.
42. Orlando E. Costas, *Christ outside the Gate: Mission beyond Christendom* (Maryknoll, N.Y.: Orbis Books, 1982), 35–36.
43. Ibid., 21.
44. Ibid., 37.
45. Ibid., 35.
46. Ibid., 34.
47. Ibid., 37.
48. Ibid., 38.
49. Ibid., 38–39.
50. David Traverzo Galarza, "The Emergence of a Latino Radical Social Ethic in the Work and Thought of Orlando E. Costas: An Ethico-Theological Discourse from the Underside of History," doctoral dissertation, Drew University, Madison, N.J., May 1992.
51. Orlando E. Costas, *Liberating News: A Theology of Contextual Evangelization* (Grand Rapids: Wm. B. Eerdmans Publishing Co., 1989).
52. Ibid., 15.
53. See Traverzo Galarza, "Emergence."
54. Costas, *Liberating News;* Orlando E. Costas, "Iglecrecimiento, el movimiento ecuménico y el evangelicalismo," *Misión* 3 (June 1984): 56–60; idem, "Evangelism in a Latin American Context," *Occasional Essays* 4:1–2 (January 1977): 3–15.
55. Costas, *Liberating News.*
56. Orlando Costas, "Christian Mission from the Periphery," *Faith and Mission* 1:1 (fall 1983): 1–14.

9

Hispanic Protestant Spirituality

Elizabeth Conde-Frazier

The term "spirituality" is of Roman Catholic origin, from French, and refers to the common experience of all Christians with God. It meant living life according to the Holy Spirit. "Gradually, it came to mean that life which was of special concern to 'souls seeking perfection,'"[1] and included individual, specialized spiritual exercises. Until the Middle Ages all theology was spiritual theology, or the reflection of one's experience of faith, and it found expression in liturgy, scripture, private prayer, and pastoral experience. In the eighteenth century spirituality emerged as a well-defined branch of theology. The Society of Jesus (the Jesuits) developed ascetical and mystical theology as a science of the spiritual life. "Ascetical theology studied the life of perfection up to the beginning of passive mystical experience. Mystical theology began with contemplation to its climax in the union with God."[2]

From a wider perspective, Christian spirituality involves the response to and relationship with God, who is revealed in the Bible and especially in the person of Jesus Christ. Our relationship with God began at creation and was broken by sin. It can be restored through faith in Jesus. Some describe the journey of spirituality as a "conformity of heart and life to the character of Jesus as Lord" (1 Cor. 12:3).[3] It is the presence and the power of the Holy Spirit working in the life of the believer that guides and guarantees our relationship with Christ.

This description of spirituality observes an interaction and weaving together of four dimensions: doctrine, discipline, liturgy, and personal action. Doctrine is what we believe about God, the world, and ourselves. Discipline deals with the form of our corporate life and the consequences of not living a Christian life. Discipline also includes the sources of our authority. Liturgy deals with the life of worship and praise of the community of faith. It is how music, prayer, the word, and the ordinances or sacraments (depending on one's tradition) are ordered in public worship to impact the attitudes, behavior, and lifestyles of those worshiping. The fourth dimension is the lifestyle of the believer, including prayer, study, devotion, work, recreation, and social involvement.

To explore the subject of Hispanic Protestant spirituality, I first look at the biblical and theological roots of our spirituality. Next I briefly discuss some of our rich roots in Spanish mysticism. This lays a foundation for identifying the characteristics of Hispanic Protestant spirituality. I also deal with the contributions and expressions that women have made to Hispanic spirituality. Finally I identify areas for expansion and renewal. Relationships and the qualities and values that direct our everyday lives are an intrinsic part and expression of Hispanic spirituality. For this reason, I also include accounts of the lives and experiences of various persons.

Biblical Roots

For Protestants, the entire biblical witness is a source for our spirituality. Scripture is the rule of our faith and practice. Passages from the Johannine and Pauline writings and the Psalms are often quoted and used as a basis for the theological foundations of Hispanic Protestant spirituality.

The Johannine writings are concerned with salvation or eternal life (John 3:16, 36; 1 John 1:2). John writes that through Jesus the world comes to know God in a new way and to live in and for him (John 1:18; 17:3). Jesus' dual nature, divine and human, and his death and resurrection enable humankind to become children of God and thus walk in the light. The term that John most often uses to describe the Christian life is "abiding" (John 15). This abiding unites us to God through Jesus and also to other Christian believers. When speaking of the experience of God, John presents a devotional and practical spirituality. Concerning worship, John understands Jesus as saying that it is Jesus' spirit that inspires worship, rather than the religious observances of the temple. Prayer is a practice that results from our abiding relationship, and it is the Paraclete who draws us to a deepening spirituality. On the practical side, service, as exemplified by Jesus in the washing of the disciples' feet (John 13), is to be done out of humility and on occasion may involve sacrifice (John 15:12–13).

The Pauline writings center on the message of the cross. Paul believed that all attempts to reach God by one's own doing are and must be crucified. Life comes only through the death of our efforts to reach God by human means. Our weaknesses and failures, and the traditions that have imprisoned salvation by tying it to a religious ritual or group, are liberated by the cross. Spiritual growth draws us to the cross, for it includes sharing in the sufferings of Christ and being like Christ in his death. Spiritual growth also consists of experiencing the power of Christ's resurrection, which enables us to live "in Christ." Day-to-day life in Christ consists of bearing one another's burdens, "giving and receiving the Spirit's gifts . . . , offering ourselves as living sacrifices . . . , [and] eating the meal of unity and love."[4] Paul includes spiritual warfare as part of the life "in the spirit," for he sees a spiritual tension between perfection and our weakness (Romans 7). Yet it is in our weakness that Christ's strength is made manifest in us (2 Cor. 12:9).

The Psalms serve as a spiritual counselor. Their rich descriptions of the varied feelings and experiences of the relationship with God through different stages in life cause readers to identify with the psalmist and to draw again and again from these wells. The many psalms we sing at worship, prayer vigils, and funerals are the most common, outward communal use of the psalms in this way. Among these are Psalms 25, 30, 116, 117, 125, 133, 136, 145, and the many versions of Psalm 23.

Theological Roots

Christian theology generally describes the Christian life as a call to live according to the Spirit and not according to the flesh (Gal. 3:3–5; Romans 8:4–13). In the pursuit of this life, Calvin identified a quest for conformity to the sovereign will of God in which "the concern was with perfection, personal experience and the means to a devout life."[5] This progression to godliness includes self-denial, cross-bearing, restraint, hope, prayer, and obedience. John Owen, a Puritan pastoral theologian, expanded Calvin's concept, developing it into a pilgrimage and battle in which God's grace renews us toward the *imago Dei*.

Pietism and Methodism are more obviously Protestant forms of spirituality. The pietists required prayer meetings and total abstinence from alcohol. Their spirituality included a familial devotion to God as Parent, rather than as Creator. Pietists claimed that it was possible to be freed from the power of sin, and they understood salvation as restoration of the *imago Dei* in humanity and the conquest of sin. This resulted in the power to do what is good. The concept of rebirth was at the heart of pietistic spirituality. Pietists believed—and believe—that hearing the gospel brings one to the experience of rebirth and transfers one from a state of nature to a state of grace. Growth follows rebirth and entails fighting and defeating actual sins through prayer. One of the first things one learns as a new believer in a Hispanic Protestant church is that the work of the Holy Spirit is to bring one to love both God and neighbor and to lead one in continual prayer. Besides prayer, one is to train the will in order to do what God wants. This can mean the breaking of the human will in order to make it surrender. This theological legacy has been passed down to us through many hymns as well as the more autochthonous *coritos*, spiritual songs, of the Pentecostal tradition.

In pietism, after the defeat of sin comes sanctification. The signs of sanctification are faith, love, humility, patience, prayer, and satisfaction with one's material situation. One must also be careful, in relations with the world, to stay away from sin. This can lead to a negative attitude toward culture.

John Wesley, the founder of Methodism, introduced the concept of a second work of grace by the Holy Spirit. According to Wesley, the first work is the new birth. The second work eliminates sinful desires, leaving only "perfect love" of God and others as the motive of one's heart. The Holiness movement grew out of this "second blessing" doctrine of the Christian life, in which the infilling of the Spirit, or the baptism of the Spirit, gives one power or spiritual gifts for service.[6] For some, glossolalia, or speaking in tongues, one of the spiritual gifts, is the point at which one goes from a lower to a higher level of spirituality in one's life.

Methodism's early rules required frequent attendance at Holy Communion, meetings for the study of the Bible, mutual encouragement in ethical conduct, regular visits to prisons, and service to the poor. A tract summarizing the rules and practices during John Wesley's time, called the *Large Minutes*, enumerated the "Means of Grace." These included public, family, and private prayer; reading and meditating on the word; fasting; the Lord's Supper; and Christian fellowship. These practices and rules are very similar to those in many of our Hispanic churches today.

Opportunities existed for growing in the faith in the early Methodist community. These included a variety of occasions for prayer such as watchnights, which were times of prayer and witness late into the night. This practice was similar to what the early church called vigils of feasts. Today in Hispanic congregations this is still a regular practice.

Three terms are key to a theological understanding of Protestant spirituality: justification, perfection, and sanctification. Justification is both biblical and dogmatic. It denotes "the action of God in re-establishing a proper relationship with fallen creation."[7] It is through faith in Christ that sinners are set in right relationship with God (Rom. 3:28). One depends not on works or other accomplishments to attain justification, but on God's action through the forgiving grace of Christ.

Simply put, perfection means striving toward a sinless life. The Puritans described it as a singleness of desire to please God. It was a process of being renewed in holiness and of purification throughout one's lifetime. Perfection is also connected with a love for God that gives one the ability to show concern and compassion for others. This is accomplished by becoming free from resentments, hatreds, jealousies, and bitterness. Modern spirituality shies away from the term "perfection," although the idea is still present; and arguments from the perspective of pastoral psychology have brought moderation to the theology of perfection. Some twentieth-century writers have drawn from the Cappadocian fathers,[8] who did not see perfection as a moral state but as continual growth brought about by the discipline of love for God and others. This perspective feels more like Paul's comment to the Philippians: "Not that I have already obtained this . . . but I press on to make it my own" (Phil. 3:12, NRSV).

In the Hebrew Bible, the term "sanctification" connotes cleansing in preparation for encountering God's presence (Ex. 19:10, 14), as well as consecration or dedication to the service of God. Besides including ritual, this meaning extends to the moral sphere. This is seen, for example, in the prophetic word of Joel 2:13: "rend your hearts and not your clothing," or in Psalm 50:13 and Psalm 51:16 in which contriteness of heart and prayer are considered more pleasing than animal sacrifice. The New Testament emphasizes other moral behavior, as we see in Jesus' confrontation with the Pharisees and scribes' rules of purification. This is why the early Christian community calls for sanctification through the cleansing of the heart and conscience (Acts 15:9; Heb. 9:14) and for living out sanctification through model conduct. This sanctification is considered to be the work of God in the believer through the Holy Spirit (Rom. 15:16; 2 Thess. 2:13; 1 Peter 1:2). In the context of the economic and sociopolitical issues facing the Hispanic community, the Hispanic Protestant church is expanding its theological understanding of the prophetic dimensions of sanctification, so that social justice, and not just social action, is becoming a growing concern of its ministry.

Roots in Spanish Mysticism

Segundo Galilea lifts up the Spanish roots of Latin American spirituality.[9] Of these, two aspects characterize Hispanic Protestant spirituality. The first is a profound sense of the presence and the action of God in all aspects of life. The second is the sufferings of Jesus, which are a part of his humanity. From these come a profound sense of and capacity to accept suffering, indigence, and death.

San Juan de la Cruz (St. John of the Cross), a Carmelite, synthesized theology and the mystic experience. This balance serves as a foundation for modern devotion, which became popular among the people and is found in the spirituality of Teresa de Ávila. Hers is a Christ-centered and affective form of devotion. In her writing about prayer she states: "La oración no es cuestión de pensar mucho, sino de amar mucho" (Prayer is not about much thinking, but about much loving).[10] Prayer and doing the will of God were inseparable for Teresa de Ávila. She urged: "Vaya doblando la voluntad, si quiere que le aproveche la oración" (Begin to bow the will, if you want prayer to be of benefit).[11] In this sense, prayer is not moving Christ to do as we ask, but becoming moved to do as Christ asks. It does not differentiate between the spiritual disciplines and Christian action; it does not substitute one for the other. Rather, out of prayer flows our direction, strength, and committed love to the work of the reign of God. The latter cannot evolve or be sustained without the former.

Segundo Galilea points out that for the Spanish mystics, the will of God was not pietism but a very demanding Christian commitment that was the root of our Christian identity. This is why Ignatius of Loyola could state, "Cristo nuestro Senor llama y dice . . . quien quisiera venir conmigo, ha de trabajar conmigo, porque siguiéndome en la pena también me sigue en la gloria" (Christ our Lord calls and says . . . whoever would follow after me must work with me, for it is by following in my suffering that he or she will also follow in my glory).[12] As we evaluate our spirituality, our Spanish mystic heritage serves as a measure and balance for our orthodoxy and orthopraxis.

Characteristics of
Hispanic Protestant Spirituality

Testimonio

Hispanic Protestant spirituality is the expression of both contemplation and action. It is knowing God not only in a cognitive way but through the affective dimension as well. This means that when we speak of a "spiritual" person we are speaking of a person who is a doer as well as a hearer of the word of God. We put things into practice as a way of coming to understand them. Understanding the sermon cognitively is one thing, but understanding the extent of its message, in order to implement it, is another. It is at this moment that a person can say, "Now I really see what it means," and can add to it a story of difficulties encountered, the grace of God in the difficult moments, and the new understanding of what that sermon means in one's life.

The change that others may observe as we live out this understanding is our *testimonio*, the outward expression, the fruit born from our seeking to obey God's word. It is living in obedience that brings an incarnational understanding of the word and reveals new things to us about Jesus manifested in that living word. This outward expression of one's faith is also the measure of one's fitness for ministry in the church since it is the church that affirms our call. The more integrity one demonstrates in one's testimony, the more powerful one's ministry, or potential for ministry, is considered.

The sharing of the joys, frustrations, and grace of God in our Christian journeys is our witness of who God is and what we are learning about God daily. This is also termed *testimonio*. It is an important part of our worship. Our testimonies are the articulation of our theology and of our faith and the internalization of that faith and theology by others. Eldin Villafañe claims that the *testimonio* of the community of faith is its creed. It follows the pattern of a creed, for it states who God is and what we believe.[13] Loida Martell-Otero describes this kind of witness:

> The witness of the believers gives insight to the community. The sharing of the Word, the oral histories conserved, the give and take among the hermanos [brothers] and hermanas [sisters], . . . allow us to "test our thoughts" and to deem our analysis of a text credible. They allow us to receive new ways of seeing a text, and new ways to experience God in our midst. . . . It is a key hermeneutical tool, which consciously or unconsciously, we use to receive theological understanding of given biblical concepts. Further, if it is invalid for the community, it becomes an invalid theological source.[14]

Testimonio is also an integral part of our preaching. It illustrates and enriches the biblical account. It is used as a way of encouraging the faith journey or the Christian life.

Daily Devotions

A distinctive emphasis of Protestant Hispanic spirituality is that it belongs to the people, or the laity, as opposed to the ordained or professional clergy. It is not leisurely contemplation, but rather, the tools of survival and struggle for those who are part of the busy rhythms of work and life. It is expressed in our believing, our giving, and in our daily lives as an example of our Christian holy living and our sacrificial service to others. The foundation is the practice of daily devotions, which varies by person or family. Some may use the early morning while others prefer the evening. It may be during the commute to work or school, shower time, or lunch time. Devotions may be an individual practice or be done as a married couple or family. However the daily devotion is done, it is considered the daily sustenance, the breathing and eating of one's life as a Christian.

The three important aspects of daily devotions are (1) abiding in and trusting God for daily surrender, (2) scriptural experience with the aid of a devotional book, and (3) prayer life.[15] Even though these three are integrally and experientially one in our spirituality, for the purposes of this presentation I look at each separately in order for us to understand the importance and impact of each aspect.

1. *Abiding and trusting.* "I am the true vine, and my Father is the vine-grower. . . . Abide in me as I abide in you. Just as the branch cannot bear

fruit by itself unless it abides in the vine, neither can you unless you abide in me. . . . Apart from me you can do nothing" (John 15:1, 4–5, NRSV). Between the vine and the branches is a union, a flow of the supply of life. To receive this life, the branch "abides" in the vine. It rests confidently in the vine in a living union. In the spiritual life, we seek this union, this trust in Jesus. We do it through our daily devotions, reading the scriptures, meditating, and praying. For some, moments of praise may also be included in this special time. We maintain our union with Jesus through our communion with him, by maintaining a moment-by-moment fellowship so that his life is flowing in us. This flowing life of Christ in us and our awareness of it enable us to bear fruit and to go beyond our limitations. For example, I am introverted and shy, yet, through my communion with Jesus, the love of Christ urges me on (2 Cor. 5:14). Instead of my fear holding sway over me, I am able to feel a passion and compassion for others. This, in turn, moves me beyond my shyness to reach out and offer what I have, and to receive from others. When I do this I discover who I am. I am dependent on God's love and life flowing in me so that I can flow out of my shell of security.

Being an instrument of God begins with coming to know God so that we can trust God. Trusting enables us to yield to God's will and in that yielding to obey God's will. God never forces God's will upon us, for God neither violates our person nor invalidates it. God works through who we are as we accept and rechannel our energies in the direction God has determined. That direction is not only for personal benefit, but for pouring out to and with others. To be united to God inevitably is to become united to others. We delight in God and therefore our desire is to please God (John 15:10–14).

2. *Scriptural experience.* The Bible is central to our spirituality, for God's word must abide in us (John 15:7). The word is a revelation of God. We come to know God by reading, studying, and meditating on the word. Before reading the scriptures we prayerfully ask God to speak to us, a form of revealing oneself to another. Commenting on how we read the scriptures devotionally, Jorge E. Sanchez says:

> Cuando leemos la Biblia, siempre pausamos un momento para dejar que el mensaje bíblico llegue muy adentro de nuestro corazón. En silencio, dejamos que las historias biblicas y su mensaje nos influyen de gran manera. El silencio, luego de la lectura, nos hace refleccionar profundamente. Nos hace que recordemos nuestra relación de amor con Dios. Comenzamos también el proceso de construir nuestra respuesta al llamado de Dios. (When we read the Bible, we always pause for a moment to allow the biblical message to penetrate deeply into our hearts. In silence, we allow the biblical stories and their message to influence us deeply. In silence, after we read it, it causes us to reflect profoundly. It causes us to remember our love relationship with God. We also begin our process of constructing our response to the call of God to be witnesses in our world.)[16]

This has considerable resonance with the centuries-old practice of *lectio divina*. To know the word is a form of loving God or abiding in God's love. To mediate on God's word also leads us to informed prayer. In the words of Warren Wiersbe, "Prayer is much more than asking. It involves giving thanks, expressing love and confessing our sin."[17] It causes us to say, with the psalmist, "Search me, O God, and know my heart; test me and know my thoughts . . . and lead me in the way everlasting" (Ps. 139:23–24, NRSV).

3. *Prayer life.* In all of this, we practice daily devotions so that we may yield to the work of the Spirit and be sustained for the work of transformation. Prayer guides and strengthens us, not only in our personal lives, but in the ministry, as individuals and as a church. Intercessory prayer demands a practiced discipline and faithful dedication. There are dedicated persons who can be called on at any time to pray, and to call others, thus forming prayer chains. Many of them are the women in our churches. They exhibit courage and determination. They pray without ceasing. They also visit and anoint the sick. This is their work in the Lord's vineyard. Their courage and strength are expressed not only in prayer but also as they do the work of the Lord.

It was through prayer, for instance, that Leoncilla Rosado Rousseau (Mama Leo), a Pentecostal minister, received a vision that redefined her ministry. María Díaz, a laywoman, volunteered to work with a drug rehabilitation center and treated each of the men served there as her own son. She fought to open the hearts of the members of her church so that they would work with the center. Each time she prayed, she would come back with a new idea to improve the work of the center. In those moments, there was no way to keep her from finding the most creative ways of implementing those ideas. Not knowing how to read or write, she learned to speak her ideas into a tape recorder so that someone else could then write proposals. Eventually, her efforts renewed the ministries of her church in the community, created bridges between the church and community agencies, and produced deep theological reflection. Her prayers led them where their traditions and theology would not. She claimed that the fervor to pray came from a deep love she felt for the young men and that her love came from her prayers. That is a spirituality for doing justice.

Prayer enables us to obey. The Hispanic devotional life seeks both a cognitive knowledge of God and an understanding of God's way. Prayer allows us to understand this way and to obediently remain on it. The Bible guides us on the way but knowledge of Jesus is essential, for he is the way (John 14:6). The stories of the lives of the biblical characters describe and illustrate the pilgrimage of others on that path, but we come to know the way only by walking in it. Therefore, as we seek to know God and as the scripture guides us in this knowledge, as we continuously walk in obedience in this path, we find ourselves in a process of ongoing transformation. It is precisely for this reason that I assert that daily devotions are a catalyst for the lifelong process of conversion. In this way conversion is intimately related to our devotional lives and especially to our prayer lives.

Conversion is initiated by the gift of God's grace. It elicits our permission and cooperation. This human response to the action of God is our faith or belief, an ongoing relationship with God. Our faith seeks an ever-growing relationship with God. As we draw nearer to God, there is a movement away from other things in our life. As Beverly Gaventa has noted, "In the Johannine gospel, birth from above implies discontinuity in the life of the one who receives this birth."[18] One also receives a new Spirit (John 20:22).

Pablo Polishuk, a pastoral counselor and ordained minister of the Hispanic community, described conversion as a series of God-initiated stages in our lives. Conversion can take various forms. It can be event, a particular moment and happening in a person's life when God intervened and led that person to changes in her or his life. It can be a process during which one is aware of God's ongoing work in a particular area of one's life. This process may take years of healing and renewal. Finally, there is the conversion of the structures of one's personhood. This is a much deeper transformation of a basic and foundational part of who we are as persons, reminiscent of the writings of St. John of the Cross, who speaks of the conversion of one's sensibilities, memory, affects, intelligence, and will. In order for God to fill us and to transmit love and liberty to us, we need to be purified and rid of what is incompatible with the Spirit of God, divested of our idols and selfishness.[19]

As Hispanic Protestants, we speak of crucifying the flesh, and we sing the scriptural *corito* (spiritual song), "No vivo yo, mas Cristo vive en mi" (It is no longer I who live, but it is Christ who lives in me; Gal. 2:20). We often lift up scriptural themes of dying to self in order to live in Christ. The purpose of this journey into death and new life is to be free to please God by serving God, which means service to others. The Holy Spirit brings the inner workings of the word of God in our lives to fruition. One of the fruits is the changing of our desires, which results in a change in our prayer requests. When our desires change we see ourselves differently in relationship to others. Our desire coincides with the will of God and our prayers envision that will. Then what we request in prayer is granted (John 15:7).

Christian Service and Sacrifice

The will of God, holy living, and Christian service are synonymous. On occasion, the sociopolitical context of the United States has tended to limit our view of the parameters of Christian service or the mission of the church.

When it dictates that because we speak Spanish, we are "less than," or that we have no voice, or when a congregation does not have the tools for interacting with the political systems controlling the community it ministers in, then spirituality has tended to be interpreted and expressed as holy living exclusively within the sanctuary of our temples and homes. Spirituality may even be reduced to a list of do's and don'ts. A community of faith that has been liberated from these lies by the message of the gospel and critical thinking is a community of faith with an integral theology of mission and outreach that combines justice and spirituality.

The idea of being holy usually evokes images and scripture passages that urge us to imitate Christ. This includes the cross and the sufferings of Jesus. The cross is always before us in our Christian life and service, as are the blessings of a life joined to Christ. The words of Jesus' prayer in the garden, "Father, if thou art willing, remove this cup from me; nevertheless, not my will, but thine be done" (Luke 22:42), was one of the first verses I learned by heart as a child through hearing it quoted in many conversations. The struggle of faith includes faith that believes in the blessings of God through healings, miracles, and answered prayer. It also includes faith that struggles toward hope in the midst of hard times.

This was the faith of my grandmother who, as a shut-in, prayed every night for the sick listed on the church bulletin. Then in the mornings she would give the list back to my grandfather with check marks next to the ones who were healed. She would place stars next to those who needed prayer in order to receive strength to accept the will of God. She discerned this because as she prayed she would see Jesus approach the bed of the ones healed. She was also the one who gathered the family together to tell us that though she prayed for her daughter to be healed, in her prayers Jesus would not come to her daughter's bedside; therefore we needed to prepare ourselves for her death. She said to us, "The God who heals the body will heal our hearts after he has taken her from us." Her faith guided us through the initial stages of the grieving process. She had not simply resigned herself, but through struggling with God in prayer, had accepted the will of God. Action, waiting, accepting, *lucha* (struggle), sacrifice, service, the reign of God, the will of God, the past, the present, and eternity are the ways that our spirituality strives to know and become like Christ. Suffering is part of the Pauline theology of the cross. To suffer for the cause of the gospel gives strength and meaning to some of the most difficult moments of Paul's life. He mentions to the Philippians: "For to me, living is Christ and dying is gain" (Phil. 1:21, NRSV).

It is necessary here to make a few distinctions about suffering as an expression of holy living. When suffering is redemptive or bears the fruit of justice it is acceptable. When, however, suffering is not redemptive and bears the fruit of injustice or further oppression, as in the case of domestic violence or any other kind of abuse, it cannot and should never be named as acceptable sacrifice before the eyes of the Lord. To accept or endure abuse is to bow down and worship the demons of brokenness. To resist abuse is to claim the power of the cross to break the power of sin and its consequences. To resist is to exorcise the demon of silence and isolation. It is to reclaim and consecrate the temple of the Holy Spirit, our bodies.

Pastors sometimes have a spirituality that seems to demand unjust sacrifice of the pastor's family and disregard of the self. It is a tremendous burden and a false spirituality that turns the pastor into an idol, denying not only the human nature of the pastor but of Christ himself, thus making it heresy. It isolates him or her from the fellowship and the communion of the saints and results in a distorted sense of the authority of the pastor in the church, denying vulnerability and thus blocking the much-needed gifts of discernment in the body. In the letter to the Romans, Paul urges us to present our bodies as a *living* sacrifice (Rom. 12:1), not a dead one. We must therefore ask what it takes to maintain life while we engage in Christian service so that our sacrifice of service may indeed be holy and acceptable to God.

Another expression of sacrifice is financial giving. Our giving is not evoked by guilt but by a sense of appreciation for our salvation as well as a biblical understanding that all we have is the Lord's (Ps. 24:1). When we say we belong to Jesus we include our personal possessions. Many even itemize these in their prayers of dedication. The practice of giving is the practice of our faith. We believe God will supply our needs when we give to cover the needs of others. Giving also arises from a sense of compassion for others. Recently I spoke to a woman who demonstrated great knowledge about refinancing loans and mortgages. Impressed, I asked how she had come to know so much about the subject. After hesitating, she whispered in confidence that she had been taking out personal loans to help numerous families who did not have citizenship. She described herself as forever in debt and forever receiving miracles from God. Her solidarity with the poor underlines those financial practices of many of us which are an affront to God. She represents the widow who gave her two mites, plus a few loans.

Tithing is part of the spiritual life of many. As our expression of thanksgiving we give a tenth part back to God. My mother had several small boxes that she labeled according to her bills. One box was labeled "El Señor." She often borrowed from one box to pay another, but she would never touch "El Señor's" box. Instead, she would become very creative in seeking ways to secure extra income. When I was baptized she brought out a dollar in pennies. After I counted all of them, she explained that they all belonged to the Lord. However, God allowed us to keep ninety of them, requiring only ten. These ten were for those who had less; they were never for us to keep. My grandfather did the same with his house. Out of the four apartments in the building, one always belonged to God. This meant that a family with little or no means of paying for the apartment lived there. A part of everything belonged to God. If you owned a car you did favors for others on your own gas. This was considered a very normal practice. It was a mark of Christian identity.

El Culto: Worship

There has always been a deep sense of community among Hispanics. Anyone traveling in the Spanish-speaking world can appreciate this sense of community in the way that the towns are laid out. There are public centers for people to gather and share. The church is a landmark in the center of the town, and it was one's identity with the Catholic church that gave one a sense of identity with the *pueblo* (people; village). This characteristic continues and can be especially felt in the growth of *comunidades de base* (base communities) throughout Latin America where persons living in the same community sit in a circle to interpret the scriptures in the light of their daily realities in order to come to a communal discernment about what the word of God means and how it addresses their current situation. This means that our spirituality has a communal dimension that is not only theologically and biblically based but also culturally based.

Theologically, we understand that to become a believer is to become a part of the community, of the body of Christ. There is a spiritual power in communal worship that is not available to the individual in private. Singing together, communal assent to the scriptures, and support in prayers are ways through which one experiences this power. Even when circumstances do not allow one to feel faith, the support and the voices lifted together fill the place of worship, and slowly one's heart feels more connected again. Others in the community may help one to utter the words of prayer or may help one to cry when one no longer has words or tears.

The *culto*, or worship, is the celebration of the victory of the cross. It is the "fiesta" expression of our spirituality, and music and testimonies reflect this. The *culto* has been described by Hispanic theologians as the place of dialogue between persons and God.[20] This dialogue takes place through verbal and symbolic expressions. It has also been called the *locus theologicus* of the Hispanic community.[21] The preaching, hymns, testimonies, and prayers all express parts of our theology. Worship is our place for using the spiritual tools for struggle and survival as a community. It is also the place for being accountable to one another and supporting one another as we grow spiritually. The theology of the *culto* explains spiritual growth and models it. It creates a culture in which one learns the practice of spirituality. The prayer times, in particular, become a gathering for support, sharing personal hardships and victories and gaining strength to go through diffi-cult situations or trials. The cross-bearing moments are shared as a com-munity. This sharing of burdens leads to a special solidarity that is expressed through prayer and informs the ministry toward others.

Another communal expression of spirituality is the intense prayer time called *vigilia*, when one prays into the early hours of the night or until day-break the next day. In preparation, some may fast. At these prayer services the focus is on intercessory prayer, seeking to become nearer to God, or seeking a special spiritual blessing or understanding. One learns the lan-guage and forms of prayer and praise. Emotions are part of the theological makeup. In the Pentecostal church, Villafañe has written, "the glossolalic experiences color all understanding of spirituality."[22] Participating in a *vigilia* is considered by some to be a sign of a person's baptism by the Spirit. It may also be a form of praise, intercession by the Spirit through the person, or, when accompanied by an interpretation, it is a prophetic message from God to the congregation or to an individual. In short, the *culto* is the place where the Spirit may be encountered as nowhere else.

A key part of spiritual life is a conversion in how we relate to others. Community life is necessary for the development of spiritual life. The con-flicts, the struggle to reconcile, telling the truth in love so that we edify each other—these are also part of the spiritual growth of the body of believers. Communal expressions of our spirituality are found not only in the *leitourgia* but in the *koinonia* and *diakonia* as well. Fellowship is a spiritual discipline that prepares us for ministry in the contexts of a PTA or a board meeting as well as the contexts of loving our neighbors in a huge urban apartment complex. Our *kerygma* needs to be more spiritual. Kerygma is the proc-lamation of the good news of Jesus in the power of the Spirit. There are broken homes and communities afflicted by social ills because of lack of many of the necessary provisions for the sustenance of life. To proclaim a liberating, Spirit-filled word is to proclaim an incarnated word, to pitch a tent in the midst of the people. Words alone, without the works of love, de-bilitate the power of the good news. When God's children are truly spiri-tual, the kerygma includes concrete evidence of the love of Christ (Isa. 61:1–2; Luke 4:18–19).

The Spirituality of
Hispanic Protestant Women

The response of Hispanic women to Christ is conditioned and struc-tured by our history as well as our sexuality. Our experience therefore is dis-tinct, although not separate, from the masculine experience with God. Our experiences are actually complementary so that we can each speak of and call forth in the other some essential aspects of responding to God.

As women, our bodies are intrinsic to how we understand our experiences of God. The routine or rhythm of our bodies in preparation for the birthing experience and the nurturing of life gives us an awareness of creation, life, and sustenance such that we experience the creator and sustainer of life in rich ways. Whether or not we have given birth, our entire person—our body, psyche, soul, and spirit—is influenced by this biological imperative.[23] This is not to say, however, that our gender sums up the totality of our spirituality. Rather, it is one of the distinct elements that make it up.

To speak of all of the ways women reflect theologically in connection with their bodies would fill a book. I will, therefore, only attempt to give a glimpse of this aspect of our spirituality.

As a young adolescent, I accompanied my mother to many bridal and baby showers. These celebratory occasions were exclusively attended by women and so there seemed to be liberty to express oneself about aspects of the otherwise taboo subjects of menstruation and sexuality. I always came away with a deep respect for life and the responsibility and care for life that women held. It was a power in us. Women dare to connect this power with the creative power of God. Salvation and creation are united in the meaning of the womb. In truth, this was the first context in which I heard God referred to in feminine images. At baby showers, women spoke of the giving of their blood and body in pregnancy in very eucharistic terms. Women connected their ministries and the image of the devotion and love a mother has for her yet unborn child with Paul's image of the faithfulness of a soldier. Faith was compared to the experience of a woman who is only a few weeks pregnant, when only she can tell that she is in such a condition; even she cannot feel the creature yet, but she feels the assurance of things hoped for and the conviction of things not seen (Heb. 11:1).

These stories were purifying. Women's bodies are constantly distorted and destroyed both physically and morally by society. Our bodies are objectified and labeled "temptation." We are forced to accept the projections of lustful desires and the resulting shame and guilt. Our slavelike servanthood, defined by others, is the cornerstone, in some, of a hunger for control and entitlement. We must therefore bear the burden and cover our shameful bodies. Doña Inez, a woman who was in her seventies when I was fourteen, was given a special time to share her words of spiritual wisdom at every shower. The room seemed to rearrange itself so that she became its center and there was a hush of reverence as she spoke. She spoke to us about our bodies, separating them from the myths and projections of others. She spoke of a woman's body as a holy sanctuary of life and the Spirit of God. From this premise, she fleshed out the biblical understanding of the worth of a woman. As she made the distinctions between our bodies as temples versus our bodies as objects and projections of sin, she seemed to bring cleansing and freedom to us.

On one occasion, she spoke to a woman who bore evidence of having been physically abused. Touching her to soothe her body and spirit, she pronounced in an authoritative, public whisper: "Because the Bible says that what we loose on earth will be loosed in heaven and what we bind on earth will be bound in heaven, in the name of Jesus I loose you from your bonds to this man who has done this to you. You are not guilty of anything he has done. Go now to your cousin's house and start a new life. Don't look back or go back like Lot's wife. In God's name, we will provide for you all you need." Her powerful words set the woman free and bound the rest of us to a commitment of support and provision.

Latina/Hispanic Protestant women are lay leaders and pastors and ordained ministers and scholars. We are teachers, evangelists, counselors, preachers, and healers. Today we are becoming more aware of the contributions we make to the church and we are learning to name these contributions as part of the process of claiming our gifts and ministries and of articulating, in a public voice, our theological perspectives in ways authentic to who we are as women. We are grounded in the church, and the expressions of our spirituality have shaped the spirituality of the church.

A woman's spirituality can be characterized by an attentiveness, a waiting, a relational connectedness, and a passionate compassion that results in courage and creativity. The attentiveness and waiting are not passive, but are an active discernment process and a wisdom. I can remember the many church meetings that became heated discussions among men. Yet it was the voice of a particular, albeit seldom heard, woman that would invariably place the issues and the choices in perspective, taking into consideration the needs and the vision of the church's mission. It was this woman who taught me that there is a time to speak and a time to refrain from speaking. It was through her listening that she was able to craft the best way to say what needed to be said in ways that others would be prompted to hear.

The courage and creativity in a woman are a strength that comes from seeking God in her struggles and finding her voice in prayer. The moans and groans of the Spirit in and through us become a power to embrace suffering and to transform it into the creative work of social action or justice. Brixeida Marquez, founder of the Free Forever Prison Ministry in Bridgeport, Connecticut, shared several years ago that she begins and ends her day with intense times of prayer in which she wails and sometimes pounds her fists on the altar as she seeks God with all her being for the strength and the vision to minister to those imprisoned and to their families. She wails because she feels their pain and God's pain for them. She pounds her fists to express her frustrations and, in so doing, rid herself of them so that she will not succumb to a sense of helplessness, cynicism, or violence. She emerges with the anger to act and the hope to persevere in her actions.

Our passion in prayer is informed by meditation and Bible study. This has been the way that women have dared to hold beliefs that differ from some of the traditions of their communities of faith about their call and about the forms of ministry. When theology has dichotomized the religious and the secular, the world and the church, women's experiences have led them to understand the scriptures in a way that prophetically moves us to go beyond those boundaries. We have sat on boards and organized the community; in short, we have taken political action. We do not articulate it that way because we are not always conscious of what we are in fact doing. We are impelled by the scriptures and a deep love for others that comes to us in prayer.

The Holy Spirit has been the one to lead us and empower us. Our sense of call is especially strong because it is centered on the authority of the Holy Spirit and because we have had to hold tenaciously and discerningly to that authority as opposed to the authorities of the church. The confrontation and conflict between these authorities and voices in the church have impacted our daily lives and our spirituality. We teach and mentor each other in connecting with and discerning the Spirit, since it is the Spirit who authorizes a woman in her call and gives evidence of that through the giving of gifts and ministries.[24] The Spirit also becomes the midwife of our ministries as they bear fruit.

Prayer is the most important tool in connecting to the Spirit. Many a friendly chat has turned into a full-fledged prayer meeting even over the miles on the telephone. Prayer has bonded us as sisters. Sharing between women bonds us rather than binds us, as the tradition has sometimes done. Connectedness with the Holy Spirit is connectedness with each other in ways that empower and edify. The spirituality and ministry of women flow from our recognition of the need for connectedness. The strength of the permeable boundaries of our self, which allows our gift of connectedness, and the gift of our compassion, which allows us to care, can also be our weakness if not nurtured by the care of others or if not accompanied by a renewed sense of the *imago Dei* of a woman. Self-denial can be wrongly understood and can lead to further low self-esteem rather than helping us achieve an understanding of our identity as servants of God. The new roles women are actively involved in, and the freedom and power of these new roles, require that as a church we reflect theologically about the feminine and masculine images of God. It is also important to revisit our relationships as women and men in the church. Does a partnership exist that brings wholeness to both? And finally, as we develop a new self-concept, what is our ministry to other women and men in society?

I have named issues that relate to encountering others because I believe that relationship is at the core of Christian spirituality. As we identify these issues, we can identify the systemic expressions of unhealthy relationships in society. Even more, a spirituality that connects us to God and to each other will teach us ways to negotiate and structure new relationships in society that will imply a fullness of life by giving relationships value and meaning congruent with the values of the reign of God. Healthy connectedness between men and women will root and ground our spiritual energy in ways that will challenge men to selfless caring for others, and women to participating in more areas of activity and power. I wonder if this would emerge into an enhanced understanding of self-denial and a transformation of power-over into mutuality?

Not all of the characteristics of women's spirituality are unique to women, but because of the traditional tasks we have done, and the constraints placed upon us by society, we have developed these qualities to an unusual degree. The spiritual challenge before women is to integrate new knowledge about the world with our spirituality in order to give expression to our faith in ways that may address not only Hispanic but global issues. For example, our skills and experiences in building and negotiating relationships in the private sphere are needed in the public sphere of peace-making and justice.[25]

Transmitting Spirituality

> But take care . . . so as neither to forget the things that your eyes have seen nor to let them slip from your mind all the days of your life; make them known to your children and your children's children. . . . Recite them to your children and talk about them when you are at home and when you are away, when you lie down and when you rise. (Deut. 4:9; 6:7, NRSV)

How have we been transmitting this spirituality, and how can we transmit it to the next generations? There is a kind of osmosis through which persons interiorize the spiritual lifestyle of another person or group. For example, the simple practice of coming to church and kneeling to pray before participating in worship and learning to carve out a time for prayer and meditation are ways in which we transmit spirituality. We learn the language of addressing God, the expressions and creeds of our faith. Our spirituality is transmitted not only through religious ritual in the formal worship of the church, but by means of a daily ritual of right attitudes and edifying conversation (Col. 3:5–17; Eph. 4:29–32). It is also transmitted through the Christian example of particular individuals or of a particular community and through our being in their presence to "watch them at work, absorb their words of wisdom, hear the accounts of their experiences and to deliberately fashion our lives after their example."[26] It is transmitted through a person who shares the failures and successes of the journey, as we often do in testimonial preaching or in a biography such as that of Ricardo Tañon.[27] It is transmitted through living the rhythms of life according to the priorities that our spirituality has ordered. Our values are informed by our spirituality and, thus, time management is ruled by a different set of priorities and activities.

Conclusion

I have mentioned some elements of spirituality that we are conscious of. There are others, however, that are a part of our practice yet we have not reflected on them or their consequences. Thus they have not been explicitly articulated or named in our teaching and preaching. I have pointed to both the priestly and prophetic dimensions of Hispanic Protestant spirituality. The priestly aspects are the cultic and contemplative tradition, the one explicitly named as spirituality. The prophetic dimension can be found in our pastoral practice, particularly in the spirituality of the laywomen of the church who are involved in the work of social action and justice. Yet, as we articulate our theology of spirituality, we do not discuss the prophetic dimension. The result is that this dimension is not being passed on to the younger generations, who therefore criticize our spirituality as being irrelevant to daily life. It is imperative that the prophetic element be integrated with the priestly in order to enlarge the scope of the mission of the church.

Consider anger, for example. Anger has not been considered a positive emotion. Like conflict, it has traditionally been considered a spiritual impediment. Anger in Spanish is *coraje*, which also means courage. Aristotle defined anger as an energy that enabled us to face difficulty. Thomas Aquinas integrated Aristotle's view into Christian thinking and "expanded this optimistic vision of anger."[28] Anger is a gift from God and also an emotion that God displays. Anger brings out resistance rather than helplessness. A person with a healthy sense of self, when harmed in any way, will be aroused to protest. That protest is anger. It is a necessary part of our survival. Beyond survival, anger also serves social transformation.[29] Anger's complement is compassion, and it fuels our mission of care. As prophets today, we must combine our anger with the spiritual discipline of temperance so that it can be cooled to a productive level and bear the spiritual fruits of justice (love),[30] hope, and peace. Anger must be respected and not used demonically; otherwise, in the end we will only have succeeded in changing the name of the oppressor into our own. Our spirituality must take the vital energy of our anger and turn it into skilled organizing and a determined love that will see us through many frustrations. Let this expression of our spiritual energies be the power that rolls the stone from the mouth of the tomb in order to liberate life for both oppressor and oppressed. Let this goal inform our sanctification and our way toward perfection as the community of the Spirit.

Spirituality is connecting to and being led by Christ through the Holy Spirit. The Spirit leads us to new truths, and this dynamic may date our theology. Theology is the attempt to define and systematize what we understand about the revelation of God as we interpret it in a given moment and context. Theology therefore conforms to the criteria of its time. But the Spirit is continually revealing new things to us about God and the reign of God—things that "no eye has seen, nor ear heard, nor the human heart conceived" (1 Cor. 2:9). It is the Spirit who reveals these things to us, for it is the Spirit who truly comprehends what is truly God's (1 Cor. 2:10–11). As women in particular have discovered, it is necessary to take on the task of spiritual discernment in order to critique our theology. This is a spiritual, communal task. As Paul reminds us, only those who are spiritual, or who have the Spirit, can handle this task (1 Cor. 2:13–15). There are places that our theology has not visited, but the Spirit is sending us there. Let us not be conformed to this age but let us be transformed by the renewing of our understanding, so that we may know, experience, connect with, and discern the will of God, that *this* may be our *spiritual* worship (Rom. 12:1–2).

NOTES

1. Mary Collins, Joseph A. Komanchak, Dermot A. Lane, eds., *The New Dictionary of Theology* (Wilmington, Del.: Michael Glazier, 1989), 972.
2. Ibid.
3. Sinclair B. Ferguson and David F. Wright, eds., *New Dictionary of Theology* (Downers Grove, Ill.: InterVarsity Press, 1988), 657.
4. Collins et al., *The New Dictionary of Theology*, 973.
5. Sister Consuelo Maria Aherne, Paul Kevin Meagher, and Thomas C. O'Brien, eds., *Encyclopedic Dictionary of Religion*, vol. 2 (Washington, D.C.: Corpus Publications, 1979), 3371.
6. For a fuller explanation of this, see Aherne et al., *Encyclopedic Dictionary of Religion*, 2732; and Gordon S. Wakefield, ed., *A Dictionary of Christian Spirituality* (London: SCM Press, 1983), 265–66, 297–99.
7. Donald W. Musser and Joseph L. Price, eds., *A New Handbook of Christian Theology* (Nashville: Abingdon Press, 1992), 271.
8. Cappadocia was evangelized by Gregory Thaumaturgus, who was a disciple of Origen. Therefore this community of fathers is influenced by Origen's theology.
9. Segundo Galilea, *El futuro de nuestro pasado: Ensayos sobre los místicos españoles desde América Latina* (New York: North East Catholic Pastoral Center for Hispanics, 1983).

10. Teresa de Ávila, "Las Moradas," IV, 1, 7.

11. Ibid., VII, 4; "Camino de perfección," XXXVI, 8.

12. San Ignacio de Loyola, *Ejercicios espirituales de San Ignacio*, in *Obras completas de San Ignacio de Loyola*, 2d ed. (Madrid: Biblioteca de Autores Cristianos, 1963), 95.

13. Conversations with Eldin Villafañe, June 2, 1995.

14. Loida Martell-Otero, "Women Doing Theology: Una Perspectiva Evangélica," *Apuntes* 14:3 (fall 1994): 82.

15. The gleanings of our daily devotions are oftentimes shared with others during the day in casual conversation, counseling, encouraging, or ministry.

16. Jorge E. Sanchez, "La educación bíblica en nuestra iglesia hispana," *Apuntes* 9:2 (summer 1989): 36.

17. Warren W. Wiersbe, *Five Secrets of Living* (Wheaton: Tyndale House Publishers, 1977), 32.

18. Beverly Roberts Gaventa, "Conversion in the Bible," in *Handbook of Religious Conversion*, ed. H. Newton Malony and Samuel Southard (Birmingham: Religious Education Press, 1992), 52.

19. Galilea, *El futuro de nuestro pasado*, 27.

20. See Orlando Costas, *El Protestantismo en América Latina hoy: Ensayos del camino (1972–1974)* (San José, Costa Rica: Publicaciones INDEF, 1975), viii; see also Eldin Villafañe, *The Liberating Spirit: Toward an Hispanic American Pentecostal Social Ethic* (Grand Rapids: Wm. B. Eerdmans Publishing Co., 1993).

21. Villafañe, *Liberating Spirit*, 124.

22. Ibid., 132.

23. For further discussion of this, see Elizabeth Dodson Gray, *Sacred Dimensions of Women's Experience* (Wellesley, Mass.: Roundtable Press, 1988); see also Ursula King, *Women and Spirituality: Voices of Protest and Promise*, 2d ed. (University Park, Pa.: Pennsylvania State University Press, 1993).

24. Martell-Otero, "Women Doing Theology," 77.

25. See King, *Women and Spirituality*.

26. Iris V. Cully, *Education for Spiritual Growth* (San Francisco: Harper & Row, 1984), 27–28.

27. Ramón Sanchez, *"El poder y la gloria de Dios": Ricardo Tañon* (San Juan, Puerto Rico: Cooperativa de Artes Gráficas Romualdo Real, 1980).

28. James D. Whitehead and Evelyn Eaton Whitehead, *Shadows of the Heart: A Spirituality of the Negative Emotions* (New York: Crossroad, 1994), 46.

29. Ibid., 47.

30. See Villafañe, *Liberating Spirit*, 211–22.

10

The Ongoing Challenge of Hispanic Theology

Loida I. Martell-Otero

In his book, *The Little Prince*, Antoine de Saint-Exupéry includes a vignette of a Turkish astronomer who discovers a new planet. He goes in his Turkish garb to the Academy of Science and brilliantly presents his findings. He is ignored. Some years later, the Turkish astronomer returns to the Academy, now dressed in a European garb of suit and tie, presents the same findings and is applauded by the august body for his brilliance.[1] Saint-Exupéry does not say more about the astronomer, since the parable within the story does not require him to do so. Yet, when I was asked to prepare a chapter for this project, with the suggestive title of "The Ongoing Challenge of Hispanic Theology," this story within a story came to mind. As I reflected on this parable, I found myself drawing parallels with the experiences of Latinos and Latinas in the United States.[2] This man was faced with the task of communicating simultaneously with two distinctively separate audiences. On the one hand, he needed to communicate to a larger audience that traditionally did not listen to people like him with anything remotely resembling respect. Still, he was acutely aware that he had knowledge that could enrich and educate precisely that audience. On the other hand, he represented an invisible audience, his own people. How much should he, could he change; how much could he mold and adapt himself without losing his soul and his own unique perspective in the process? Hispanic Americans, particularly those in theology, are in a quandary similar to that of the character in Saint-Exupéry's story. This chapter will, therefore, reflect on some challenges facing Hispanics doing theology today, keeping in mind the above-cited vignette. In addition, I will also explore the challenges that Hispanic theology poses to the larger theological community.

The Challenge of Our Praxis

To begin with, Hispanic theology presents a challenge to the traditional methods of theological reflection. It is distinctive from the traditional methods in various aspects. First, Latino theology is a contextualized endeavor seeking to carry out theological reflection in light of the praxis and life of faith of the community. This emphasis on praxis is the result of a paradigm shift emerging from a process of conscientization in the 1960s and 1970s, a time in which Hispanic, as well as Latin American, theology began to focus on the "nonperson" in history as the subject of theology.[3] In Latin America, the nonperson was identified as the mass of overwhelmingly poor people. In the United States, Hispanic theology acknowledges that the "nonpersons" are the ethnic minorities, the poor and women who live at the political and socioeconomic periphery; they are the voiceless, the powerless and the invisible, marginalized by the centers of power and injustice.[4] This new way of doing theology has challenged the traditional method—with its insistence on orthodoxy over orthopraxis, its emphasis on a Cartesian model of knowledge and a historicist penchant for declaring its analyses objective and value-free—declaring it bankrupt, a fallacy that has only served to sustain the oppression of the two-thirds world.[5] Traditional theological methods had only succeeded in sacralizing injustice and obfuscating the social structures of sin, allowing racism, sexism, and the exploitation of peoples to continue unchallenged. Latino theology's challenge stems from its paradigm shift, a "turn to the new subject" if you will, that views all "reflection, including theological reflection" as "situated" with emphasis now on orthopraxis over orthodoxy.[6] Theology is, therefore, a second step, a reflection on the praxis and life of faith lived in the community.[7] To be situated implies that it is done from a particular social location, from a defined perspective. Theology is not an objective subject impassively analyzing an object "out there."[8] It does not pretend to be "value-free" or neutral. Theological reflection in a Latino context is similar to Justo González's description of biblical truth:

> Biblical truth, the truth in which the people of God are called to live . . . is concrete, historical truth. It does not exist in a world of pure ideas but rather is closely bound with bread and wine, with justice and peace, with a coming Reign of God—a Reign not over pure ideas or over disembodied souls but over a new society and a renewed history.[9]

Theological reflection is "embodied love." It is intersubjective.[10] We reflect on the God we have come to know within the context of the community of faith, in the midst of the community of which we are a part. For Hispanic Protestants this means that our reflection is related to our *pastoral*, our pastoral praxis, our ministry in the church.[11] This is why our theological reflection is carried out *en conjunto*; it is a collaborative venture carried out by the community of faith.

Hispanic theology also poses a challenge to traditional theological methodology because of our distinctive spirituality. Our theology is intimately linked with our spirituality, which in turn is rooted in our Iberoamerican, Amerindian, and African heritage.[12] Gustavo Gutiérrez has defined spirituality as a "following of Jesus" in light of an "encounter with the Lord."[13] For Latino theology, the point of departure of this following is from a place of marginality, from the underside of history. To follow Jesus is no longer perceived as a private, individualistic endeavor, but a communal praxis: it is struggling for justice and for the liberation of the oppressed and voiceless in order to be faithful to the call of the One we seek to follow. Our spirituality is experienced within the context of the Hispanic community, particularly within the community of faith. Thus our theological reflection is no longer separated from our spiritual experience; there is an intimate integration of mind and spirit.[14] For the Hispanic Protestant community in particular, the Holy Spirit plays an important role in our spirituality. It is the Holy Spirit who guides us, empowers us, and transforms us. The Holy Spirit is in the midst of the community, pouring the love of God into our hearts (Romans 5:5), granting us the passion and the ability to discern the vision that allows us to struggle from the underside and for the reign of God. If indeed Latino theology is carried out *en conjunto*, it can only do so because the Holy Spirit has created a new community, making it one body, one equipped to grow to the stature of the fullness of Jesus Christ (Ephesians 4:11–13).

The challenge is not only to the traditional theological community. The Latino community is also challenged, especially those involved in institutions that provide theological education. As Hispanic Americans, we live between two cultural worlds, with two diametrically opposed worldviews. On the one hand, we are a community whose cultural and religious heritage is one with a distinctively nonmodern worldview. This is the world in which we worship, where we encounter the Lord we seek to follow, where we sing and pray to the One who would heal our wounds. This community is our *familia* (family). On the other hand, we study and work in an environment whose understanding and philosophical insights are predicated on a modernist (or postmodernist) worldview. Torn between these two worlds, we want to join in with the Mexican singer Marco Antonio Muñiz, who popularized the phrase "No soy de aquí, ni soy de allá" (I am not from here, nor am I from there).[15] It is difficult to maintain one's balance: on the one hand, the academic environment dismisses certain biblical narratives as mythological while, on the other hand, our church communities rejoice in the lived experiences of healing and miracles based on those same narratives. It is difficult to hear our communities being dismissed as "quaintly naive" and our academic colleagues touted as "knowledgeable." We are not sure whether to reject our traditions or to reject the opportunities of theological education. In the long run, the danger lies in forgetting our heritage, and uncritically accepting the values of dominant culture as the "intellectually honest" thing to do.

Our ongoing challenge is to live within this contradiction. We are challenged to grow theologically as well as spiritually. We are also challenged not to be on the defensive. Defensive postures are conducive to the ghettoization of theological reflection. There is a propensity for consructing theological idols and for defending unacknowledged ideologies.[16] Idols do not permit us to hear the "other" in theological discourse, and they impoverish the theological endeavor. Idols are destroyed only to the degree that we "listen to, and be with, others in the Christian community."[17] For example, Latino theologians must be careful not to defend sexist positions, but learn to listen to their Latina colleagues and sisters.[18] We Latinas must also carefully listen to the "other" in our communities.[19] We are each called to be aware of the sexist, racist, ethnic, or other "idols" that prevent us from serving the living God as we seek justice and liberation for all people.

Even as we are challenged not to encase ourselves in defensive idols, even so we are also challenged to uphold what is good and beautiful in our culture, in our communities, in our churches, and not discard them as passé. We do this by revisiting our roots, by remembering and passing on the stories of our *abuelitas* and *abuelitos* (grandmothers and grandfathers), the cloud of witnesses of our faith, who nurtured us, taught us, and gave formation to who we are today. This is the *adobo* (seasoning), the *sofrito* (herbs and spices), that gives *sabor* (flavor) to our theology, and which imbues us with the passion of our faith.[20]

Tradition and Tomorrow:
The Challenge of the Spirit

To live in this contradiction creates another challenge for Latino and Latina theologians: how to keep the dynamic tension between tradition and tomorrow. How can we preserve our traditions without falling into traditionalism? How can we be open to the creative possibilities of tomorrow, and ensure our relevancy to the life of the church as well as to the life of our *pueblo* (people), without becoming followers of fads and trends? This challenge demands that the theological community in general, and the Hispanic theological community in particular, deal with some difficult issues. Let us first deal with those related to our traditions.

Part of our tradition is the recognition of our voicelessness and invisi-

bility. Neither the existence of Hispanic American theology nor its relevance to the North American context has been recognized. Its theological
voices do not fit the "norm" according to the present standards of academia. Latino Protestant theology is articulated from our pulpits and in our
Sunday school classes. We have learned theology in the worship experiences of our churches. But this is only part of our tradition. For the past
forty years we have had extraordinary women and men who, at great cost
to themselves and their loved ones, have risen among the ranks of the more
traditional academic halls to acquire the credentialing that would allow
them to better serve the Hispanic American community and the church at
large. These men and women carved out paths that others could follow.
They encouraged younger Hispanics to seek further education, to write,
to become scholars in various fields. Not all fields were open to them, but
nonetheless they knew how to do much with few resources. My mother
called that "haciendo blusas nuevas de las camisas viejas de papá" (making
new blouses from papa's old shirts). They struggled, and continue to
struggle, against injustice, racism, and sexism to ensure our visibility and
our viability in the life of the church. These pastors, missiologists, historians, and social ethicists are, in reality, our "systematic theologians." In
their writings, and in their teachings, they have left us a theological legacy
that has articulated, in a credible way, our faith and our witness to the
living God who is present among an oppressed people. Nonetheless, the
voices of these theologians—and therefore part of our traditions—are in
danger precisely because their voices are not recognized by the larger
theological community as being relevant or valid. According to Justo L.
González,

> North Atlantic male theology is taken to be basic, normative, universal the-
> ology, to which then women, other minorities, and people from younger
> churches may add their footnotes. What is said in Manila is very relevant for
> the Philippines. What is said in Tübingen, Oxford, or Yale is very relevant
> for the entire church.[21]

A new generation of Latina and Latino scholars seeking to study this tradition of Hispanic scholarship are discovering that these writings are either
out of print or not found in their local libraries.[22] Publishing houses
have deemed such books "unmarketable," and therefore not worthy of being reprinted.[23] Seminaries challenge the validity of their scholarship or
question their academic quality. The present theological community,
which cherishes Bonhoeffer and Barth, must also realize that there are
other "classics" that do not come from Germany or Switzerland. As
Nathanael found out about Nazareth, this community must realize that
good things can come even from the South Bronx, or from South Central
Los Angeles. The ongoing challenge for Latina and Latino scholars is that

we must not allow our past mentors and teachers to disappear into the past. We must tell their stories and share their wisdom. They are part of our cloud of witnesses.

Having said that, we must also recognize the danger of traditionalism. As theologians, we are called to celebrate and honor the traditions of our communities, and particularly our communities of faith. But, we must walk the fine line between honoring that tradition and being prophetic and exercising discernment. Hispanic American churches today are a particular mix of the old and the new: recent arrivals from the Caribbean and Latin America, together with those who are part of the founding mothers and fathers of our Hispanic Protestant congregations from as far back as the early 1900s, together with new church members who were born and raised in the United States.[24] This mix presents us with vast opportunities of creating new scholars, new leadership, new ministries, and new vistas together with the historical roots to keep us grounded in the good things of our traditions. However, such a mix also presents us with a great danger: that of having the traditionalists of our churches close the doors to new leaders because they speak little or no Spanish, or because "that is not the way things are done." Too often in churches I have seen practices which make little theological sense but are carried out because that is how things have been done for the past fifty years. The other danger is from those who would transplant Latin American theology unreflectively to the United States, without recognizing the Hispanic American context. We are a people who speak Spanish in English, and speak English in Spanish. We are not Latin Americans, nor do we live in Latin America. Our reality here is very different. If our churches are to survive, and if our theology is to have any relevance for the future, our theology must reflect that reality. In short, the ongoing challenge is to have a contextual theology. This, in turn, presents us with a twofold challenge: one is at the level of theological education, which needs to create an academic environment that will prepare scholars not just for academia but also for the church (and, in the case of Latino and Latina theologians, specifically for the Hispanic American church); and the other is at the level of the church, which must be open to changes, to become contextualized, and to realize that its future is not in the past nor in Latin America, but that its future lies in its ability to be obedient to the leading of the Holy Spirit who, behold! makes all things new (2 Cor. 5:17).

Encouraging New Scholars:
The Challenge of Multicultural Equity

One other issue is related to this tension between tradition and tomorrow: the place for present and future generations of Latina and Latino scholars. A recent conversation with one such future academic underscored the importance of this issue. This theological student agonized over the future. Once one finally acquires a doctoral degree, what can one do? Full-time work in the pastorate is a possibility, but the nature of pastoral work often precludes full use of one's acquired skills (for example, the ability to do research or to write scholarly papers). The other possibility is to find a teaching position in a seminary or institution of higher learning. However, there one is faced with the possibility of being disconnected from the Hispanic community because of the lack of Latinos or Latinas in traditional seminaries, or of findng oneself embroiled in the many conflicts one has already faced as a student trying to get the institution to acknowledge the presence of Hispanics.[25] Many future scholars are dismayed by the latter possibility: the struggle is exhausting, and many already suffer from "battle fatigue."

As we seek to better prepare the church for tomorrow, how are we to face the challenges in theology if we do not encourage future generations to become creative and growing scholars? And how can we encourage future scholars if there is no sense of hope? The ongoing challenge for academia, then, is to create an environment that is as welcoming and nurturing to Latina and Latino theological scholars as it has been to more traditional groups in the past. It will not suffice to include a book on Latin American liberation theology in a class list of required reading. It will not suffice to grudgingly accept two or three Hispanics who have had to jump through the hoops just to apply. The tent must be enlarged. Seminaries must become truly multicultural centers of learning. What is said in Manila, the South Bronx, or San Juan must be seen as relevant to all the church. For theological discourse to become truly engaging, truly challenging, truly dynamic, all voices must be heard equally, with the same respect. We have belatedly begun to realize that inclusive language does not necessarily guarantee a spirit of inclusiveness; it only means we have discovered ways of speaking that do not commit us to new ways of living! Or, as it is expressed in popular jargon: it is not enough to talk the talk, if one does not learn to walk the walk.

Robert Pazmiño, professor of religious education at Andover Newton Theological School, asserts that an educational institution demonstrates true multicultural equity when all representative groups are granted the same access to resources, respect, space to be heard, appropriate role models, and shared power.[26] Thus, the challenge for theological institutions is to "walk the walk" and implement those elements of equity. It is to understand that Latina and Latino theologians speak English in Spanish. It is to be open to different methods of theological reflection. It is also to be open to accept those whom the Hispanic community identifies as theologically credible scholars and not measure them solely by the traditional standards of academia. It means not lumping us together with, as if indistinguishable from, Latin American liberation theologians, and it means recognizing that Hispanic Americans have a long theological history on this continent, and that we are rooted in our places of origin. It means creating a space where we no longer have to choose between the church of our faith and the places where we teach. Jürgen Moltmann sounds a similar warning when he reminds his readers:

> Theology is a "Christian" and a "spiritual" affair, and it is only as such that it is one of the church's tasks. . . . If it were to lose the fellowship of the church, it would stop being Christian theology and turn into a kind of science of religion. As Christian theology, theology has to remind the church of the lordship of Christ and has to insist that the church's form be an authentic one. As the Christian church, the church must remind theology of God's people and insist on a theology which has relevance for that people.[27]

These timely words should be remembered to avoid constructing unfortunate dichotomies that adversely affect Hispanic scholars. It means allowing us to exist as a people, with respect; to be heard, with respect; and to be acknowledged, with respect. What a challenge, indeed!

The Hispanic community is also challenged: to continue to support future scholars, to mentor the new generation rising. Our church communities must make churches a nurturing place for theological reflection, and allow for openness for creative and new possibilities. As I mentioned earlier, it too must realize that we speak Spanish in English, and that accents do not imply ignorance. We must begin to pool resources and make them available for young people who seek to enter the ministry, or who seek to enter theological education. Contrary to popular thought, "la letra *no* mata el espíritu" (learning does *not* kill the spirit). To think otherwise is to distort the meaning of Paul's words (2 Cor. 3:6b). Those who are now presently engaged in theological training must not lose hope, and must continue to work *en conjunto*, not just for the *pueblo*, but for the life of the church and for our faith.

Creating New Paradigms:
The Challenge of New Visions

Living in this tension between tradition and tomorrow has led Latina and Latino theologians to demonstrate great creativity. This creativity has given expression to the various paradigms that we have used to articulate the depth of our faith experiences. Paradigms are "models" that represent the values and beliefs shared by a community.[28] They function as "interpretive frameworks for understanding reality" by providing a broad context "for interpretation or meaning."[29] Paradigms, like metaphors, are powerful in evoking both affective and cognitive effects because they reflect the experiences and the shared worldview of a community. Consequently, they also help shape that worldview and the experience of that community.[30]

Certainly, the paradigms presented by Hispanic theologians evoke powerful images for us. Virgilio Elizondo, for example, speaking from the experience of Mexican Americans, developed his paradigm of *mestizaje*, while Orlando Costas expressed the experience of being a Puerto Rican in the United States by reflecting theologically "from the periphery," from the underside of history.[31] Recently, Justo González has provided us with the imagery of reading the Bible "through Hispanic eyes," and Ada María Isasi-Díaz has given us the rallying cry of *en la lucha* (in the struggle) as she articulates a *mujerista* theology.[32] The power of paradigms was experienced at the 1995 *Encuentro* of Theology and Ethics held at Princeton when one of our presenters, Elizabeth Conde-Frazier, spoke on Hispanic spirituality. As she spoke about the spirituality of women, she commented that women measure time differently from men. "Women," she said, "measure time with their bodies, according to their menstrual cycle, to their life cycles (the onset of puberty, the monthly menstrual cycle, pregnancy, menopause, and so on)." Not only did her words resonate with many of us at the conference, allowing us to see ourselves in a new yet familiar way, her words also revealed the possibilities of a new paradigm: one as relevant as it is powerful for women. This is part of the power of paradigms: they allow us to ask questions, explore new vistas, and see things in a new light.

However, even as they open up new vistas and new possibilities, paradigms also prove to be limited and partial. They cannot account for all experiences, for all perspectives. When a given framework proves to be inadequate for interpreting experience, then there is an "anomaly." The paradigm cannot adequately account for the experience.[33] When an anomaly is sufficiently powerful, the old paradigm is left aside as a new one is created; a paradigm shift has occurred.[34] This is precisely what happened in the 1960s and 1970s, when Latin and Hispanic American theologies became increasingly aware that the paradigms of traditional theology were inadequate to express the experience of suffering, marginalization, and poverty of the two-thirds world. At that time a significant paradigm shift took place and the *locus theologicus* for liberation theology became the nonperson of history. Presently, Latina feminist and *mujerista* theologians have expressed the inadequacy of the paradigm focusing exclusively on the poor, because they bypass the issue of gender oppression and can also bypass the issues of racism and ethnocentrism.[35] Hispanics from the Caribbean have indicated that *mestizaje* does not sufficiently account for the African heritage in their cultural roots. They have suggested *mulatez* as a more appropriate paradigm for their context.[36] It will be a continual challenge for

Latino theology to discover and articulate new paradigms that can reflect the rich experiences of Hispanic Americans, raise new questions, and lead to new avenues of thought and action.

New paradigms are created, therefore, when we listen to those voices silenced for too long and allow them to speak. Some time ago, while attending a conference for Latina American Baptist pastors in San Juan, Puerto Rico, a talent show was held to celebrate the gifts of these extraordinary women. A sizable delegation from California, which included a significant number of Mexican American women, presented a dance called *La Malinche*. *La Malinche* was originally the name given to a fourteen-year-old Aztec girl. Her true name was Malintzen but she was renamed Doña Marina by the Spaniards when she was given as a peace offering to Hernán Cortés by the Aztec emperor. A highly intelligent girl (she knew various indigenous dialects and quickly learned the language of her captors), Malintzen not only suffered at the hands of the *Conquistadores*, who misunderstood the nature of the gift, but has since then also suffered the interpretive ravages of historians, sociologists, and theologians who have propagated the legend of *La Malinche:* folklore has identified her as the one who betrayed her people and helped the Spaniards conquer Mexico. Chicana feminists have begun to revisit this story and to seriously question traditional interpretations of *La Malinche*.[37] The dance reflected the more traditional view of *La Malinche*. The audience was asked to identify who, among the dancers, was the designated *Malinche*: she would be the one always subtly out of step with the rest of the dance group. Many of us, especially those of us who pursue higher theological education in traditional programs and seminaries, often feel like *La Malinche*. We are made to feel that we do not quite belong, that we are not quite in step. Many of us have stories of growing up in non-Hispanic neighborhoods, our mothers *yelling* at us to "keep quiet" so that the neighbors would not think we were noisy Puerto Ricans, or Dominicans, or Mexicans, or whatever ethnic group we represented. We are never quite in step with the dominant group, and we are made painfully aware of that.[38] When we do theology, we do theology with the pain of that reality. *La Malinche* is a powerful image, especially in the Mexican American context. It is also a reminder of how new paradigms arising from the voices of the silenced in history can deconstruct the traditional modes of thought, granting us new and liberating insights. Such paradigms allow us to see the world with new eyes.

We are, therefore, not only challenged to create new paradigms but also reminded that the present ones must be revisited and examined anew. We must identify those which have enriched our theological reflections. It is equally imperative that we identify the ones that have been exclusionary, sexist, or racist. We are challenged to create paradigms that empower, and to be wary of those which only serve to sustain oppressive practices.

Recently, in a conversation with a professor, I spoke about being a "bridge generation." Such a phrase is certainly not original to me. I have heard that phrase on the lips of many of my colleagues and friends. Yet as I spoke, the imagery of a bridge came to mind: it not only connects two disparate areas that would not otherwise communicate, it can do so *only* by being trodden upon. What does it mean to do theology as a "bridge generation," we who speak Spanish at home and in our food, and speak English in our jobs and in our schools? Do we get trodden upon in the process? We are challenged to weigh our words as well as our silences, and to ensure that the images we convey bring life, and not death, to the Hispanic community.

Between Tradition and Tomorrow:
The Challenge of Relevance Today

I began this chapter describing the distinctive characteristics of Hispanic theological reflection: it is a contextualized endeavor reflecting on the praxis and life of faith of the community. Theology is a second step whose subject is the nonperson in history. It is intimately related to our spirituality, to the life of a community that follows Jesus. I then made reference to our need to uphold our traditions, as well as to be open to the creative possibilities of our tomorrow—a tomorrow that is opened by the power of the Holy Spirit, who is creative life. In this way, I maintained, Latino theology seeks to be contextual, and relevant to the life of a *pueblo*. This issue of relevance, however, is not only defined by tradition and tomorrow. Indeed, a theology is only an intellectual exercise, a process of knowledge like philosophy or mathematics, if it only seeks to learn what yesterday's teachers said, and what tomorrow's teachers might say. If theology is intimately related to the truth of God that is discovered in our following Jesus, then theology must have a relevant word to say to all people today. In particular, the whole of the theological community must have a relevant word for Latinos and Latinas today, and Hispanic theology must have a relevant word for the whole church, and not just for the Hispanic American church.[39] Thus, I would be remiss if I ended this chapter without speaking of the ongoing challenge of Hispanic theology articulating a relevant word for our people today.

In order for theology to be relevant, it must not only be a reflection of our faith as we follow Jesus but also reflect our walking with *our people*. This is precisely what Luke demonstrates in the closing chapter of his Gospel (Luke 24:13–35): Jesus is to be found with the disciples who are in crisis on their journey. It is in this context that he speaks an empowering word that is able to change the direction of their journey. From being disciples without understanding, they now have come to understand. From being disciples who are fleeing, they now return precisely to the place that poses danger in order to give witness to the Risen Christ. In order for us to be relevant, we must walk on the road that our *pueblo* traverses. In order to do that, we must first be keenly aware of that road and what it entails. We must understand the community in which our churches work and exist, the community from which our church members come, the community for which we are seeking to find a word that gives understanding to our faith. We must know *who* they are. I believe that sometimes we are working with the premise that we are dealing with the church of our mothers and fathers. On the contrary, this is a radically different church, and we are living in a radically different world.

Presently, there are an estimated 27.5 million Hispanics (10.3 percent of the total population) living in the United States.[40] Of the 30 percent of Latinos and Latinas living in poverty, 41.5 percent are children.[41] Given that the Latino population is relatively young (the median age is 26.2 years), and that almost 30 percent are under the age of 15, it is obvious that young children bear the brunt of the effects of poverty.[42] This cycle of poverty is compounded by other interrelated factors. For example, in 1995 only 53.4 percent of our children graduated from high school, only 9 percent graduated from college, and less than 3 percent entered graduate school.[43] In today's extremely competitive job market, these statistics indicate that the cycle of poverty, unemployment, and underemployment will only worsen. Health care is ever more out of the reach of Hispanics, AIDS is on the increase, and more and more children are having children.[44] However, we do not need to see the statistics to know that we are a community in crisis. Those of us who pastor witness daily to the brokenness and pain of our communities: in addition to the poverty, lack of adequate health care, poor educational attainment, and underemployment, we have also seen a rising tide of resentment against "illegals," an increase in substance abuse, and an escalation in spousal and family violence. These are just some of the many crises we face within our churches and within our communities. These crises have led to a crises in our pulpits: more and more pastors are leaving the ministry, suffering professional and spiritual burnout, and more and more congregations are resenting ministerial leadership which they perceive to be inept and ineffective against such seemingly insoluble problems. Clearly, this is not the church of fifty years ago.

It is imperative that we grapple with these issues today. The single most critical challenge of Hispanic American theology is to find the courage and discernment to make God, Jesus Christ, the reign of God, salvation, and so forth, not just interesting topics of philosophical reflection, but most urgently issues of life and death. Hispanic theology must present a word of hope and life in the face of the death-dealing powers and principalities that daily assault humankind. To do that, we must ensure that we are connected to the source of life that imparts new life, abundant life, to us. There are no easy answers. It is certainly beyond the scope of this chapter to attempt to provide them. But it is imperative that together, *en conjunto*, we ensure that we do not fall into a facile, superficial, and anesthetizing kind of theology.[45] We are challenged to see that the church does not do so either.

Taped to a wall in my office is a three-by-five-inch index card on which I copied the following sage advice by Orlando Costas:

> The preacher-teacher needs to be a person of prayer, because prayer is the means by which we express our dependence on the Holy Spirit, seek his guidance and submit to his will. Thus, through submission and intense supplication we may claim the empowering presence of the Spirit in our preaching and teaching and thus we may anticipate believers being motivated for witness.[46]

I remember hearing my seminary classmates and teachers criticizing those "mystics" who think that they can change the world with their prayers. These, I was assured, are only pacifists who are partly responsible for the oppression of people. Since then, after seven years of pastoral work in an inner-city church, I have discovered that Costas's words ring true for battling the realities of our communities. I have discovered that the most powerful act I can participate in is to pray and to cry out to the Lord. If theology is truly a reflection of our "following Jesus," then we must encounter this Lord of life daily. Theologians, especially Latina and Latino theologians, should take heed of Costas's advice. Whether we teach, or preach, or write, we must begin by encountering the God of our faith on God's terms. That, I believe, is done through prayer. And that, I believe, will help us as we seek to articulate a theology that is relevant for our *pueblo* today.

There is a particularity of our spirituality which enlivens our life of faith, and therefore our theology. We have many names for this: our passion, our joy, our deep love for the Lord.[47] Non-Hispanics are often nonplussed by it. They call us "emotional," or ask us if we are angry, or comment on how "intense" we are. Many of us have sought to tame our passion in order to make our presence more palatable to the dominant theological community. However, I think that our passion is a gift that we bring to society and to the church. It is our passion which makes us care deeply for our people. It is our passion which makes us hunger for the fullness of God's presence in our lives and in our communities. It is our passion which helps us to hope, and to dream, and to struggle, rather than to give in to despair. It is our passion which helps to keep us relevant. Our passion is as empowering as is our prayer life, because for Christians, the two go hand in hand. It is our passion which allows us to identify with the pain of our communities; it is our passion which enables us to push our communities for something better. It has helped us survive; it has helped us live. Our passion colors our theology in a particular way. Our challenge is to keep the fire of our passion from dying out. We must continue to think with our hearts and feel with our brains. It is only in this way that our theology will continue to have a heart of compassion and a vision of hope.

Conclusion:
The Challenge to Follow Jesus

In this chapter I have mentioned only a few of the vast challenges before Hispanic American theologians as we face a new millennium. It is a time of hope and a time of vigilance. It is a time to march and a time to pray. It is a time to discover the fullness of what we are and a time to realize that we still see as through a glass darkly (1 Cor. 13:12). We are challenged to live with the contradictions of our existence, to live between the traditions of yesterday and the possibilities of tomororw. We are challenged to be obedient to God's call to follow Jesus, and to allow the wind of the Spirit to blow in the midst of our lives as a believing people. As Jesus warned Nicodemus, this implies that we must go where the Spirit blows (John 3:8). It is only then that we can maintain our prophetic edge. It is in responding to this challenge that we can be transformed. We are called, as Costas so eloquently reminded us, to be with Christ outside the gate, and there to suffer with him. We are thus called to go to the margins, where we will find those who suffer, where life is not comfort and prestige but tears and struggle. It is only from this position of marginality, of being on the periphery, that we can then go to the centers of power and challenge them with a prophetic Word of God.[48] We are not called to become a part of the center, however, or to replace the center. If we are called to challenge the center, it is to participate in the building of the reign, where there are no "in" or "out" people. "Nobodies" do not exist there. We will find neither the powerless nor the powerful. In the spirit of this reign, we will seek to do God's will on earth as it is done in heaven. It is for this reign that we are called to love all, to be servants and friends. Our challenge is therefore to place our theology at the service, not of our egos, but of the Lord and the reign of God. Is not this truly faith seeking understanding, and obedience?

NOTES

1. Antoine de Saint-Exupéry, *El Principito*, trans. Bonifacio del Carril (San Diego: Harcourt Brace Jovanovich, 1973), 22–23.
2. I will alternate the use of "Hispanics" or "Latinas and Latinos" throughout this chapter. Much has already been said as to the inadequacy of these titles imposed

on us by the dominant society. For further discussion, I refer the reader to the Introduction of this book, note 3, as well as to Fernando F. Segovia, "Hispanic American Theology and the Bible: Effective Weapon and Faithful Ally," in *We Are a People! Initiatives in Hispanic American Theology*, ed. Roberto S. Goizueta (Minneapolis: Fortress Press, 1992), 25–27.

3. Eduardo Mendieta, "From Christendom to Polycentric Oikoumené: Modernity, Postmodernity, and Liberation Theology," *Journal of Hispanic/Latino Theology* (May 1996):74.

4. Virgil Elizondo, "Toward an Hispanic-American Theology of Liberation in the U.S.A.," in *Irruption of the Third World: A Challenge to Theology*, ed. Virginia Fabella and Sergio Torres (Maryknoll, N.Y.: Orbis Books, 1983), 53.

5. Roberto S. Goizueta, "In Defense of Reason," *Journal of Hispanic/Latino Theology* (February 1996):16–17; Mendieta, "Christendom," 72.

6. Mendieta, "Christendom," 72–73.

7. Gustavo Gutiérrez, *A Theology of Liberation: History, Politics, and Salvation*, 15th anniversary ed., trans. and ed. Sister Caridad Inda and John Eagleson (Maryknoll, N.Y.: Orbis Books, 1988), xxxiv, 8–9. It must be noted at this juncture that as Protestants, many Hispanic theologians, especially those identifying themselves as "radical evangelicals," add the caveat that scripture, as the rule of practice and faith—not praxis—continues to be the *starting point* and foundation of a Latino Protestant theology. For a fuller discussion of this, see Orlando E. Costas, *Christ outside the Gate: Mission beyond Christendom* (Maryknoll, N.Y.: Orbis Books, 1984), 13–131; Beatriz Melano Couch, "New Visions of the Church in Latin America: A Protestant View," in *The Emergent Gospel: Theology from the Underside of History*, ed. Sergio Torres and Virginia Fabella (Maryknoll, N.Y.: Orbis Books, 1976), 213–14.

8. Goizueta, "Reason," 18.

9. Justo L. González, *Mañana: Christian Theology from a Hispanic Perspective* (Nashville: Abingdon Press, 1990), 50.

10. Goizueta, "Reason," 20–21.

11. I do not believe it is a coincidence that many Latina and Latino Protestant theologians are, or have been, pastors (lay or ordained), teachers, deacons, or church elders. Most continue to exert leadership in their communities of faith.

12. Orlando O. Espín, "Pentecostalism and Popular Catholicism: The Poor and *Traditio*," *Journal of Hispanic/Latino Theology* 3:2 (November 1995): 20–21; Ada María Isasi-Díaz, "'Apuntes' for a Hispanic Women's Theology of Liberation," in *Voces: Voices from the Hispanic Church*, ed. Justo L. González (Nashville: Abingdon Press, 1992), 28–29.

13. Gustavo Gutiérrez, *We Drink from Our Own Wells: The Spiritual Journey of a People*, trans. Matthew J. O'Connell (Maryknoll, N.Y.: Orbis Books, 1988), 55.

14. Goizueta, "Reason," 18–20.

15. Fernando F. Segovia has described this condition as our being a diaspora people, always translating from one cultural world to another, but never belonging to either, in "Towards a Hermeneutic of the Diaspora: A Hermeneutics of Otherness and Engagement," in *Reading from This Place*, vol. 1, *Social Location and Biblical Interpretation in the United States*, ed. Fernando F. Segovia and Mary Ann Tolbert (Minneapolis: Fortress Press, 1995), 61, 64.

16. David Tracy defines ideologies as "unconscious but systemically functioning attitudes, values, and beliefs produced by and in the material conditions of all uses of language, all analyses of truth, and all claims to knowledge," in *Plurality and Ambiguity: Hermeneutics, Religion, Hope* (Chicago: University of Chicago Press, 1987), 77. Idols are the constructs of our ideologies; they are "idologies."

17. Justo L. González and Catherine G. González, *The Liberating Pulpit* (Nashville: Abingdon Press, 1994), 117.

18. Feminist and *mujerista* theologians have underscored that the theological debate in Hispanic theology, upon focusing on the poor, have rendered the issue of sexism peripheral to the debate, or even invisible. See, for example, María Pilar Aquino, *Nuestro clamor por la vida: Teología latinoamericana desde la perspectiva de la mujer* (San José, Costa Rica: DEI, 1992), 211.

19. Jill Martínez reminds us that listening is one of our strengths; see "In Search of an Inclusive Community," in *Voces*, 66. Segovia, in "Diaspora," 55, recommends ways in which the Hispanic theological community can ensure a critical dialogue that is open to listening to the voices of the "other."

20. *Adobo* is a seasoning; *sofrito* is a mixture of spices which is added to soups and sauces while cooking to enhance the flavor of the meal.

21. González, *Mañana*, 52.

22. In other instances, invaluable documentation such as letters, unpublished manuscripts, and lecture notes are stored in boxes, or other insecure places, in the homes of family members because libraries are unable to process such documents. Consequently, they are unavailable to scholars doing research.

23. I realize that this problem is not faced only by the Hispanic American community. This is a growing problem in theological education as "downsizing" and "profit margin" become the watchwords of our present context. It is a critical issue, however, in the Latino community because there is such a serious dearth of material to begin with. In light of technological advances, I will dare to present a challenge to publishing houses. Is it possible to retain such books in computer disk or CD-ROM format? When a professor or researcher requires a copy of such a book, rather than undertaking all the prohibitive expenses entailed in printing, binding, and mailing such books (which in turn requires that this need be done in large amounts in order to justify such an expense), the commercial establishment need only to produce the required amounts of CD-ROMs from the master disk. The advantage of such a system is that storage is minimal, as are the shipping costs; there would be no need to undergo costs of printing and binding; and such material is protected by the existing copyright laws of this country.

24. The history of the American Baptist mission among the Hispanic immigrants in New York City is chronicled by S. Soto Fontánez in *Misión a la puerta/Mission at the Door: Una historia del trabajo bautista hispano en Nueva York/A History of Hispanic Baptist Work in New York* (Santo Domingo, Dominican Republic: Editora Educativa Dominicana, 1982). It is the first fully bilingual book, that I am aware of, dealing with Hispanic Americans in the history of the church in the United States.

25. González has made note in his landmark study for The Fund for Theological Education, and in *Mañana*, as to the low percentage of Hispanics in schools

accredited by the Association of Theological Schools. Justo L. González, *The Theological Education of Hispanics* (New York: The Fund for Theological Education, 1988), 74–75. After noting that in 1985–86 only four Hispanics had completed Ph.D, Th.D., and S.T.D. degrees, and that in the following year there were no Hispanics graduating from Ph.D. programs, González notes in *Mañana*, 35, that "Hispanics constitute only 2.5% of seminarians, both Catholic and Protestant." In sharing with other professionals, it seems that this trend extends to many professional degrees. I am most familiar with the statistics in Veterinary Medicine, in which less than 2.9 percent of all veterinarians in the United States are minorities. This is a decrease of 1 percent from the late 1970s.

26. Class conference, Andover Newton Theological School, Newton Centre, Mass., spring 1988. Cf. Robert W. Pazmiño, "Double Dutch: Reflections of an Hispanic North American on Multicultural Religious Education," in *Voces*, 144.

27. Jürgen Moltmann, *The Church in the Power of the Spirit*, trans. Margaret Kohl (Minneapolis: Fortress Press, 1993; originally published 1977), 7.

28. Thomas S. Kuhn, *The Structure of Scientific Revolutions*, 3d ed. (Chicago: University of Chicago Press, 1996), 10, 175. Sallie McFague in *Metaphorical Theology: Models of God in Religious Language* (Philadelphia: Fortress Press, 1982), 70, defines paradigm as "an entire set of assumptions about what we believe we do, ought to do, or would like to do."

29. Letty M. Russell, "Unity and Renewal in Feminist Perspective," *Mid-Stream* 27 (January 1988): 58–59.

30. McFague, 80, 108. I want to thank Father Thomas R. Kopfensteiner, Professor of Moral Theology, Department of Theology, Fordham University, Bronx, New York, for reviewing this section for me. His feedback and insights on paradigms and metaphors, which I have incorporated into this chapter, were of great value to me.

31. Virgilio Elizondo, *Galilean Journey: The Mexican-American Promise* (Maryknoll, N.Y.: Orbis Books, 1983). For an excellent survey of Orlando Costas' theology and paradigms, see Belén González y Pérez, "The Gospel Mandate and a Theology of Contextual Evangelization: An Essay in Honor of Dr. Orlando E. Costas," *Apuntes* 15:3 (fall 1995):83–99.

32. Justo L. González, *Santa Biblia: The Bible Through Hispanic Eyes* (Nashville: Abingdon Press, 1996); Ada María Isasi-Díaz, *En la Lucha/In the Struggle: Elaborating a Mujerista Theology* (Minneapolis: Fortress Press, 1993).

33. McFague, 70. Anomaly here is not used in a pejorative manner. It simply refers to those experiences that do not fit into the framework of a given paradigm. See also, Kuhn, 52, 82–89.

34. Kuhn, 89, 111; McFague, 74.

35. The term *mujerista* was coined by Ada María Isasi-Díaz in "Mujeristas: A Name of Our Own," *Christian Century* (May 24–31, 1989): 560. Daisy Machado and Elizabeth Conde-Frazier have begun to write from the perspective of Latina Protestant women, creating richly suggestive paradigms for Hispanic theology. Daisy L. Machado, "A Borderlands Perspective," in *Hidden Stories: Unveiling the History of the Latino Church*, ed. Daniel R. Rodríguez and David Cortés-Fuentes (Decatur, Ga.: AETH, 1994), 49–65. Elizabeth Conde-Frazier, "Hispanic Protestant Spirituality," chapter 9 in this book.

36. Margarita Sánchez de León has written from an African Caribbean perspective in her article "Las mujeres negras latinas: las voces no escuchadas," in *Púlpito cristiano y justicia social*, ed. Daniel Rodríguez and Rodolfo Espinosa (South Holland, Ill.: Ediciones Borínquen, 1994), 113–21.

37. For a fuller discussion of the legend and history of *La Malinche*, see Irene I. Blea, *La Chicana and the Intersection of Race, Class and Gender* (Westport, Conn.: Praeger Publishers, 1992), 27; José E. Limón, "La Llorona, the Third Legend of Greater Mexico: Cultural Symbols, Women and the Political Unconscious," in *Between Borders: Essays on Mexicana-Chicana History*, ed. Adelaida Del Castillo, La Mujer Latina series (Encino, Calif.: Floricanto Press, 1990), 401–7.

38. David T. Abalos, *Latinos in the United States: The Sacred and the Political* (Notre Dame, Ind.: Notre Dame University Press, 1986), 43.

39. I am not referring here to a "universal truth" which is to be somehow articulated and applied generally to all people, regardless of their context. In fact, I am referring to the "scandal of particularity" wherein a relevant and relevantly contextual word that speaks truth to a particular people, often speaks in some concrete way to all people. See González, *Mañana*, 52–53; also Justo L. González, *Out of Every Tribe and Nation: Christian Theology at the Ethnic Roundtable* (Nashville: Abingdon Press, 1992), 18–37.

40. U.S. Bureau of the Census, *Statistical Abstract of the United States: 1996*, 116th ed. (Washington, D.C.: U.S. Government Printing Office, 1996), tables 13 and 53, 14, 51.

41. Ibid., tables 730–31, 472–73. Also Carey Goldberg, "Hispanic Households Struggle amid Broad Decline in Income," *New York Times*, January 30, 1997, A-1, reports that the median income of Hispanics dropped 6.9 percent from its levels in 1989 (from $26,000 to $22,000 in 1997) while median income for non-Hispanic whites increased 2.2 percent during the same period (to its present level of $35,766).

42. Ibid., table 22, p. 23; also, Jorge del Pinal, U.S. Bureau of the Census, "The Hispanic Population," March, 1993, Internet posting, URL: http://www.census.gov/population/www/pop-profile/hisppop.html.

43. As a comparison, it should be noted that in that same year 83 percent of non-Hispanic whites completed high school, 24 percent went on to graduate from college, and more than 8 percent completed postgraduate work. The data was obtained from the U.S. Bureau of the Census Internet posting at the following addresses: "Educational Attainment Level by Ethnicity Population," at http:www.census.gov/population/socdemo/hispanic/ed94.txt; also at http://www.census.gov/population/socdemo/education/table01.txt and /table03.txt as well as /table 18.txt. Tables 1 and 3 are published in the Current Population Report Series P70-32. For similar data, refer to the U.S. Bureau of the Census, Current Population Reports P23–183, *Hispanic Americans Today* (Washington, D.C.: U.S. Government Printing Office, 1993), 10–11.

44. In 1991, Antonia Novello et al. reported that "Injuries and violent death are also tragically elevated among Hispanic children. . . . [In 1987] more than 7.5 million Hispanics lacked health insurance for at least part of the year. . . . High levels of poverty, a disproportionate reliance on employment that provides no health insurance, and inadequate public coverage imply the issue of access to

health care will remain of central importance to Hispanic communities in the years to come." Antonia C. Novello, Paul H. Wise, and Dushanka V. Kleinman, "Hispanic Health: Time for Data, Time for Action," *Journal of the American Medical Association* 265:2 (Jan. 9, 1991):253–54. In that same issue of the *JAMA*, which was dedicated to Hispanic American health, the Council on Scientific Affairs in "Hispanic Health in the United States, 248–49, reported that approximately 30 percent of Mexican American and Puerto Rican girls between the ages of 15 and 19 years had given birth; they also found that even though at the time of the report Hispanics comprised only 7.9 percent of the population, they accounted for 14 percent of all AIDS cases reported, 21 percent of AIDS among women, and 22 percent of all pediatric AIDS. It should be noted that none of the recommendations in that issue has been followed through, as far as I can determine. In fact, the sociopolitical climate has militated against those recommendations, and even the frail safety nets of Medicare and Medicaid are now under fire.

45. The phrase *en conjunto* may be translated into English as "conjoined," bringing forth the imagery of the joints of the body, the place where two bones meet. Part of the integrity of the body depends on its various bones being "conjoined" in appropriate places, such that movement is fluid and without friction. A fracture is one way the integrity of the skeletal system, and therefore of the body, may be compromised. The closer such a fracture is to the joint, the more difficult it is to stabilize and set, in order to allow healing. There are different kinds of fractures. Most people know about simple fractures, where a bone breaks in two. But there are other kinds of fractures. For example, there is the "compound fracture." It is so called, not because the bone is broken in various places (that is a comminuted fracture), but because the bone fragment has broken through the skin. Such a fracture causes much soft tissue damage, and compromises the circulatory and sensory (nerve) supplies to the area. It is therefore damage that has been "compounded" by various other trauma: to the skin, muscle, nerves, blood vessels, etc. The greatest danger of such a fracture is that it exposes the area to infection which can spread throughout the blood system (septicemia), possibly causing death. The brokenness of our community is a "compound fracture" and cannot be treated as a "simple fracture" with simple and minimal solutions. Much damage has occurred at a social, spiritual, familial, emotional, and physical level. The problem has been compounded, and has become generational as well. It is imperative that we realize that the compound fracture of our present community demands that as a Christian people we must be "conjoined" to seek ways of healing the brokenness of our communities. Perhaps it is this that the author of Ephesians was alluding to (without, of course, the complicated medical diagnostics) when in 4:12–13 he refers to the Spirit's giving gifts to "equip" the saints for the building up of the body, to bring it to the fullness of unity. The Greek term used for "equip" is *katartismos*, a term which also refers to the setting of broken bones. Clearly, as a people we cannot reach the height of the stature of Jesus Christ if our body is suffering from the "broken bones" of racism, sexism, oppression, poverty, violence, exclusion, and the like. Salvation brings precisely "healing." It is the Holy Spirit who "effects" this healing in our midst. Theology, and Christian theologians, must be

conjoined to be part of this ministry of healing and salvation, to witness, in effect, to the reign of God in our midst. See Markus Barth, *Ephesians 4–6*, Anchor Bible (Garden City, N.Y.: Doubleday & Co., 1974), 439.

46. Orlando E. Costas, *The Integrity of Mission* (San Francisco: Harper & Row, 1979), 34.

47. This passion is a result of our particular mestizo Iberoamerican Catholic, Amerindian, and African worldview. See Martínez, "Inclusive Community," 66; Goizueta, "Reason," 20–22.

48. Orlando E. Costas, *Christ outside the Gate: Mission beyond Christendom* (Maryknoll, N.Y.: Orbis Books, 1984), 186–94; Orlando E. Costas, *Liberating News: A Theology of Contextual Evangelization* (Grand Rapids: Wm. B. Eerdmans Publishing Co., 1989), 57.

Index